THE
PR⬤CⅅISE
OF
GⵕD

God's Unchangeable Purpose
Through Human History

THE
PROMISE
OF
GOD

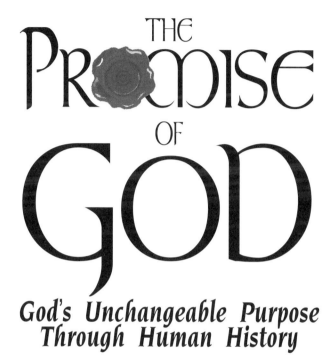

God's Unchangeable Purpose Through Human History

GEORGE BRISTOW

GOSPEL FOLIO PRESS
P.O. Box 2041, Grand Rapids, MI 49501-2041
Available in the UK from
JOHN RITCHIE LTD., 40 Beansburn, Kilmarnock, Scotland

THE PROMISE OF GOD
by George Bristow
Copyright © 1997
George Bristow
All rights reserved

Published by Gospel Folio Press
P. O. Box 2041,
Grand Rapids, MI 49501-2041

ISBN 1-882701-29-1

Cover design by J. B. Nicholson, Jr.
Graphics by D. Lein and M. Donahue

Printed in the United States of America

CONTENTS

FOREWORD

It is a pleasure to commend to the reader this most succinct, but detailed guided study of the Old Testament. *The Promise of God: God's Unchangeable Purpose through Human History* meets a real need in that it demonstrates quite conclusively that there is a unified plan to the whole of the testament that has a precise fit with the New Testament as well. Few have packed so much in so little space with such good judgment on what to include.

In choosing the theme of the "promise-plan" of God in the Old Testament, George Bristow has followed a similar theme that I have been emphasizing in my own teaching at the college and graduate theological seminary level. Not only is the theme of the "promise" one of the most promising integrating concepts of the whole Bible, it is the one that the writers of Scripture appear to espouse themselves, and the one that yields the highest dividends on the meaning and current relevance of the Bible.

The study of each chapter, along with the suggested readings and study questions at the conclusion of each chapter, will yield one of the most exciting adventures that any person committed to the truth of Scripture could ever imagine.

All too many believers today have forgotten how rooted their faith is in the whole of the canon and history of Scripture. Without an understanding of the Old Testament, the believer is left without any roots, suspended in mid air, and without any meaningful context in which in ground his or her faith. But that condition will cease to exist once one has gotten into the study of this book.

May each one who opens the covers of this book experience the joy of his or her life in one of the most fascinating investments of their time that

I could recommend. And may the power of the Word of God grip each one in new and living way to the honor and glory of our great God and Saviour Jesus Christ.

WALTER C. KAISER, JR.
Colman M. Mockler Distinguished Professor of Old Testament
Gordon-Conwell Theological Seminary
S. Hamilton, MA 01982

PREFACE

e moved to Istanbul in 1987. During the past nine years, I have had the privilege of discussing issues of faith with many Turkish Muslim friends and acquaintances. I can affirm that most of them have genuine respect for our biblical Scriptures. In their own way, they believe in these books. For this reason we have found common ground on subjects such as the oneness and eternity of the Creator, and the respect which we owe Him as creatures.

At the same time, I have found myself in disagreement with these friends on essential points. One of these issues demonstrates the importance of the focus of this book, *The Promise of God*. According to Islamic teaching, God, whom they call "Allah," gave four holy books in succession to four great prophets:

> The *Tavrat* (Torah) to *Musa* (Moses).
> The *Zabur* (Psalms) to *Davut* (David).
> The *Injil* (Gospel) to *Isa* (Jesus).
> The *Quran* to Mohammed

They claim that the authority and validity of each divine book lasted only until its successor was given. So each book has in turn replaced and, for all practical purposes, abolished the preceding books. Of course, the conclusion of this line of reasoning is inescapable: the last book in the series, the Quran, is the only valid law of God today. Islam thus cleverly claims to rest on the foundation of the Old and New Testament Scriptures, while in fact ignoring and denying their message. Muslims view the Scriptures as outmoded books that have been changed by deceitful rabbis and priests who refused to accept Mohammed.

I try to explain that the truth is far from this: "Look, you're working with faulty information. The writings of David never invalidated those of Moses! They take their place alongside and confirm them completely, continuing the same divine revelation. Nor does the Gospel of Jesus abolish the earlier scriptures, but fulfills them. These are not three separate books sent to three different nations as you've heard—they are chapters in the inspired series of writings which reveal God's single, unchangeable purpose. The God in whom I believe is unchanging and utterly trustworthy. He is more than able to protect His own revelation from all such attacks."

But in spite of the truth of my arguments, few of these friends are persuaded, because they have never read these scriptures and have never heard of any "unchangeable purpose of God." These concepts mean nothing to them.

These friends, who say they believe in the books of Moses, David, and Jesus, often ask, "What do you think of the Quran?" to which I respond, "Well, I've read and studied the Quran. But I can't accept it as the Word of God. It contradicts much of what the earlier books have revealed in perfect harmony."

Their answer? "Well, of course it conflicts with them! Those books have been corrupted and changed!" Such futile arguments arise because they really know nothing of God's Word and the great divine purpose and plan it reveals.

The Lord Jesus described His own relationship with the books of Moses, David, and the other prophets with these words:

Do not think that I came to destroy the Law or the Prophets. I did not come to destroy but to fulfill. For assuredly, I say to you, till heaven and earth pass away, one jot or one tittle will by no means pass from the law till all is fulfilled (Mt. 5:17-18).

Then He said to them, These are the words which I spoke to you while I was still with you, that all things must be fulfilled which were written in the Law of Moses and the Prophets and the Psalms concerning Me (Lk. 24:44).

If He spoke the truth, then by studying these holy writings we should be able to discover many things written about Jesus there, and see that the earlier prophets testified about Him. One of my purposes in preparing this series of studies was to clearly present the things which are written about Christ in the Old Testament. If you read all of the recommended Scripture readings given at the beginning of each study, you will at least be acquainted with most of the "Messianic"[1] passages of the Old Testament.

A second purpose in writing was to give a general introduction and overview of all the Old Testament scriptures. Many Christians have never read through the entire Bible even one time, especially the Old Testament. I want to encourage such believers in Christ to deepen their faith and knowledge of Him. As the apostle Paul wrote to his young assistant, Timothy,

All Scripture is given by inspiration of God, and is profitable for doctrine, for reproof, for correction, for instruction in righteousness, that the man of God may be complete, thoroughly equipped for every good work (2 Tim. 3:16-17).

We will begin with a general introduction to the Old Testament (OT). Then we will divide OT history into thirteen periods or eras, extending from the creation of the world to the birth of Christ, and try to show the beautiful progression and unity of these scriptures as God's purpose is unfolded through the ages. Finally, we will look briefly at the New Testament to see how these accumulated promises are being perfectly fulfilled in Christ.

These studies have also been prepared as a complete course on the Old Testament for use by individuals or study groups. At the end of each study, the reader will find comprehensive study questions intended to make him think through the Bible passages discussed in the study. Obviously the student who works through, and tries to answer, these study questions will benefit far more than one who only reads the book. We all understand and remember best the things God's Spirit has taught us during our own personal study. The Lord is still looking for serious men and women like Ezra:

> *For Ezra had prepared his heart to seek the Law of the Lord, and to do it, and to teach statutes and ordinances in Israel* (Ezra 7:10).

For those wishing to do further study, additional cross-references and more details are provided in the footnotes from time to time. At the end of the book, an index of scripture references and a subject index have also been included to make the studies more useful for future reference.

In this survey of the Old Testament, focusing on the promise of God, I make no claim to complete originality. I owe a great debt to Walter C. Kaiser, Jr., whose excellent book, *Towards an Old Testament Theology*, I first read in Chicago in 1982. I learned much at that time.

Seven years later, in Istanbul, I was giving a young Turkish Jewish believer an overview of the OT, and found myself referring to Dr. Kaiser's work frequently. Studying God's Word with the aid of *Towards an Old Testament Theology* for the second time was a blessing to my soul and greatly enlarged my grasp of the *"unchangeableness of His purpose"* as God has revealed it in the OT Scriptures. I began to think that his approach would make an excellent basis for an introductory course on the OT.

So I began to prepare these studies in 1989, attempting to make this great theme of God's Promise more accessible to the average believer. Although I have revised it many times since then, adding two eras and much new material, the original outline of this course (and some of the content) was drawn from Dr. Kaiser's work with his kind permission.

I owe special thanks to God's beloved people in Turkey. Their eagerness to be taught the OT strengthened my resolve to complete this work. Thanks to the hard work of brother Ali Simsek and the staff of Yeni Yasam (New Life) Publishers, the book was published in Turkish in October 1995 under the title *"VAAT"* (*The Promise*).

There is no shortage of Bible study materials in the English language. Nevertheless widespread unfamiliarity with much of the Old Testament persists. My prayer is that these studies will challenge God's people to rededicate themselves to meditating day and night in the law of the Lord, and that together we *"do not become sluggish, but imitate those who through faith and patience inherit the promises"* (Heb. 6:12).

The movement called "PROMISE KEEPERS" is the latest wave among many evangelical believers today. Yet at times one wonders if it could grow into a dangerous tidal wave before running its course. There is the danger of surrendering vital truth in the quest for unity and reconciliation, especially if finding allies in the struggle against decaying moral values becomes top priority. There is also the danger of focusing too much on men keeping their promises. Unquestionably God's people should be keepers of their word. Our "yes" should remain "yes," no matter the personal cost. Still, all man-centered covenants are marked by frailty. Remember Israel's eager affirmation: *"All the words which the Lord has said we will do"* (Ex. 24:3). The Lord's answer to their promise is relevant today: *"O that there were such an heart in them, that they would fear me"* (Deut. 5:28-29). But they did not have such a heart; none of us do; *"The heart is deceitful above all things, and desperately wicked: who can know it?"* (Jer. 17:9). God calls hasty promises *"the sacrifice of fools"* and warns, *"For in the multitude of dreams and many words there is also vanity. But fear God"* (see Eccl. 5:1-7).

Our focus should be on the only true Promise Keeper, God Himself, and on knowing and believing *"His precious and magnificent promises,"* through which we can become *"partakers of the divine nature, having escaped the corruption that is in the world through lust"* (2 Pet. 1:4).

The Lord Jesus had been risen from the tomb for less than twenty-four hours when He approached two of His distressed disciples on the road to Emmaus. After listening to their confused words for a while, He gently rebuked them for not believing what the prophets had written about the Messiah's sufferings and resurrection from the dead. They should have expected the tomb to be empty! *"And beginning at Moses and all the prophets, He expounded unto them in all the Scriptures the things concerning Himself"* (Lk. 24:27). Later, the stunned disciples, hardly able to believe their eyes and ears for joy, asked each other, *"Did not our heart burn within us while He talked with us on the road, and while He opened the Scriptures to us?"* (Lk. 24:32). We could all use a good dose of this kind of "heart-burn"!

May the living Lord be our Teacher as well.

GEORGE BRISTOW
August 1997
Istanbul, Turkey

---

1 By the term *Messianic* we refer to things related to the promised Messiah, or "Christ."

THE PROMISE OF GOD
INTRODUCTION TO THE OLD TESTAMENT

Recommended Readings: Psalms 1 & 19; Luke 24:44-49; Hebrews 6:11-20

Our world is changing at mind-boggling speed. "We live in an unprecedented day with unprecedented problems."[1] Electronic mail, satellite communication, and international networking are reducing the distance between nations to the point where we speak of a "global village." Every convenience is ours to command. At the same time, we are haunted by the specters of racial tension, financial collapse, and mindless terrorism. At any given moment, dozens of wars are going on around the world. The following is a shocking but realistic summary of our situation:

> With the aid of progress, perils now encircle us. No matter which direction we turn, yet another crisis stares us in the face. Not only has progress been unable to solve these crises, it has not even been able to slow them...We are immersed in a crime and prison crisis; a drug-abuse crisis, a national debt and international-trade-deficit crisis; a savings-and-loan and banking crisis; a health-care system and Medicare crisis; a sexually-transmitted-disease crisis, including AIDS; an adolescent-suicide crisis; a liability-and-litigation crisis; an ethics crisis at every level of personal and public life; and the inexorably deepening environmental crisis. Our families are relentlessly torn apart by divorce, abuse, incest, and teenage pregnancies...Inner cities are war zones. Breakdown on a large scale is now within our reach. Each day we awake to a world that appears more confused and disordered than the one we left the night before.[2]

Confronted with this daunting reality, many people struggle with deep fears and uncertainty when they pause long enough to ask themselves life's more serious questions: Why are we really here? Where are we going at such a breakneck pace? How will it all end? Does mankind's sad history have no real meaning or direction? Are world peace, brotherhood, and lasting prosperity nothing but dreams after all? What is the true purpose of life? Or is man condemned to appear for a brief moment on the world's stage only to burn to ashes and smoke as the whole theater goes up in flames? (A. E. Wilder-Smith)

For centuries philosophers, scientists, and pioneers have searched for answers to these questions and even thought they had found them. Great men have dreamed of ideal societies and labored to create conditions where all men would live together in happiness, peace, and equality. Words such as "Life, liberty, and the pursuit of happiness" express these lofty ideals, but today they ring hollow. On the world scale, little of substance has really changed. The contradictions have only reached greater proportions than ever.

Thankfully the living God, who alone knows the answers to all such questions, has given us the sure hope of a coming glorious age, even of new heavens and a new earth full of righteousness, peace, and joy:

> *And in this mountain the Lord of hosts will make for all people a feast of choice pieces, a feast of wines on the lees, of fat things full of marrow, of well-refined wines on the lees. And He will destroy on this mountain the surface of the covering cast over all people, and the veil that is spread over all nations. He will swallow up death forever, and the Lord God will wipe away tears from all faces; the rebuke of His people He will take away from all the earth; for the Lord has spoken* (Isa. 25:6-8).

The Creator who makes such promises is a trustworthy God who cannot lie. He has an unchangeable and good purpose for mankind. He has promised to fulfill this purpose and has even begun to put it into operation. What is His plan? How and when will He carry it out? How do we fit into His plans? Does He have a purpose for me? These are some of the questions we will be examining in this series of fifteen studies.

God began to reveal His plan in the ancient Hebrew writings we call the Old Testament. If we will commit ourselves to read them seriously, these sacred Scriptures will not only enable us to understand where our world is going but, even more importantly, discover the eternal value and essential purpose of our own lives.

THE PROGRESS AND UNITY OF THE SCRIPTURES

The foundation of this course is that the living God has revealed Himself to mankind. In addition to the wordless testimony of the created universe to the power and wisdom of its Creator, God has also spoken in written form. These collected writings form the "Holy Bible," and are the very "word" or "oracles" of God.

The Bible is a *progressive* book. God has chosen not to reveal everything at once. Instead, He has done so progressively, over many ages. Just as the education of a child proceeds from simple lessons to more complex, God's revelation begins with fundamental truth and gradually adds deeper insight to these basics. We must understand the beginning lessons well before proceeding to more advanced ones. Otherwise we may badly misunderstand the later revelation. In mathematics, you must know the numbers before you can do addition. You must understand the rules of addition before attempting multiplication, and so on. Likewise, for a clear grasp of God's wonderful plan, we must understand well the first chapters of the Scriptures.

The Bible is also a *unified* book. Its later sections may be more complex and full, but they do not invalidate or replace the earlier ones. Rather they expand and deepen the same essential truth. Each stage of God's revelation builds on and reinforces the preceding ones. We can use this as a test: if "revelation" is truly from God, it will be consistent with what He has already taught us. If an idea claims to be from God, yet conflicts with what He has previously revealed, it must be steadfastly rejected.

One of the main goals of this course, then, will be to discover both the progress and the unity of God's Word, the Bible. As we proceed through the coming lessons, we will return to these two elements again and again.

THE VALUE OF THE OLD TESTAMENT

The Bible is a *unique* book, meaning "different from all others; having no like or equal." It is unique in its continuity, its circulation, its translation, its survival, its teachings, and its influence.[3] It is also a *reliable* book, meaning that we can trust it completely. History and archaeology confirm its accuracy in great detail. But the perfect fulfillment of hundreds of predictive prophecies made centuries before is the greatest evidence that the Bible is God's Word. No other ancient writings contain such accurate predictions of distant events relating to specific nations, cities, and even individual people. Only God can reveal the distant future with perfect accuracy, and His prophets openly challenge all other "gods" to do likewise: *"Let them bring forth and show us what will happen…Show the things that are to come hereafter, that we may know that you are gods"* (Isa. 41:22-23).

There is also nothing in all literature to compare with the *style* of the Bible. The great Jewish Christian scholar, Adolph Saphir, wrote:

> The simplicity, the perfect objective calmness of its narratives, its power, its lucidity, its attractiveness, its terseness, everyone has felt whether he believes or not. Where is there in the whole realm of literature a narrative like that of Abraham taking Isaac to Mount Moriah, or of the raising of Lazarus, or of Joseph making himself known to his brethren?…Indeed it is God's Word, while all other books evince only human skill…As nature is above art, so is inspiration above nature."[4]

The Old Testament contains the portions of God's written Word which were revealed before the birth of Jesus Christ. Together with the New Testament, these Holy Scriptures are of priceless value and will endure forever. The psalmist David, who meditated on the early parts of these writings, marveled at their transforming power in Psalm 19:7-10:

> *The law of the Lord is perfect, converting the soul:*
> *The testimony of the Lord is sure, making wise the simple.*
> *The statutes of the Lord are right, rejoicing the heart:*
> *The commandment of the Lord is pure, enlightening the eyes.*
> *The fear of the Lord is clean, enduring forever:*
> *The judgments of the Lord are true and righteous altogether.*
> *More to be desired are they than gold, yea, than much fine gold:*
> *Sweeter also than honey and the honeycomb.*

Sadly, the Old Testament (OT) is sometimes neglected or thought of as the "Jewish" Bible which has been made obsolete by the "Christian" New Testament (NT). But this is like saying that once a building is complete, its foundations and lower stories are no longer necessary! No, on the contrary, these ancient Hebrew words are *"the Holy Scriptures, which are able to make you wise for salvation"* (2 Tim. 3:15). *"For whatever things were written before were written for our learning, that we through the patience and comfort of the Scriptures might have hope"* (Rom. 15:4).

> Here the foundations of [true] religion are laid in the revelation of the one and only true God. Here the origin of…the curse which separates man from God [is disclosed]…Here is anticipated the saving purpose and plan of God…Here the Saviour Himself is promised…Here we find men at grips with great moral problems…Here all the chords of the human heart are swept in immortal songs.[5]

Like all of the Bible, the Old Testament is God's authoritative Word given to us for our good. It is like a deep gold mine which will richly reward all our efforts. As Gregory the Great said, "Holy Scripture is like a stream of running water, where alike the elephant may swim and the lamb walk."[6] But it must be studied prayerfully and reverently because it will condemn all who trifle with it.

THE DIVINE AND HUMAN QUALITY

A widespread misconception regarding prophets and their writings is that the process of revelation was similar to dictation. According to this view, prophets simply wrote down God's messages word-for-word and brought them to the people. So when Muslims, for example, read the biblical Scriptures, they expect to find nothing but "Thus saith the Lord." They are often shocked to find not only history, poetry, and other literary forms, but even the prophets' own personal pondering, prayers, and problems mingled with direct statements of the Lord. We need to grasp two related biblical ideas: "revelation" and "inspiration."

Revelation is God personally disclosing Himself to man. God is so far above man that unless God reveals Himself, man cannot see Him, find Him, or know His thoughts (Ex. 33:20; Job 11:7; Isa. 55:8-9). God has revealed Himself through His physical creation (Ps. 19:1-6) and through His actions in history (Ps. 145), as well as in the written Scriptures (Ps. 119). The fullest revelation of God was when *"the Word became flesh, and dwelt among us"* as the divine man, Jesus of Nazareth (Jn. 1:14).

Inspiration is God enabling men to express His revelation in words. God's Holy Spirit caused prophets, psalmists, wise men, and apostles to record His revelation in written scriptures: *"All scripture is given by inspiration of God"* (2 Tim. 3:16). The books of Moses, the historical books, the wisdom books, and the prophetic books are all equally the Word of God. Yet while the words are God's own words, each biblical book is also the literary creation of its human author. "Inspiration was not mechanical dictation which suspended the action of the human writer's mind. God did not eliminate the personality, style, outlook, and cultural conditioning of His penman, but His perfect control produced the inerrant written Word of God."[7] *"For prophecy never came by the will of man, but holy men of God spoke as they were moved by the Holy Spirit"* (2 Pet. 1:21).

> We must acknowledge the twofold nature of Scripture: on the one hand it as a God-breathed book, but on the other hand it has a human character. God used living men, not dead tools. He did not set aside human personality, but rather used the very personality of the human authors in the penning of His revelation.[8]

Thus we will study history, genealogical and legislative material, poetry, songs, and prophecy written by political leaders and military generals, shepherds, kings, captives, and cup bearers. The OT records both the great exploits and the sinfulness of many heroes of faith. But it is this very humanness and variety which makes God's Word so relevant to us. "This is its unspeakable value: thoroughly and entirely divine...yet perfectly and divinely adapted to man as being by man."[9]

THE CONTENT AND STRUCTURE

In the index of your Bible, you will see 39 books in the OT, running from Genesis through Malachi. The Lord Jesus referred to the Hebrew Scriptures in three parts: *"the law of Moses...the prophets...the psalms"* (Lk. 24:44), which in Hebrew are called the *Tôrah*, the *Nevî-îm*, and the *Ketûvîm* (see Appendix 1). In the first century these writings were divided into only 24 books, but the content was exactly the same as the 39 books of today's OT. Only the order and grouping of the books was different.

Today's OT follows a generally chronological order, with two main sections. In simplest terms, the books from Genesis through Esther record God's *historical* dealings with mankind from the creation of the world until the stage was set for the coming of His Redeemer, Jesus Christ. The

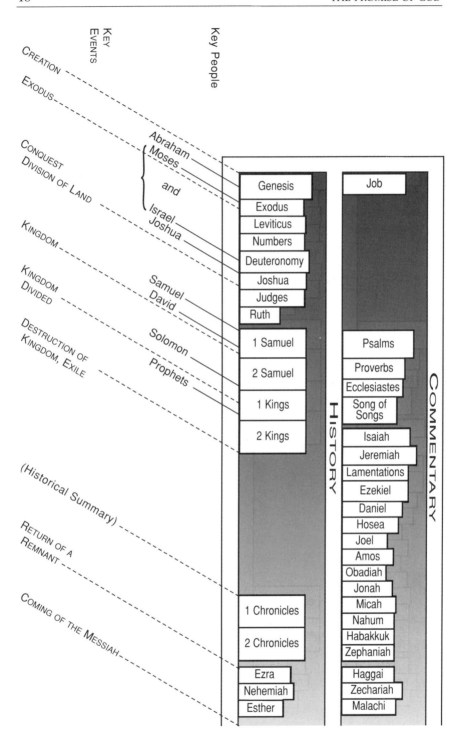

Key Events

Key People

CREATION

EXODUS

CONQUEST
DIVISION OF LAND

KINGDOM

KINGDOM
DIVIDED

DESTRUCTION OF
KINGDOM, EXILE

(Historical Summary)

RETURN OF A
REMNANT

COMING OF THE MESSIAH

Abraham
Moses
and
Israel
Joshua

Samuel
David

Solomon

Prophets

HISTORY

COMMENTARY

Genesis
Exodus
Leviticus
Numbers
Deuteronomy
Joshua
Judges
Ruth
1 Samuel
2 Samuel
1 Kings
2 Kings

1 Chronicles
2 Chronicles
Ezra
Nehemiah
Esther

Job
Psalms
Proverbs
Ecclesiastes
Song of Songs
Isaiah
Jeremiah
Lamentations
Ezekiel
Daniel
Hosea
Joel
Amos
Obadiah
Jonah
Micah
Nahum
Habakkuk
Zephaniah
Haggai
Zechariah
Malachi

books from Job through Malachi records God's own *commentary,* as at various key points He clarifies and further reveals His own purposes behind and beyond that history. Think of it as two shelves of books, the lower a "history" shelf and the upper a "commentary" or "prophecy" shelf. The diagram on page 18 shows approximately how the "commentary" books relate to the key events and characters of the historical narrative.

This two-part division shows us an important principle: God's revelation is not in word only, but in historical action. God has intervened in human history to reveal Himself. In fact, He is the very Architect of the ages. His written Scriptures first record what He has done, then explain why He has done it. We are called to trust God on the basis of what He has done in history. Man's relationship with God depends on His initiative, not ours. He is doing something tremendous. We must know what that "something" is and get in line with Him.

To better understand the beautiful structure of the Scriptures, we should notice that it moves through four general stages of revelation:

(1) First the foundation is laid and the people of God are created and redeemed. (2) Second, the developing history of this people and God's dealings with them are recorded. (3) Third, God's people pour out their hearts in written form, revealing their inner life and struggles, while addressing God in prayer and praise. (4) Fourth, God speaks from His heart, often in the first person, appealing to and warning His people, as well as comforting them with glimpses of the future fulfillment of His promises to them. We can overlay these four stages on the bookshelf diagram as shown below:

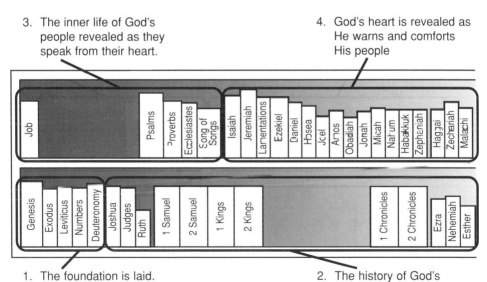

3. The inner life of God's people revealed as they speak from their heart.

4. God's heart is revealed as He warns and comforts His people

1. The foundation is laid. God redeems His people.

2. The history of God's people develops.

The same general structure is seen in the New Testament as well. In the Gospels the foundational revelation is given. In the Acts of the Apostles the early history of God's people is recorded under the direction of the Holy Spirit. Then the letters of the Apostles reveal to us the inner life of men and women in Christ. Finally, in the Revelation the Lord addresses His churches directly, warning them and unfolding to them the things to come in the future. Such consistency in structure testifies clearly to the wisdom of the one divine Author of both Testaments.

THE CENTRAL IDEA

In spite of great variety of form and content, and a multitude of authors, there is a central theme to the books of the OT. An inner unity runs from Genesis to Malachi and reveals one ongoing, developing purpose. This center is the Promise of God. "It was a definite singular plan of God to benefit one man [Abraham] and through him [and his *"seed"*] to bless the whole world."[10]

In your seed all the nations of the earth shall be blessed (Gen. 22:18).

This promise forms a core or focal point around which the OT revelation grows. Walter C. Kaiser compares this idea to "the relation of a seed acorn to the full-grown oak tree. Just so, the central idea matures as revelation progresses into the NT era…The emphasis is on unity with plenty of room for expansion and development."[11] The Bible does not simply repeat the same ideas in different ways, but records one progressively advancing plan.

This central idea is known in the OT under a collection of terms, beginning with *"blessing,"* and including *"promise," "pledge," "oath"* and *"covenant."* The heart of God's promise is a divine *"seed"* through whom all the various facets of His purpose would be fulfilled.

The NT apostles preached *"the covenant which God made with our fathers"* (Acts 3:25-26; 13:32). Their epistles also confirm this unified purpose, referring to it as "the gospel" or "the blessing of Abraham":

The Scripture, foreseeing that God would justify the Gentiles by faith, preached the gospel to Abraham beforehand, saying, "In you all the nations shall be blessed"…that the blessing of Abraham might come upon the Gentiles in Christ Jesus, that we might receive the promise of the Spirit through faith (Gal. 3:8, 14).

This *"seed"* would be not only a single, unique descendant, but also a collective group of descendants. On the one hand, the "seed" referred to the Messiah: *"Now to Abraham and his Seed were the promises made. He does not say, "And to seeds," as of many, but as of one, "And to your Seed," who is Christ"* (Gal. 3:16). On the other hand, the "seed" was the vast body of spiritual offspring whom the Messiah would represent and redeem: *"If you are Christ's, then you are Abraham's seed, and heirs according to the promise"* (Gal. 3:29). We will trace this theme of "the one and the many" throughout the Old Testament.

In the development of this promise, "the two pivotal characters were, no doubt, Abraham and David. Their respective covenants are initially recorded in Genesis 12:1-3 and 2 Samuel 7:11-16."[12] Throughout the long ages of OT history, and in spite of their many sins, failings, and weaknesses, God sovereignly selects and preserves this line of descendants which He calls *"the holy seed"* (Isa. 6:13).

THE HISTORICAL ERAS

In this series of lessons we will survey the entire Old Testament. But instead of merely surveying the contents of the books, we will focus on the promise of God as it is progressively revealed and expanded throughout Old Testament history. Again, we want to examine both the unity and the development of God's central purpose as revealed in His Word. Each successive era or age brought "fresh branches of teaching" which strengthened and "continued the unbroken, continuous chain in the emerging details of the plan of God...Each writer added to the theme."[13]

> These books were written at different times, and by different persons, across a period of some sixteen hundred years, yet...through all these ages "one increasing purpose runs," a way is being prepared for the feet of the Redeemer.[14]

We will divide the OT into thirteen historical eras and devote one study to examining the promise of God in each. In a final lesson we'll consider the fulfillment of the promise as revealed in the New Testament. Let's look at the outline of our studies and note the key items in each historic period:[15]

STUDY 2—Roots of the Promise: Pre-Patriarchal Era
(*Genesis 1-11*)
From Adam to Noah to Abraham, God states His intention to "bless" all mankind. At three different points, man's disobedience leads to disastrous judgment. But each judgment is followed by new hope as God promises a redeeming "seed."

STUDY 3—Faith in the Promise: Patriarchal Era
(*Genesis 12-50*)
In Genesis 12, God chooses one family through whom He would bless *"all the families of the earth."* God's promise of an heir, an inheritance, and a heritage is unveiled during the lifetimes of the patriarchs: Abraham, Isaac, and Jacob.

STUDY 4—People of the Promise—*A Redeemed People:* Moses' First Era
(*Exodus 1-18*)
By the time of Moses, the "seed" had grown from a family into a peo-

ple. In a six-act "Drama of Redemption," God demonstrates His faithfulness to His promise. With great power He punishes Pharaoh's arrogance and delivers Israel from Egyptian slavery under Moses' leadership.

STUDY 5—People of the Promise—*A Holy People:* Moses' Second Era
(*Exodus 19–Leviticus*)

At Mount Sinai, God enters into a unique relationship with Israel, involving great responsibility and the high privilege of His personal dwelling among them in the tabernacle. The principles of a holy relationship between God and His people are established.

STUDY 6—The Law and the Promise: Moses' Third Era
(*Numbers–Deuteronomy*)

When God gave His holy Law to Israel, He made a covenant with them. His holy character was the basis of that standard or "testimony." Yet no sooner is the Law received than Israel breaks it. Forty years of wandering in the desert demonstrate their inability to keep the Law. Moses' era ends as he brings them to the border of the promised land and renews the covenant.

STUDY 7—Entering the Promised Rest: Pre-Monarchical Era
(*Joshua–Ruth*)

The transition from Moses to Joshua brought a new focus: the inheritance of the promised land. Through repeated cycles of success, failure, and restoration, Israel receives the promised God-given *"rest"* by obedience and faith, yet repeatedly loses it through sin and unbelief.

STUDY 8—King of the Promise: David's Era
(*1&2 Samuel; Psalms*)

The ancient plan of a "seed," a world-wide "blessing," and a "rest" would now be focused in a "king." Using His great prophet, Samuel, God anointed David, "a man after His own heart," and promised him an everlasting dynasty, dominion, and a kingdom involving the future of all mankind.

STUDY 9—Life in the Promise: Solomon's Era
(*1 Kings 1-11; Job–Song of Songs*)

The major emphasis of Solomon's era was *"the fear of the Lord."* This was the foundation of the wisdom and righteous living the Lord intended for His people. It gave meaning and fullness to all of life. Great questions such as the suffering of righteous people and the true purpose of life find their ultimate answers in God's intimate love and discipline of His people.

STUDY 10—Prophets of the Promise: First Pre-Exilic Era
(*1 Kings 12–2 Kings 14; Hosea–Obadiah*)

The division and sinfulness of the kingdom after Solomon led God to send prophets to warn of a coming *"Day of the Lord."* The ultimate establishment of God's everlasting kingdom must be preceded by His judgment of sin, both in Israel and in the wicked kingdoms of man.

STUDY 11—The Promised "Servant of the Lord": Second Pre-Exilic Era
(*2 Kings 15-20; Micah; Isaiah*)

In Isaiah's magnificent book, he calls us to behold God Himself, the Holy One. The Lord's promise to Abraham and David is expanded and clarified, and His Messiah revealed in amazing detail as *"Emmanuel," "the Branch," "the Cornerstone,"* and the *"Servant of the Lord."*

STUDY 12—Renewal of the Promise: Third Pre-Exilic Era
(*2 Kings 21-25; Jonah; Nahum–Zephaniah; Jeremiah*)

Despite the dark times preceding the fall of Jerusalem, beyond the repeated warnings by the prophets of God's coming wrath, the joyous prospect of a *"New Covenant"* shines for a righteous remnant who will live by faith in God's promise.

STUDY 13—Kingdom of the Promise: Exilic Era
(*Lamentations; Ezekiel; Daniel*)

From Babylonian exile, Ezekiel and Daniel continued to sharpen the picture of the coming *"Son of Man."* This One was the focus of God's promise, who as *"the Shepherd"* and the Davidic *"King"* would give *"a new heart and a new spirit,"* fulfill the *"everlasting covenant,"* and establish an *"everlasting kingdom."*

STUDY 14—Triumph of the Promise: Post-Exilic Era
(*Chronicles–Esther; Haggai–Malachi*)

These 8 books, which focus particularly on God's temple, form the "final note of revelation in the OT…They move from the despondency of conditions in Israel after their return from the 70 years of Babylonian Exile to the complete triumph of God's Person, word and work."[16]

STUDY 15—Fulfillment of the Promise: Present and Future Eras
(*New Testament*)

In Jesus the Messiah, God's promise is fulfilled. But while some of the fulfillment is linked with His first coming, and particularly with the accomplishments of His death, resurrection, and exaltation, much still awaits His second coming in power as the King of Glory.

THE GOAL

The Islamic religion requires Muslims to believe in the existence and inspiration of the "Tavrat" and the "Zabur," which are Arabic names referring generally to the OT writings. Yet for various reasons these books are not read today. Sadly, there is no content to a Muslim's belief in these books and they remain simply unknown "holy books."

But even worse, many Christians have never read the Old Testament of their Bible one time, and some not even all of the New Testament. The inevitable result is a shallow, uncertain faith, and an inconsistent, discouraged life. On the contrary, *"Blessed is the man...(whose) delight is in the law of the Lord; and in his law he meditates day and night. And he shall be like a tree planted by the rivers of water, that brings forth its fruit in its season; whose leaf also shall not wither; and whatever he does shall prosper"*(Ps. 1:1-3). Which of these persons are you?

God's purpose in giving His Word is not simply to give us information, but to cause us to know Him and trust Him fully. In particular, He wants us to know the unchangeableness of His purpose for us personally, and by faith to take hold of *"exceeding great and precious promises"* (2 Pet. 1:4). The goal is stated in Hebrews 6:11-12:

> *And we desire that each one of you show the same diligence to the full assurance of hope until the end, that you do not become sluggish, but imitate those who through faith and patience inherit the promises.*

ENDNOTES

1   Richard A. Swenson, MD., *MARGIN—Restoring Emotional, Physical, Financial, and Time Reserves to Overloaded Lives,* NavPress, 1992, p. 41.

2   Ibid., pp. 25-26.

3   Josh McDowell, *Evidence That Demands a Verdict—Vol. 1,* Here's Life Publishers, 1986. p. 30,

4   Adolph Saphir, *Divine Unity of Scripture,* Kregel, 1984, pp. 21-22.

5   W. Graham Scroggie, *Know Your Bible,* Revell, pp. 13-14.

6   *Expositor's Bible Commentary,* Zondervan, Vol. 1, Preface, p. vii.

7   J. I. Packer, in *The New Bible Dictionary,* Eerdman, 1962, pp. 565-566.

8   Reference unavailable.

9   J. N. Darby, *A New Translation,* Revised Preface to Second Edition, p. xix.

10 Walter C. Kaiser, Jr., *Towards an Old Testament Theology,* Zondervan, p. 264.

11 Ibid., p. 22.

12 Ibid., p. 35.

13 Ibid., p. 52.

14 Scroggie, pp. 14-15.

15 This outline has been adapted from Kaiser, pp. 43-49.

16 Ibid., p. 49

1. Choose the correct view of the Old Testament from the following choices:
   a) The Jewish Holy Book (as the New Testament is the Christian Holy Book).
   b) God's Word for the BC generation, no longer valid for us today.
   c) The foundational part of God's Word, able to make us wise for salvation.
   d) The first of four Holy Books sent by God through various prophets.

2. According to this lesson what are two important qualities of the Old Testament?
   a)   b)

3. In Psalm 19:7-9 (see pp. 15-16) the psalmist David describes the value of the Holy Scriptures. In each line he gives one quality of the Word of God and the result it produces on the believer. List these qualities and effects:
   (7a)
   (7b)
   (8a)
   (8b)
   (9a)
   (9b)

4. What are some of the types of writing found in the OT?

   How would you explain the fact that the Scriptures contain such a variety of materials? Is it reasonable to you that all these types of "literature" equally be called "God's Word"?

5. How many books are in the Old Testament as we have it today?
   a) 24   b) 39   c) 66   d) 45

6. Study the diagram of Old Testament books on page 18. What are the two main divisions (types) of books?
   a)   b)

25

What period of world history is covered by the Old Testament writings?

What are the first and last "historical" books in the OT?

What are the first and last "commentary" books in the OT?

7. Explain in your own words the central idea of the Old Testament Scriptures.

8. Who were the two most important OT characters in the giving of God's promise?
    a) Moses and Abraham
    b) Adam and Moses
    c) David and Solomon
    d) Abraham and David

9. Read Psalm 1 completely. How will the Scriptures affect the life of one who reads and meditates on them? What are some differences between the two groups of people in the psalm?

10. In the space below, write Hebrews 6:11-12 in your own words:

11. What do you think this passage means in practical terms? How can we carry it out?

12. Have you ever read completely through the OT scriptures?

    If not, are you ready to commit yourself to doing so during the next year? Why or why not?

ROOTS OF THE PROMISE
PRE-PATRIARCHAL ERA

Recommended Readings: Genesis 3; 6; 9; 11:1-9; 12:1-3

The book of Genesis gives us our "roots" as members of the human race. It is the book of origins or beginnings, and lays the foundation for all of God's revelation to follow. The truth about God and man, good and evil, responsibility and punishment, and divine judgment and salvation is first revealed here. It is quite impossible to make sense of the Bible without Genesis. For this reason we are devoting two entire lessons to this one key book.

Genesis divides simply into two major sections. Chapters 1 through 11 trace the history of *all mankind* from creation to the division into many nations at Babel. Chapters 12 through 50 narrate the history of *one family*, from God's choice of the first "patriarch," Abraham, to the migration of his grandson Jacob's family to Egypt. The first period is called the "Pre-Patriarchal Era." It covers at least 2000 years of our world's history, and lays the essential groundwork for the plan which God reveals through His "Promise."

Following their creation and blessing by God, mankind was overtaken by three great catastrophes or judgments. Each was a result of man's disobedience to God. However, each disaster was followed quickly by a promise from God, who was determined to bless man in spite of his rebellion. Notice this pattern of man's revolt and God's grace:

MAN'S REVOLT		GOD'S GRACE
The FALL (Gen. 3)	⇨	PROMISE of a Seed (Gen. 3:15)
The FLOOD (Gen. 6–8)	⇨	PROMISE to dwell with Shem (Gen. 9:25-27)
The SCATTERING (Gen. 11)	⇨	PROMISE to bless All Nations (Gen. 12:1-3)

We want to consider some fundamental truths that emerge from these chapters. In particular we must grasp the desperate condition of mankind today in relation to our Creator, and lay hold of the same single remedy which God began to reveal to the ancients. We'll begin where the Bible does—with God Himself. It has been truly said that what comes into your mind when you think of God is the most profound thing about you.

THE TRUTH OF GOD: The Creation

"'In the beginning God...' These first four words of the Bible form the foundation for faith. Believe these words, and you can believe all that follows in the Bible."[1] There is a personal, living God who is the Creator of all things. He was there before *"the beginning"* and He will be there after time has run its course. He is infinite, eternal, all-powerful, all-knowing, unchanging, self-existent, and self-sufficient. Yet He is also "personal."

Not only does God exist, but what kind of God exists? The [biblical] God is completely different from all the other gods in the world...God is a personal-infinite God. The gods of the East are infinite by definition, in that they contain everything, including the male and the female equally, the cruel and the non-cruel equally, and so on. But they are never personal. In contrast, the gods of the West, the Greek and the Roman gods, the great god Thor and the Anglo-Saxon gods, were personal but always limited and finite. So the [biblical] God is unique: He is infinite, and He is, at the same time, personal.[2]

As Creator, God deserves and requires our fullest honor, allegiance, and worship:

> *Thou art worthy, O Lord,*
> *To receive glory and honor and power:*
> *For Thou hast created all things,*
> *And for Thy pleasure they are and were created* (Rev. 4:11, KJV).

Anything short of thankfully honoring God as God with our whole heart is sin. When mankind's downward history is summarized in the book of Romans, the indictment is: *"Although they knew God, they did not glorify Him as God, nor were thankful…Who exchanged the truth of God for the lie"* (1:21, 25). Men have willingly rejected the knowledge of God.

"And God said…" Ten times this statement is repeated in Genesis 1-2. The world began "by the divine word of a personal, communicating God."[3] In six majestic days He commanded light (Gen. 1:3-4a), order (4b-19), and life (20-31) for the heavens and the earth. It is common to ridicule the Genesis creation account as unscientific, but no solid scientific evidence has ever refuted it. Instead, *"Through faith we understand that the worlds were framed by the word of God"* (Heb. 11:3).

> *By the word of the Lord were the heavens made;*
> *And all the host of them by the breath of His mouth.*
> *For He spoke, and it was done;*
> *He commanded, and it stood fast* (Psalm 33:6, 9).

MAN: In the Image of God

God is unique. There is none like Him. He asks, *"To whom then will you liken God? Or what likeness will you compare to Him?"* (Isa. 40:18). Yet amazingly God said, *"Let Us make man in Our image, according to Our likeness"* (Gen. 1:26). Distinct from the rest of creation, man was made a personal and *spiritual being,* created for a rich, deep relationship with God. Man was given qualities such as creativity, personality, love, reason, and righteousness in God's own image and likeness. For this reason every human being has tremendous value and dignity, and may not be murdered (Gen. 9:6) or cursed (Jas. 3:9).

Francis Schaeffer points out that on the side of God's infinity there is a vast chasm between the Creator God and all creation, including man. But on the side of God's personality, there is a chasm between man and the rest of creation, because man is made in God's image.

> Only He is infinite and only He is the Creator; everything else is the creature and finite. Only He is independent; everything else is dependent. So man, the animal, the flower, and the machine are equally separated from God in that He created them all…But there is another side—the personal. Here the animal, the flower, and the machine are below the chasm. On the side of God's infinity everything else is finite and equally separated from God; but on the side of His personality God has created man in His own image. Therefore, man's relationship is upward rather than downward…Man is separated, as personal, from nature because he is made in the image of God. That is, he has personality and as such he is unique in the creation, but he is united to all other creatures as being *created…*and finite.[4]

Schaeffer illustrates man's relationship "upward" to God and "downward" to creation in the following diagram:[5]

THE PERSONAL	INFINITE GOD
Man	Chasm
Chasm	Man
Plant	Plant
Animal	Animal
Machine	Machine

In accordance with his unique place in creation, man was also made a *responsible being*. God blessed mankind and charged them with dominion and leadership over God's creation (Gen. 1:28; Ps. 8:3-8). Man was given the right and ability to choose, and would be held responsible for the consequences of his decisions (Gen. 2:15-17). God gave the man *"a helper comparable to him"* originating *"from man"* (2:18-23; 1 Cor. 11:8-9). As male and female together, they reflected the likeness of God (Gen. 1:27), and their marriage union pictured the intimate relationship the Lord intends to have with His people: *"They shall be one flesh"* (Gen. 2:24; see Isa. 54:5-8; Hos. 2:19-20; 1 Cor. 6:16-17; Eph. 5:22-33; Rev. 19:7).

"THE GENERATIONS OF THE HEAVENS AND THE EARTH"

The awesome work of creation was finished. *"God saw everything that He had made, and indeed it was very good"* (Gen. 1:31). The Creator then *"rested"* on the seventh day (Gen. 2:1-3). Of course, this was not the rest of fatigue; *"The everlasting God, the Lord, The Creator of the ends of the earth, neither faints nor is weary"* (Isa. 40:28). Rather this was the rest of completion, satisfaction, and enjoyment of His creatures. His desire was for man to enjoy this "rest" with Him.

The seven-day creation account (Gen. 1:1-2:3) forms a preamble to the five books of Moses, known as the Pentateuch. In fact it is the introduction to the whole Bible. The subsequent history opens in Genesis 2:4 with a remarkable phrase: *"These are the generations of the heavens and the earth"* (NAS margin). This is the first of ten occurrences of a formula used throughout Genesis as a title to mark the beginning of new narrative sections. Rather than simple genealogy, the meaning is something like "This is what happened to..." We learn what became of the ones mentioned in the title, especially in the ensuing generations. So, for example, the narrative beginning in 6:9 has the title, *"These are the generations of Noah"* and it records the story of the great flood. The section beginning with the words, *"These are the generations of Terah"* in 11:10 deals primarily with Abraham's life (11:27–25:11).

In the same way, the section beginning in 2:4 records what became of the heavens and the earth. The chapters following this title tell us how enmity was introduced between heaven and earth and the intimate relationship between them was severed.

Examine the chart below. It shows the general structure of Genesis that emerges from the ten occurrences of the title formula. The ten sections are grouped in five pairs of related themes or characters. (The final occurrence of this formula opens the NT.[6])

God keeps careful record of who we are and what we do. Our actions

THE STRUCTURE OF GENESIS

Preamble: *"In the beginning God created*
the heavens and the earth" 1:1–2:3

---

1. *"These are the generations of **the heavens and the earth"**** 2:4–4:26
   (Primarily the record of the Fall and Adam's first sons)

2. *"The book of the generations of **Adam"*** 5:1–6:8
   (Primarily the record of Seth's descendants)

---

3. *"These are the generations of **Noah"***...................... 6:9–9:29
   (Primarily the record the flood)

4. *"These are the generations of **Ham, Shem** and **Japheth"*** 10:1–11:9
   (Primarily the record the original nations)

---

5. *"These are the generations of **Shem"***...................... 11:10-26

6. *"These are the generations of **Terah"*** 11:27–25:11
   (Primarily the record of Abraham's life—15 chapters)

---

7. *"These are the generations of **Ishmael"*** 25:12-18

8. *"These are the generations of **Isaac"***.................... 25:19–35:29
   (Primarily the record of Jacob's life—11 chapters)

---

9. *"These are the generations of **Esau"*** (twice)......... 36:1-8; 36:8–37:1

10. *"These are the generations of **Jacob"***.................... 37:2–50:26
    (Primarily the record of Joseph's life—14 chapters)

---

have far-reaching consequences in the generations which follow. God often deals with whole nations on this basis. Obedience to Him is more important than we may imagine.

MAN'S FIRST REBELLION AND ITS CONSEQUENCES: The Fall (Gen. 3)

God's relationship to man was in the form of a covenant. The central elements of this covenant were two trees in the middle of the garden: *"the tree of life...and the tree of the knowledge of good and evil"* (Gen. 2:9). In emphatic terms[7] man was commanded to eat of all the trees of paradise, especially the tree of life which represented communion with God, the Source of all life (2:16).

Equally emphatically, God established the principle of responsibility and punishment for His free creatures: *"Of the tree of the knowledge of good and evil you shall not eat, for in the day that you eat of it you shall surely die"* (2:17). This knowledge of good and evil was the right and ability to decide right and wrong for themselves.[8] God had reserved this privilege for Himself, and the inevitable outcome of rebellion against this restriction was clearly stated: *death.*

God had definitely said, *"You shall surely die."* Now Satan, the serpent (see Rev. 12:9), subtly asked the woman, *"Has God indeed said..."* Then, having sown the first seeds of doubt in her mind, he added, *"You will not surely die"* (3:1, 4). The deceiver works to undermine faith in God's goodness and His word. He is *"he is a liar, and the father of it"* (Jn. 8:44). Satan's lie was successful; man broke the covenant (see Hos. 6:7). This revolt against God's command and its consequences is known as "the Fall." Its lasting effects on all mankind were disastrous:

1. DEATH—As God had warned, that very day man "died." *"Just as through one man sin entered the world, and death through sin...thus death spread to all men, because all sinned"* (Rom. 5:12). It is important to understand what is meant by death. We can identify three separate aspects of death.

First, *physical death.* Although Adam did not die physically that day, the dying process began. He was condemned to die, like a branch cut off from the trunk of the tree. The progressive decay of man's body ends in its separation from his spirit and soul (Gen. 5:5). Death, the great enemy, reigns over all the sons of Adam. *"In Adam all die"* (1 Cor. 15:22).

Second, *spiritual death,* or separation from God. When Adam rebelled against God, his spirit was alienated from the life of God and he came under the sentence of death. All men are by nature *"dead in trespasses and sins...by nature children of wrath"* (see Eph. 2:1-3).

Third, if man is not made alive spiritually before physical death occurs, this separation from God becomes eternal. This awful, unending anguish is called *"the lake of fire...the second death."* (Rev. 20:14).

2. SINFUL NATURE—Not only is man under a death sentence, like branches of a condemned tree, but he is also in deep bondage to sin. We inherit a nature prone to sin: " *The heart is deceitful above all things, and desperately wicked"* (Jer. 17:9). Like streams of a polluted fountain, we sin because we are sinners from birth (Ps. 58:3; Gen. 8:21). As a dented mold produces cakes with the same bent shape, so man is fatally bent by the Fall. God's Word describes all human beings as *"man, which drinketh iniquity like water?"* (Job 15:16).

3. GUILTY CONSCIENCE—In the Fall, man also received a conscience, a knowledge of both good and evil. *"The eyes of both of them were opened, and they knew that they were naked"* (3:7). Adam and Eve were filled with shame and fear of their Maker (3:10). Their attempt to cover themselves with leaves and to hide are like all human attempts to cover up or make up for our sins—futile. We know good but lack the power to do it, and know evil without the power to avoid it! Our guilty conscience cannot truly rest until God provides the covering, as He made garments of skin for Adam and his wife by the death of an animal (Gen. 3:21; Heb. 9:14).

4. BONDAGE TO SATAN—By choosing to believe the serpent rather than God, man became the slave of Satan. *"The whole world lies under the sway of the wicked one"* (1 Jn. 5:19), and He is called the *"prince of this world"* (Jn. 12:31; 16:11). Only God's salvation can transfer man *"from darkness to light, and from the power of Satan to God"* (Acts 26:18).

GOD'S FIRST WORD OF PROMISE: "The Seed" (Gen. 3:15)

All seemed lost, but even before passing sentence on him, God gave guilty, fallen man hope. In Genesis 3:15, He intervened with the promise of a future *"seed"* (descendent) who would deliver man from Satan's newly-gained grasp.

> This verse [Genesis 3:15] is known as the *proto-evangelion,* meaning the first gospel. It predicts the perpetual hostility between Satan and the woman (representing all mankind), and between Satan's seed (his agents) and the woman's seed (the Messiah). The woman's seed would crush the devil's head, a mortal wound spelling utter defeat. This wound was administered at Calvary when the Saviour decisively triumphed over the devil. Satan, in turn, would bruise the Messiah's heel. The heel wound here speaks of suffering and even of physical death, but not of ultimate defeat. So Christ suffered on the cross, and even died, but He arose from the dead, victorious over sin, hell, and Satan.[9]

As we will see in this course, this "seed" promise ran on through the ages until, *"when the fullness of the time was come, God sent forth his Son, made of a woman"* (Gal. 4:4).

MAN'S SECOND REBELLION AND ITS CONSEQUENCES: The Flood (Gen. 4-8)

Two ways diverge from Genesis 4. The two seeds (Satan's and the woman's) begin with Adam and Eve's two sons, then become two separate lines of humanity, and end in two different destinies. Scripture describes these two ways:

The path of the just is like the shining sun, that shines ever brighter unto the perfect day...There is a way that seems right to a man, but its end is the way of death (Prov. 4:18; 14:12).

These two ways are illustrated by the offerings brought by Cain and Abel (4:3-5). Cain's offering represented his own labor in the fields and was rejected by God. Abel brought a lamb in faith and was accepted. God's fundamental principle of forgiveness was pictured here: *"Without shedding of blood there is no remission"* (Heb. 9:22).

Following the murder of Abel, Genesis 4 describes the development of Cain's proud, self-centered, restless line, walking without God. In contrast, Genesis 5 records the descendants of Seth, the son given to Adam and Eve by God in place of Abel. This line of faithful men *"began...to call on the name of the Lord"* (4:26) and *"walked with God"* (see 5:21-24; 6:9).

By Noah's day, human society was so corrupted that *"every intent of the thoughts of his heart was only evil continually...the earth also was corrupt before God, and the earth was filled with violence"* (6:5, 11). God was, and still is, deeply grieved by the terrible effects of sin, yet His patience delayed the inevitable judgment which His holiness demanded (6:3). Finally, after long years of warning, the threatened flood came suddenly with awful, inescapable fury. *"All in whose nostrils was the breath of the spirit of life, all that was on the dry land, died"* (7:22). Let's take note of this: If God promised once to judge the world, and then did so, we ought to listen when He has promised to do so again (2 Pet. 3:3-13)!

GOD'S SECOND WORD OF PROMISE: The God of Shem (Gen. 9)

Following the flood, God blessed mankind again (8:17; 9:1, 7). The basis of this blessing was His covenant, ratified through an altar on which Noah offered burnt sacrifices. Despite the Fall, man still carried the divine image. As such his life is precious, and God declared death to be the penalty for murder (9:6). In God's order for the world even today, the state is charged with enforcing this penalty (Rom. 13:4).

In addition to the grace shown to Noah's family by rescuing them from the flood (6:8-18), and by His covenant with all creatures never to destroy the earth by flood again (9:8-17), God followed this second crisis with a second element in His plan. In Noah's prophetic word, after he learned what his son Ham had done to him and cursed Ham's son, Canaan (9:18-25), God revealed His intention to be *"the Lord God of Shem"* in a particular way (9:26). He further said, *"He* (in all probability referring to God) *shall dwell in the tents of Shem"* (9:27), which seems to be a promise to dwell in a unique way with the Semitic peoples (the Shemites), who were the ancestors of Abraham (11:10-26).

MAN'S THIRD REBELLION & ITS CONSEQUENCES: Confusion (Gen. 10-11:9)

Chapter 10 is known as "the table of nations." Beginning with Noah's three sons, the origins of the nations of the earth are given in amazing detail. In all, the roots of seventy families are listed, *"and from these the nations were divided on the earth after the flood"* (10:32).

Yet in spite of great numerical growth, man had not changed. "The third and final crisis to hit the earth during this period of mixed blessing and curse was the concerted effort put forth by the human race to organize and preserve their unity around some architectural symbol."[10] God had commanded Noah and his sons to fill the earth: *"Be fruitful, and multiply, and fill the earth"* (9:1). But when the migrating descendants of Noah reached the Mesopotamian land of Shinar, they made their own plans in open defiance to this command:

> *Let us build ourselves a city, and a tower whose top is in the heavens; let us make a name for ourselves, lest we be scattered abroad over the face of the whole earth* (Gen. 11:4).

Mankind planned to secure a "name" here apart from God. The roots of astrology, sorcery, and false religion can be traced to this ancient tower. In fact, throughout Scripture Babel or Babylon symbolizes deceptive and even demonic religion. In the list of names in chapter 10 special note is made of Nimrod, the founder of Babel (10:8-12). His name means "rebellion" and in the ancient Sumerian religion he and his mother were deified.[11] A final judgment of the false religious "Babylon" which grew out of this lie is yet to come (Rev. 17-18).

After the first rebellion in the garden, God drove Adam and Eve from the garden so they wouldn't eat from the tree of life and live forever in sin (3:22-24). He now came down and *"scattered them abroad from there over the face of all the earth"* by confusing their language (11:5-9). This prevented the unified defiance of God and opened the way *"That they should seek the Lord"* (Acts 17:26-27).

The map on the following page shows the most significant of these ancient civilizations which affect biblical history.

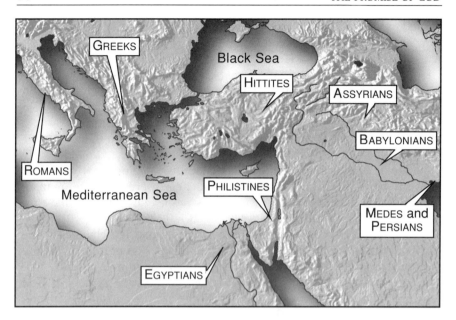

GOD'S THIRD WORD OF PROMISE:
All nations shall be blessed (Gen. 12:1-3)

Following this third judgment, God again brought His word of grace and blessing for the scattered families of the earth. As promised, through the line of Shem we are led to Abraham (11:10-27), whom God calls and gives the great promise of blessing for himself and for the whole earth: *"I will bless you and make your name great; and you shall be a blessing…in you all the families of the earth shall be blessed"* (12:2-3). The great name the nations vainly tried to gain without God (11:4) would be freely given by grace to Abraham and his seed. This next stage in the purpose of God will be the focus of our next study.

CONCLUSION

Three important truths stand out in the early chapters of Genesis. First, God's great desire is to *bless*. Genesis 1 to 11 reveals this fact clearly. At the beginning (Gen. 1:28), at key points during the story (Gen. 5:2; 9:1), and at the conclusion (Gen. 12:3), He promises to bless. God loves mankind, whom He has made in His own image, with a deep, eternal love.

Second, mankind is fallen and alienated from God. Through the first man's sin we and our world are under the *curse* of God instead of His blessing. Man's early history is marked by little but repeated failure and rebellion. Sin and death reign over us, and Satan, the god of this world, has dominion over us. God clearly summed up the human condition in

Genesis 8:21, *"the imagination of man's heart is evil from his youth."* The first critical step in deliverance is to accept the awful fact that we are sinners, separated from the life of God. Left to ourselves we're utterly lost, with no hope of pleasing God or regaining the lost image with which we were created.

Third, because of the rich mercy of God, there is *hope* for mankind. After each crisis and judgment, God intervened with a gracious promise of deliverance. There was to be a redeeming "seed" who would ultimately crush Satan's head and bless all the scattered nations of the earth. Jesus Christ has fulfilled this through His death and resurrection. As God clothed Adam and his wife with the skins of an animal that gave its life, so He provides garments of righteousness for all who come to Him through Jesus, the Lamb of God.

We're called to believe and grasp this single, secure remedy. If we will like Noah obey Him in faith and walk with God, we will *"find grace in the eyes of the Lord"* (Gen. 6:8-9). He will transfer us from the dominion of Satan into His own kingdom and remake us in His own image. The glorious vision at the end of God's Word sums up the sure results of God's purpose for man.

> *He showed me a pure river of water of life, clear as crystal, proceeding from the throne of God and of the Lamb. In the middle of its street, and on either side of the river, was the tree of life, which bore twelve fruits, each tree yielding its fruit every month. The leaves of the tree were for the healing of the nations. And there shall be no more curse, but the throne of God and of the Lamb shall be in it, and His servants shall serve Him. They shall see His face, and His name shall be on their foreheads* (Rev. 22:1-4).

ENDNOTES

1 William MacDonald, *Old Testament Digest,* Vol.1, p.11.

2 Francis A. Schaeffer, *Pollution and the Death of Man—The Christian View of Ecology,* Tyndale, 1973, p. 49. Schaeffer provides tremendous insight into the biblical relationship between man and nature, in which nature has value because God made it.

3 Kaiser, p. 72.

4 Ibid., pp. 49-50.

5 Ibid., p. 49.

6 *"The book of the generation of Jesus Christ, the son of David, the son of Abraham"* (Mt. 1:1, AV). The word "generation" here is "genesis," indicating both genealogy and what follows from a certain origin. This final occurrence tells us that all that follows is what becomes of Jesus and all who belong to Him through spir-

itual birth. Significantly, the birth of Jesus is the last physical birth recorded in Scripture. He is the last Adam, the Seed of Abraham and David, and the true Israel. God is gathering *"together in one all things in Christ, both which are in heaven, and which are on earth; even in Him"* (Eph. 1:10).

7 Literally the two key phrases regarding these two trees are *"Eating you shall eat"* (2:16) and *"dying you shall die"* (2:17). See Henri Blocher, *In the Beginning,* IVP, p. 122.

8 Blocher, p. 132.

9 MacDonald, p. 16.

10 Kaiser, p. 82.

11 According to Alexander Hislop, author of *The Two Babylons,* this mother-infant cult of ancient Babylon formed the basis of the Roman Catholic worship of Mary and the infant Jesus. Hislop gives evidence to show that Roman Catholicism has become the second "Babylon," the head of the great apostate religious body referred to in Revelation 17:5 as *"Babylon the Great, the mother of harlots and abominations of the earth. "*

1. Into what two major sections can we divide the book of Genesis? Whose history is given in each section?

    a)

    b)

2. What three disasters overtake mankind in Genesis 1-11? Identify the cause of each one.

    a)   (Gen. 3)

    b)   (Gen. 6-8)

    c)   (Gen. 11)

3. What can we learn about God and man's relationship to Him from Genesis chapter 1?

4. When God says, *"Let Us make man in Our image, according to Our like-ness"* (1:26), which of the following statements best explains His meaning?

    a) Man was created to look like God.

    b) God can be understood by looking at man.

    c) Man is like God in that he is a spiritual being with the capacity to create, love, and reason.

    What can you add to the explanation?

5. According to Genesis 1:26-30, what was God's purpose in creating man?

    What does this tell you about the value of a human being?

6. In Genesis 2, God warned Adam that if he ate the forbidden fruit he would surely "die." Yet he did not die that day. How can you explain this fact? What kind of "death" was the Lord referring to? What effects has this "Fall" had on you?

7. Read Genesis 3:15 carefully. What two "seeds" are referred to here? How did this promise give hope to Adam and Eve?

8. How does God assess the nature of mankind in the following verses?
    (Gen. 6:5)
    (Gen. 6:11-12)
    (Gen. 8:21)

    Does this accurately describe your own condition? Explain:

9. In Genesis 9:25-27, Noah makes an inspired prophecy? With which of his sons was God's name to be associated in the future?
    a) Ham   b) Shem   c) Japheth

    Trace the family tree of this son in chapter 11:10-27. What connection can you make between Noah's prophecy in 9:25-27 and God's call of Abraham in chapter 12:1-3?

10. In Genesis 10 and 11, we learn how mankind came to be divided into many nations and families. How does God's promise to Abraham in Genesis 12:3 show that God has not lost interest in these nations?

11. What have you learned about man and God from the repeated giving of a promise following man's failures?

    How can you apply this lesson to your own relationship with the Lord?

FAITH IN THE PROMISE
PATRIARCHAL ERA

Recommended Readings: Genesis 12:1-9; 13:14-18; 15; 17; 22:11-19; 26:2-5, 24; 28:10-17; 35:9-15; 48:3-4; 49:10

In the first eleven chapters of Genesis we have seen God dealing with mankind as a whole. The scattering of mankind at Babel marks the end of this period, and from this point on, Old Testament history is concerned with one nation: Israel. Other nations have importance primarily as they come into contact with Israel. A new era began in Genesis 12 as God selected one family through whom He would extend His blessing to all mankind. We can diagram the book of Genesis this way:

Chapters		Chapters	
1	11	12	50
ALL MANKIND		ONE CHOSEN FAMILY	
Creation ⇨	Babel	Call of Abraham ⇨	Egypt

Few men are revered by so many as the patriarch Abraham. Jews, Muslims, and Christians all look to him as their "father"—either physically through his sons, Isaac (Jews) and Ishmael (Muslims), or spiritually, as *"father of all those who believe"* (Rom. 4:11). In this "Patriarchal Era" God revealed Himself and His purposes first to Abraham, then to his son Isaac, and finally to his grandson Jacob. It was a period rich in God's revelation, as He opened His heart to mortal men and entered into eternal agreement with them. We begin to see the gracious provisions of God's promise and the far-reaching scope of His purposes.

This era was so important that from then on God identified Himself as *"the God of your father—the God of Abraham, the God of Isaac, and the God of Jacob"* (see Ex. 3:6, 15). Throughout the ages to come, in difficult times

God's people would plead the unchangeable commitment of God to these three patriarchs. This was the reason why God should not fail them, as Moses argued when Israel had sinned:

> *Remember Abraham, Isaac, and Israel, Your servants, to whom You swore by Your own self, and said to them, `I will multiply your descendants as the stars of heaven; and all this land that I have spoken of I give to your descendants, and they shall inherit it forever* (Ex. 32:13).

Genesis 12 to 50 is organized around the lives of these patriarchs as shown below. The horizontal lines in the diagram represent their lifetimes as recorded in the book:

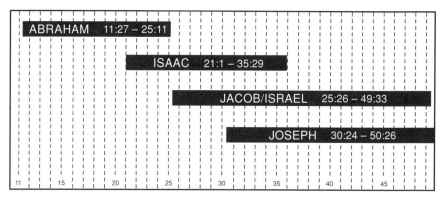

Genesis chapters 11–50

The story told in these chapters is as simple as it is profound. Although it has changed the world, it spans just four generations. God appears to Abraham in Mesopotamia and calls him to move to a strange land in Palestine. Obeying God in faith, Abraham spends his life as a nomadic stranger in that land, living in a tent. His son Isaac and grandson Jacob follow in his ways, never owning even an acre of land. Only Jacob's son Joseph ever gains any political power. After being sold into slavery by his brothers, he rises miraculously to the second highest seat in the Egyptian kingdom. The story ends after the family is reunited in Egypt, where Jacob and his eleven sons have been driven for survival during a great famine.

THE PATRIARCHS AND THEIR NEIGHBORS

These patriarchs live among pagan nations. Their interaction with these nations is interspersed at various points in the narrative, and forms a significant part of the drama:

Abraham
- Migrates temporarily to Egypt during a famine, and deceives Pharaoh about his wife Sarah's identity (12:10-20).

- Forced to intervene in a war between two alliances of local kingdoms to rescue his nephew, Lot; he is blessed by Melchizedek (king of Salem and priest of the Most High God) and refuses the reward offered by the king of Sodom (ch. 14).
- Intercedes with God for the condemned city of Sodom where Lot is living; witnesses the destruction of the city by God (18:16–19:29).
- Lives among the Philistines and deceives their king, Abimelech, also about his wife Sarah's identity (ch. 20).
- Makes a treaty with Abimelech, who has seen that God's blessing is with Abraham (21:22-34).
- Purchases a burial ground for Sarah from the sons of Heth (ch. 23).

Isaac
- Like his father, deceives Abimelech about his wife Rebekah's identity and makes a treaty with him (26:1-17, 26-33).

Jacob
- Moves to Egypt with his sons to meet Joseph and escape the famine (ch. 46).
- Meets and blesses Pharaoh (47:1-11).
- Dies in Egypt; mourned by Egyptians and buried in the place purchased by Abraham back in the land of promise (50:1-14).

Joseph
- Is sold into slavery in Egypt (ch. 37).
- Is blessed by God as a slave and in prison in Egypt; rises to the highest post next to Pharaoh; marries an Egyptian woman and has two sons (chs. 39-41).
- Dies in Egypt; embalmed by Egyptians (50:22-26).

These nations stand in the book of Genesis as ungodly representatives of all the scattered nations. Sodom in particular is given as an example of the depravity into which mankind descends when they turn from the knowledge of God (see Jude 7). Abraham hopes God will find at least 10 righteous people in that wicked city, but they cannot be found (18:16-33)! Even hesitant Lot, who is considered "righteous" by God on the basis of faith in His promise to Abraham, must be dragged from the city (19:1-22). Abraham stands and looks down at the smoke rising after God's fiery judgment falls on the wicked Sodomites (19:27-29).

From these narratives we also learn the origin of five future enemies of God's people: the *Ishmaelites, Moabites, Ammonites, Edomites,* and *Amalekites.* These nations were born out of the sinful mistakes of the patriarchs and their relatives.[1]

SINS OF THE PATRIARCHS AND THEIR FAMILIES

What can we learn from Abraham's and Isaac's repeated deception of Gentile kings (12:10-20; 20:1-18; 26:1-11)? The book of Genesis actually catalogues many disgraceful incidents in the lives of the patriarchs and their families, as well as the sins of unbelieving mankind before the flood (4:16-24; 6:1-13), at the tower of Babel (11:1-9) and in Sodom (13:10,13; 14:21-23; 18:20-21; 19:1-26). Here is an additional list:

- Adam listens to Eve and leads all mankind into sin (3:1-5).
- Cain murders his brother Abel and denies it to God's face (4:1-15).
- Noah disgraces himself by lying naked in a drunken stupor in his tent (9:20-23).
- Abraham listens to Sarah and sleeps with her slave-girl Hagar (16:1-6).
- Lot is debased by his two daughters after being reluctantly delivered from Sodom (19:30-38).
- Jacob deceives his brother Esau twice, first buying his birthright, then stealing his blessing in disguise (chs. 25; 27).
- Jacob deceives his father-in-law Laban by not telling him that he was leaving (31:17-21).
- Rachel steals her father Laban's household idols and then lies to him to hide it (31:19, 33-35).
- Jacob's sons, Simeon and Levi, wipe out a whole clan in revenge for the rape of their sister (ch. 34).
- Joseph's brothers sell their own brother into slavery and deceive their aged father about it (37:18-36).

All of this shows that there is nothing in man, even in the "righteous," to be proud of. The failure of even Abraham, the father of the faithful, is all too evident. Their sins are disgraceful and repugnant. Israel, reading their holy Torah, would constantly be confronted with the sins of their forefathers, and be reminded that only by the sovereign grace of God were they saved. The patriarchs were not chosen because they were holier than other men. Only "by faith" were they justified.

At the same time, as C. H. Mackintosh points out so beautifully, the contrast between the way the world looks at God's people and the way God Himself looks at them is very striking:

> God sees His people in Christ. He looks at them through Christ; and hence He sees them "without spot or wrinkle or any such thing"...But in themselves, they are poor, feeble, imperfect, stumbling, inconsistent creatures; and it is what they are in themselves...that the world takes knowledge of...Yet it is God's prerogative to set forth the beauty, the dignity, and the perfection of His people. It is His exclusive prerogative, inasmuch as it is He Himself who has bestowed those things.
>
> ...In Abraham's case, he might lower himself in the view of Abimelech, and Abimelech might have to rebuke him, yet when God comes to deals with the case, He says to Abimelech, "Behold, thou art a dead man;" and of Abraham He says, "He is a prophet and he shall

pray for thee" (20:3, 7). Yes, with all "the integrity of his heart and the innocency of his hands" the king of Gerar was "but a dead man;" and moreover, he must be a debtor to the prayers of the erring and inconsistent stranger for the restoration of the health of his household. Such is the manner of God. He may have a controversy with His child, on the ground of his practical ways, but directly the enemy enters a suit against him, Jehovah ever pleads His servant's cause. "Touch not Mine anointed, and do My prophets no harm" (Ps. 105:15).[2]

Yet the heart of the patriarchal story is not in the often dismal inter-tribal relationships nor in the sinfulness of the patriarchs themselves. Rather it is found in the unique and holy relationship between these very human men and the Almighty God who chose to use them to carry out His purposes.

How God Promised—The Word of Revelation

Throughout Genesis 12-50, the patriarchs receive divine revelation. They are called "prophets" (20:7; Ps. 105:15), that is, "men who had immediate access to the word and ear of the living God."[3] We find God using at least four ways to reveal Himself to them:

1. At certain key points the patriarchs are addressed directly in spoken words by God—*"The Lord said to him"* or *"The word of the Lord came to him"* (Gen. 12:1, 4; 13:14; 21:12; 22:1).

2. More startling was the fact that the Lord *"appeared to"* these men. This appearing is sometimes called a theophany (see Appendix 8). God's awesome presence marked major turning points in their lives as He blessed, renamed, or sent them (12:7; 17:1; 18:1; 26:2-5, 24; 35:1, 7, 9).

3. Linked with these theophanies was the appearance of "the Angel of the Lord" (16:7-11; 21:17; 22:11-18; 24:7, 40; 31:11, 13; 32:24-30; 48:15-16; see Appendix 8 for a full summary). "Frequently He receives the respect, worship, and honor reserved only for God, yet He was consistently distinguished from God...He carried an identity with God; yet He was also sent from Him!"[4] In the light of the New Testament we recognize Him as the eternal *"Word"* and *"Son," "the Image of the invisible God"* (Jn. 1:1, 14; Heb. 1:2-3; Col. 1:15).

4. God also spoke to them (and others) through *dreams* (20:3; 28:11-17; 31:10-11, 24; 37:5-10; 40:5-16; 41:1-32) and *visions* (15:1; 46:2).

The essential point is that God drew near to reveal Himself to men in such a way that they could comprehend, allowing them to know Him, the Almighty. He becomes *their* God, not just the God of all creation and all nations. He is *"not ashamed to be called their God"* in spite of their many failures and sins (Heb. 11:16). He reveals to the patriarchs His own purposes and intentions for the nations as well as for them. This closeness is particularly illustrated in God's relationship with Abraham (18:17-19), whom he calls a "friend of God" (2 Chron. 20:7; Isa. 41:8; Jas. 2:23). God is not an unknowable force but an infinite, personal Being who wants us to know Him personally and live in vital partnership with Him.

THE THREE-FOLD PROMISE

Abram[5] was still in Mesopotamia when the God of glory appeared to him and said, *"Get out of your country, from your family and from your father's house, to a land that I will show you"* (Gen. 12:1).

Believing that God had commanded him, Abraham set out, traveling first to Haran, a city in the southeast of present-day Turkey. He later moved on to the land of Canaan in what is known today as Israel.

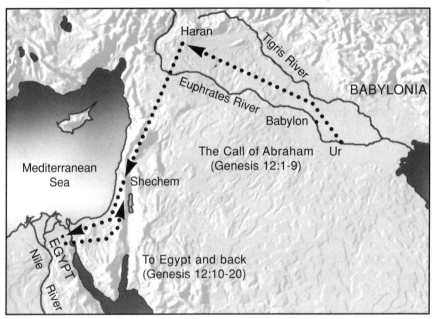

The importance of God's promise to Abraham can hardly be overestimated. It is central to the message of the Scriptures. "The content of this promise was basically threefold: a seed, a land, and a blessing to all the nations of the earth."[6] It began with God entering into a personal agreement with Abraham, which formed the foundation for all that followed:

> *I will make you a great nation; I will bless you and make your name great; and you shall be a blessing. I will bless those who bless you, and I will curse him who curses you; and in you all the families of the earth shall be blessed* (Genesis 12:2-3).

The emphasis here was simply God's intention to bless and to do it through this one man. But as time went by, more specifics became clear. There would be an heir, an inheritance, and a heritage.[7]

A. An Heir—A "Seed"

Beginning from 12:7, the gift of a child who would inherit the promises became a key theme (13:16; 15:3, 5; 17:7, 9-21; 21:12; 22:17-18; 26:3-4, 24; 28:13-14; 32:12; 35:12; 48:3-4). God was going to give to Abraham a seed. While this *"seed"* often referred to the great numbers of descendants, it also referred to the individual sons of the patriarchs. In Genesis 15:3, Abraham said to the Lord, *"Thou hast given no seed,"* meaning that he had no child. God replied, *"He that shall come forth out of thine own [body] shall be thine heir."* He took Abraham outside and showed him the star-studded sky, promising him, *"So shall thy seed be!"* Then He ratified His covenant with an unforgettable sacrifice ceremony (see 15:13-16).

So the whole seed was sometimes seen in a single person who was to obtain victory for the whole group he represented. This concept or plan of God is sometimes called "the one and the many." He dealt with the whole *"seed"* through their representative *"Seed."* Ultimately this principle was fulfilled in Christ: *"For as by one man's* [Adam's] *disobedience many were made sinners, so also by one Man's* [Christ's] *obedience many will be made righteous"* (Rom. 5:19).

Much of the drama of Genesis is found in the obstacles and difficulties which threatened to block this intention. Abraham was too old (17:17); Sarah, Rebekah, and Rachel were all barren (16:1; 17:15-21; 25:21; 30:1). Abraham and Isaac's wives were nearly taken from them by Egyptian and Philistine kings (12:10-20; 20:1-18; 26:1-11). Famine threatened their lives several times (12:10; 26:1; 41:53-57). God Himself tested Abraham's faith by asking him to sacrifice the son of promise (22:1-10). The substitutionary ram provided by God demonstrated clearly that this "seed" (Christ) would be God's supernatural gift, and not man's doing (22:11-18).

"The elder shall serve the younger"

God also made it clear that this seed was not being selected according to normal rules. He said, *"The elder shall serve the younger"* (25:23). Repeatedly the youngest, least important brother or sister is chosen in place of the firstborn to carry out His purposes.[8] Throughout Genesis the story or genealogy of the firstborn is first briefly recorded, and then that of the chosen one. This principle or order is picked up in the NT: *"That was not first which is spiritual, but that which is natural; and afterward that which is spiritual"* (1 Cor. 15:46).

Yet God's sovereign choice never invalidated man's freedom of choice. Cain is the first example of the firstborn rejecting God's purpose for him. But God told him clearly, *"If you do well, will you not be accepted? …sin lies at the door. And its desire is for you, but you should rule over it"* (Gen. 4:7). Isaac's firstborn son Esau likewise despised his privilege and *"for one morsel of food sold his birthright"* (Gen. 25:34; Heb. 12:16).

"YOU MEANT EVIL...BUT GOD MEANT IT FOR GOOD."

Another characteristic of the history of this seed is the strife between brothers, which is in fact just the continuation of the conflict predicted in the garden: *"And I will put enmity between you and the woman, and between your seed and her Seed"* (Gen. 3:15). Over and over in Genesis, brothers deceive, fight, and even kill one another.[9] Yet in spite of the repeated effort of the enemy to undermine the developing plan, God's will is ultimately done. Joseph knew this and could comfort his worried brothers who had sold him into slavery: *"You meant evil against me; but God meant it for good, in order to bring it about as it is this day, to save many people alive"* (Gen. 50:20).

"UNTIL SHILOH COMES"

By the end of Genesis, the promise of a seed is centered in Jacob's son *Judah,* and it has become clear that this would be a "royal" seed, from which God's chosen king would spring. The "scepter," symbolizing royal authority, would continue in Judah's line *"until Shiloh comes"* or *"until he comes whose right it is"* (49:10; note Ezek. 21:27). To Him all the nations would yield obedience. In this way God clarifies His purpose a bit further: His plans include a world ruler who will establish God's perfect kingdom over all the earth.

B. AN INHERITANCE—"All the land of Canaan"

The second element of the promise was the land of Canaan (13:15, 17; 15:7-8, 18; 17:8; 24:7; 26:3-5; 28:13-14; 35:12; 48:4; 50:24). After leaving Haran (in southeast Turkey) Abraham arrived in the land of Canaan (Palestine). *"The Lord appeared to Abram, and said, Unto your seed will I give this land"* (12:7). After Lot chose the rich Jordan valley for himself, *"All the land which you see I give to you and your descendants forever"* (13:15). In Genesis 15:18, the Lord further defined the borders of this land: *"From the river of Egypt to the great river, the river Euphrates."*

Yet the patriarchs themselves never possessed the land, except for a burial site purchased by Abraham in faith (ch. 23). *"By faith he (Abraham) dwelt in the land of promise as in a foreign country, dwelling in tents with Isaac and Jacob, the heirs with him of the same promise"* (Heb. 11:9).

The Lord made a formal covenant with Abraham in chapter 15 that the land was his. But He told him that it would be over 400 years before his descendants took possession, because *"the iniquity of the Amorite is not yet full"* (15:13-16). God would endure the wicked idolatry, child sacrifice, immorality, and cruelty of the people of Canaan for a few more generations before purging the land of them (see Lev. 18:24-28).[10] The fact that God doesn't punish immediately does not mean He won't punish at all.

When Abraham was ninety-nine years old, the promise was made into *"an everlasting covenant"* (17:7, 13, 19), The promised land would be *"an everlasting possession"* for his descendants (17:8; also 48:4).

C. A HERITAGE—"All the nations of the earth…"

The greatest element of the promise was that Abraham and the successive heirs of promise would be the source of blessing to all other peoples on earth. On five separate occasions, the patriarchs were designated as a blessing for all nations: to Abraham in 12:3; 18:18; 22:17-18; to Isaac in 26:3-4; and to Jacob in 28:13-14.

The apostle Paul would later point to this phrase and declare that it was the same "gospel" he preached. Simply put, the good news was that "in [the promised seed] all the nations of the earth shall be blessed" (Gal. 3:8). Thus the embryo of God's good news could be reduced to the…word "blessing."[11]

We see this channel of blessing illustrated as Abraham mediates for Sodom (18:16-33) and prays for the pagan king Abimelech (20:7, 17), as well as in God's blessing on Laban's flocks because of Jacob, and on the Egyptian's household because of Joseph (30:30; 39:5). In fact, Joseph's entire life beautifully pictures God's plan to bless the nations through Abraham's greater Seed (the Messiah). Both Joseph and Messiah were, or will be…

- Beloved by the father
  (Gen. 37:3; Isa. 42:1; Mt. 3:17; 17:5)
- Rejected by his brothers
  (Gen. 37:12-36; Isa. 53:3; Jn. 1:11)
- Endured betrayal and sufferings
  (Gen. 37, 39; Isa. 53:3-10; Mt. 26-27)
- Became deliverer of the nations
  (Gen. 41; Isa. 49:5-13; Lk. 24:46-47)
- Revealed to his brothers
  (Gen. 45; Zech. 12:10; Rom. 11:11-29)

D. RESPONSE TO THE PROMISE—Faith

In these chapters we surely see the *sovereignty* and *grace of God*, choosing Abraham for this role out of the nations, choosing Isaac instead of Ishmael, and Jacob rather than Esau, *"that the purpose of God according to election might stand, not of works, but of Him who calls"* (Rom. 9:11).

We also see that God has determined to bless those who believe Him—beyond all human comprehension. He granted them not only the land of Canaan but also a heavenly inheritance, *"a city which hath foundations, whose builder and maker is God"* (Heb. 11:10). One might have few possessions on earth, but if he is an heir of God, he has everything! It is infinite wealth to be a partaker of His holy calling; we should be filled with thanksgiving!

But what did God require in response to His promises? Simply to believe what He said and obediently, patiently trust Him. It is critical to understand this—we are saved and made righteous in God's sight simply by believing God's promise, just as Abraham in Genesis 15:6: *"He believed in the Lord; and He counted it to him for righteousness."* This verse provides the initial foundation for the crucial doctrine of justification by faith alone, apart from religious works. The apostle Paul carefully expounds this truth from Genesis 15:6 in Romans chapter 4.

We too are called to believe God. Faith is the channel of blessing. He works out His sovereign plans through man's believing response, and in fact *"Without faith it is impossible to please Him"* (Heb. 11:6).

However, this faith must be real or living faith. There is such a thing as "dead" faith: *"For as the body without the spirit is dead, so faith without works is dead also"* (Jas. 2:26). God's promise is certain only to *"that also which is of the faith of Abraham"* (Rom. 4:16). Let's look at Abraham's faith and ask ourselves a simple question: Does my faith resemble his?

1) Real faith is *obedience*. When God called Abraham, he didn't ask questions, he went (Heb. 11:8). When told to sacrifice his own son, he did it. If he'd said, "Lord, I believe. Thank You for the glorious inheritance You want to give me!" and then stayed in Mesopotamia, would that have been faith? No.

Likewise, if we say, "Lord, Thank You for Your wonderful salvation and eternal life," and then live as we like, it is not real faith. Real faith obeys.

2) Real faith is *forsaking*. Abraham left his country, his roots, and his father's house—all that gave him security and status in life—to live in tents. Clearly faith means relinquishing our rights to an inheritance in this world for the sake of an eternal inheritance. An apostle writing to Christian believers in the first century said, *"You had compassion on me in my chains, and joyfully accepted the plundering of your goods, knowing that you have a better and an enduring possession for yourselves in heaven"* (Heb. 10:34). True disciples gladly forsake other allegiances to follow Jesus, knowing that all who forsake anything for Christ's sake *"shall receive a hundredfold, and inherit everlasting life"* (Mt. 19:29).

3) Real faith is *life-long*, not something you dabble in for a while. Abraham lived the rest of his life as a stranger in Canaan. He could have returned, but he was looking for God's promise. Genuine faith results in a life-long journey toward heaven, during which we are no longer "at home" here. It endures, maintained by the faithfulness of God.

4) Finally, Abraham's faith was characterized by *worship*. He and his family lived in *tents*, and the only permanent structures he built were *altars*.[12] Wherever he went, except during his misguided journeys to Egypt, he built altars to worship the Lord (Gen. 12:7-8; 13:4, 18; 22:9), and his sons continued the practice (26:25; 33:20; 35:7). Abraham's perspective were right. He left behind no real estate other than a tomb, but his example of worshipping faith inspires his spiritual heirs to this day.

CONCLUSION

Could these things be said of us? Does our faith resemble Abraham's? Jesus Christ said, *"If ye were Abraham's children, ye would do the works of Abraham"* (Jn. 8:39).

ENDNOTES

1 **Ishmael,** born to Abraham by his wife Sarah's Egyptian slave, Hagar (16:1-16); driven out after Isaac was born (21:9-21); descendants recorded (25:12-18).

   Moab and **Ammon,** born of Lot's drunken, incestuous acts with his two daughters (19:30-38).

   Jacob's twin Esau (also known as **Edom**) despises his birthright and loses his blessing to his scheming brother (ch. 25); marries two pagan Hittite women and Ishmael's daughter (26:34-35; 28:6-9); descendants recorded (ch. 36).

   Amalek was Esau's grandson (36:12, 16).

2 C. H. Mackintosh, *Notes on Genesis,* Loizeaux Inc., pp. 214-216.

3 Kaiser, TOTT, p. 84.

4 Ibid., p. 85.

5 God changed his name to Abraham in Gen. 17:5.

6 Ibid., p. 86.

7 Ibid.

8 Examples in Genesis are Abel (4:1-8), Seth (5:3-4), Isaac (17:18-19), Jacob (25:23), Rachel (29:18), Joseph (37:3), Judah (49:8) and Ephraim (48:19). Both Saul (1 Sam. 9:21) and David are examples of this principle (1 Sam. 16:4-13).

9 Cain and Abel (4:3-8)
   Noah's sons (9:24-27)
   Abraham's and Lot's servants (13:7-12)
   Isaac and Ishmael (21:9)
   Jacob and Esau (25:20-34; 27)
   Jacob and Laban (chs. 29-31)
   Joseph and his brothers (chs. 37-50)

10 See Appendix 7 for discussion of the annihilation of the Canaanite peoples.

11 Kaiser, p. 91.

12 I am indebted to my friend and co-worker Michael Maletich for this insight.

QUESTIONS FOR STUDY THREE

1. What significant change occurs in the book of Genesis at the beginning of chapter 12? Keep in mind that up to this point the history of all humankind has been traced.

2. What four men's lives form the focus in Genesis 12-50?
   a)   c)
   b)   d)

3. In Exodus 3:6 and 3:15, how did God identify Himself to Moses?

4. Through what means did God reveal Himself to the patriarchs in the following passages?
   a) Gen. 12:1, 4
   b) Gen. 12:7; 17:1
   c) Gen. 16:7-13; 18:1-2, 9, 13
   d) Gen. 20:3

5. What were the three provisions of God's great promise to Abraham?
   (1)
   (2)
   (3)

6. Explain the promise of a "seed" in your own words. Through whom would this seed come? Does the seed refer to a group of descendants or to a single person among them? Explain the connection with Genesis 3:15.

7. Read Genesis 15 carefully. Then write out verse 6 below.

   What does the phrase, *"The Lord reckoned it to him as righteousness"* mean to you? What does *"it"* refer to?

How do the following New Testament passages explain this verse? (Rom. 4:3, 9; Gal. 3:6)

In what ways did God confirm His covenant with Abraham in this chapter?

What specific events did the Lord foretell to Abraham in verses 12-16, and what did He covenant to give him in verses 18-21?

8. The most important element of the promise to the patriarchs was repeated five times (Gen. 12:3; 18:18; 22:17-18; 26:3-4; 28:13-14). Write out this promise below and explain, in your own words, God's plan. If necessary, refer to Galatians 3:8 for help.

9. In what ways was the life of Joseph a picture or illustration (type) of the Messiah's career?

10. Define *"faith"* as fully as you can. According to the lesson, what four elements are found in real faith.
   1)
   2)
   3)
   4)

Based on these insights would you be willing to say that you live "by faith"? Why or why not?

PEOPLE OF THE PROMISE
MOSES' FIRST ERA

Recommended Readings: Exodus 1—18

INTRODUCTION TO THE MOSAIC ERA

Moses may be the most notable character in the Old Testament. More chapters of Holy Scripture are devoted to the events of his era than to those of any other until the coming of the Messiah Himself. The period from Moses' birth to his death fills four large books of the Bible, totaling 144 chapters (Exodus, Leviticus, Numbers, and Deuteronomy).

The events of this era carry great importance for our understanding of the progressive revelation of God's plan. Therefore He has given us a detailed record of the great things accomplished through His prophet. Deuteronomy 34:10-12 summarizes Moses' career this way:

> *Since then there has not arisen in Israel a prophet like Moses, whom the Lord knew face to face, in all the signs and wonders which the Lord sent him to do in the land of Egypt, before Pharaoh, before all his servants, and in all his land, and by all that mighty power and all the great terror which Moses performed in the sight of all Israel.*

During Moses' lifetime, God powerfully delivers Israel from Egyptian slavery and adopts them as His own people or "congregation." He then gives them His holy Law or Commandments to live by, and comes down to dwell personally among them and lead them to the land He promised to the patriarchs. Certain key events form the chronological backbone of Moses' era:

STUDY 4	
EXODUS	ISRAEL'S BONDAGE IN EGYPT
chs. 2-3	⇨ Birth & call of Moses to lead Israel Pharoah's resistance and the plagues
chs. 12-15	⇨ The Passover & the Red Sea deliverance Wilderness provisions

STUDY 5	
chs. 19-20	⇨ The Covenant (10 Commandments) Tabernacle construction
LEVITICUS	THE SACRIFICIAL SYSTEM, PRIESTHOOD, AND LAW ARE ESTABLISHED IN DETAIL

STUDY 6	
NUMBERS	FIRST CENSUS, ASSIGNMENTS
chs. 9-10	⇨ Moving out from Sinai Journeying & complaining
chs. 13-14	⇨ The failure of Israel to enter the land 40 years wandering in the desert
chs. 22-24	⇨ Arrival in Moab, Baalam's prophecies Second census, Preparations for inheriting Canaan
DEUTERONOMY	MOSES REVIEWS ISRAEL'S HISTORY
ch. 5	⇨ The Covenant Renewed (10 Commandments) The Law expounded and applied in detail
ch. 34	⇨ The Death of Moses

We will devote three studies to the era of Moses. Our present study (Study 4) will focus on the period from Israel's deliverance out of Egypt to their arrival at Mount Sinai. Studies 5 and 6 will cover the rest of Moses' lifetime and the books of the Pentateuch as shown above.

EXODUS 1–18: THE DRAMA OF REDEMPTION

Exodus contains some of the richest, foundational theology of all the books of the O. T. Preeminently, it lays the foundations for a theology of God's revelation of His person, His redemption, His law, and His worship. It also initiates the great institution of the priesthood and the role of the prophet, and formalizes the covenant relationship between God and His people."[1]

In particular, the first eighteen chapters of Exodus record the most dramatic demonstration of God's power in all the Old Testament as He intervenes in human history to deliver and take possession of Abraham's descendants. We can think of these events as a "drama of redemption" in six stages or "acts."

ACT I—GOD REMEMBERS HIS COVENANT (EX. 1–2)

When He changed the name of Abraham's grandson Jacob to "Israel," God told him, *"I am God Almighty: be fruitful and multiply; a nation and a company of nations shall proceed from you"* (Gen. 35:11). Now, more than 400 years later, as the book of Exodus opens, we see that God has kept His word: *"The children of Israel were fruitful and increased abundantly, multiplied and…the land was filled with them"* (Ex. 1:7). The promised seed was now more than a family; it had become a "people" (Ex. 1:9).[2]

But the scene is dark when Act I opens. The Israelites are in bondage, groaning under the weight of ever-increasing forced labor. The latest Egyptian king or "Pharaoh" knows nothing of the blessing which came to Egypt through Israel's great ancestor, Joseph (Gen. 41; 47:13-26). In an effort to reduce what he perceived as a threat to Egypt's security from the massive Israelite population, Pharaoh orders the execution of all Israelite boys under two years of age.

At this dark hour Moses is born. With his birth and miraculous protection by Pharaoh's own daughter, God begins His intervention on behalf of His suffering people. Forty-year-old Moses is rejected when he attempts to help his own people: *"Who made you a prince and a judge over us?"* (Ex. 2:11-14; see Acts 7:23-35). He is forced to flee to the Sinai wilderness where he will live and learn for another forty years. During that long period Israel began crying to God for help, and He *"heard their groaning, and God remembered His covenant with Abraham, with Isaac, and with Jacob"* (Ex. 2:24).

We should take courage in the fact that God remembers His promises in even the most difficult, and apparently hopeless and endless, situations.

ACT II—THE LORD AND MOSES (3:1–7:5)

The focus of Act II is God revealing Himself and calling a reluctant Moses to be His messenger to Pharaoh. Appearing in flaming brightness in the famous "burning bush," the Lord tells Moses to remove his shoes, *"for the place where you stand is holy ground. Moreover He said, I am the God of your father—the God of Abraham, the God of Isaac, and the God of Jacob"* (Ex. 3:5-6). Then He tells Moses in 3:7-8 what is on His heart:

> *I have surely seen the oppression of My people…So I have come down to deliver them out of the hand of the Egyptians, and to bring them up from that land to a good and large land, to a land flowing with milk and honey!*

Moses asks His name, and God reveals for the first time His own unique proper name: "Yahweh" (usually written "the LORD"), which means *"I am that I am"* (3:14). He is the absolutely self-existent God. After much resistance, Moses finally consents to go to Pharaoh with the message to let God's people go free (Ex. 4:1-17).

While instructing Moses on what to say to Pharaoh, the Lord says in passing, *"Israel is My son, My firstborn"* (4:22). This phrase contains in seed form much of God's eternal purpose for mankind, who were created in God's image to worship and enjoy the heavenly Father forever as His sons and daughters. The word "firstborn" hints at the ultimate goal of redemption: *"Whom He foreknew, He also predestined to be conformed to the image of His Son, that He might be the firstborn among many brethren"* (Rom. 8:29). God is at work *"bringing many sons to glory"* (Heb. 2:10).

The first round in the confrontation with Pharaoh goes badly. Pharaoh refuses to obey God's command, arrogantly asking, *"Who is the Lord, that I should obey His voice to let Israel go? I do not know the Lord, nor will I let Israel go"* (5:2). His only response is to increase the Israelite's, already heavy burden. The Israelites in turn accuse Moses and his brother Aaron of only making things worse for them (5:21). Moses pours out his complaint to the Lord, *"neither have You delivered Your people at all"* (5:23). However, God acts according to His own time schedule, not ours.

The Lord, in a very important passage linking the past age of patriarchal promise to the coming deliverance, re-commissions Moses. As He had done at the burning bush, He again declares His Name, *"I am Yahweh. I appeared to Abraham, to Isaac and to Jacob as God Almighty (El Shaddai), but by My name Yahweh I was not known to them. I have also established My covenant with them...and I have remembered My covenant"* (6:2-5 NASB).

Then in a seven-fold "I will" statement, God commands Moses to declare again to the Israelites His unchanged purpose:

I will bring you out from under the burdens of the Egyptians,
I will rescue you from their bondage,
I will redeem you with an outstretched arm, and with great judgments:
I will take you as My people, and I will be your God:
Then you shall know that I am the Lord your God, who brings you out from under the burdens of the Egyptians.
I will bring you in unto the land, which I swore to give it to Abraham, Isaac, and Jacob; I will give it to you as a heritage: I am the Lord. (6:6-8)

Nothing will stop Him. The Lord again sends Moses and Aaron to Pharaoh (6:10-13, 28–7:2).

ACT III—THE LORD AND PHARAOH (7:6–11:10)

For God's people to be set free, the power that held them in bondage must be broken. In Act III, the Lord begins to deal with His enemies. His declared purpose is that *"the Egyptians shall know that I am the Lord, when I stretch out My hand on Egypt and bring out the children of Israel from among them"* (7:5).

After receiving a preliminary warning and the sign of Aaron's rod becoming a snake, Pharaoh's heart becomes hard and he refuses to listen. So the Lord begins to bring plague-judgments on Egypt as warnings not to resist God.

Three cycles of plagues begin in 7:14. Each cycle is made up of three plagues. The cycles increase in severity, and each is preceded by an early morning confrontation at the Nile River.[3] Pharaoh receives stern declarations of Yahweh's inescapable presence, His incomparability, and His awesome, universal power. During each cycle of plagues the Lord states His purpose clearly: to reveal His identity as Yahweh, the only Sovereign of the earth.

CYCLE 1—IRRITATIONS, affecting river and land

1. Water turned to blood (7:14-25)	*"In this you shall know*
2. Frogs cover the land (8:1-15)	*that I am Yahweh"*
3. Dust becomes lice (8:16-19)	(7:17; 8:10 and 8:19 NASB)

CYCLE 2—DESTRUCTIONS, upon man and beast

4. Insects (8:20-32)	*"You may know that I am*
5. Pestilence (9:1-7)	*Yahweh in the midst of the earth"*
6. Boils (9:8-12)	(8:22 NASB)

CYCLE 3—DEATH, from above (sky and wind)

7. Hail (9:13-35)	*"That you may know that there is*
8. Locusts (10:1-20)	*none like Me in all the earth. (9:14)*
9. Darkness (10:21-29)	*"That you may know that the earth*
	is Yahweh's" (9:29)

Again and again Pharaoh hardens his heart, stubbornly refusing to acknowledge the Lord's authority and supremacy. A careful study of the references to Pharaoh's hardening heart shows that the Lord hardens Pharaoh's heart only after the king's own refusals to listen. In fact, in the Exodus account, 10 times Pharaoh hardens his own heart, and 10 times the Lord hardens Pharaoh's heart.[4]

The royal magicians at first succeed in imitating the plagues (7:11, 22; 8:7), but by the third plague they are forced to admit: *"This is the finger of God"* (8:19). And before long they are unable to stand before Moses because of the agonizing boils covering their bodies (9:11). Yet Pharaoh would not listen.

Finally the Lord warns Pharaoh of a tenth and final plague or judgment. All the firstborn males of Egypt were to die (11:5). God had told him long before, *"Israel is My son, My firstborn. So I say to you, let My son go that he may serve Me. But if you refuse to let him go, indeed I will kill your son, your firstborn."* (4:22-23). Now the time has come. But not a single Israelite would die if they accepted God's provision.

In all these dreadful "acts of God," we see His wrath against the idolatry and false religion which lead people to destruction. Quite a number of the plagues were "judgments" directed at Egypt's so-called gods.[5] In particular, the execution of the firstborn showed the falseness of the Egyptian deities, which often took the form of animals, and of Pharaoh himself, who was deified as the son of the sun-god Ra: *"I will...strike all the firstborn in the land of Egypt, both man and beast; and against all the gods of Egypt I will execute judgment: I am the Lord"* (12:12; see also Num. 33:4).

The conflict between the Lord and Pharaoh was admittedly one-sided. Pharaoh's stubborn refusal to bow to the Lord's command was permitted by God to demonstrate the foolishness of hardening one's heart against his Maker. It is a fatal misjudgment to make the Lord force you to acknowledge His supremacy. Much better to bow willingly. But ultimately, one way or the other, *"You will know that I am the Lord."*

ACT IV—THE LORD AND THE FIRST-BORN (12:1–13:16)

"Exodus chapter twelve is the birth chapter of Israel as a nation. The birth-pangs are over and the deliverance is at hand."[6] Even the year is changed to mark this new beginning (12:1-2). The Lord commands each Israelite family to select a flawless lamb, then to slaughter it and put its blood on the doorposts and lintel of their house. His promise is, *"When I see the blood, I will pass over you, and the plague shall not be upon you to destroy you, when I smite the land of Egypt"* (12:13).

The lamb died in place of the firstborn son, clearly establishing the unchanging principle of redemption from God's wrath through the bloody death of an innocent substitute. To benefit from this deliverance each family had to personally apply the lamb's blood to the door of their own house, trusting God to keep His promise.

The annual Passover and Feast of Unleavened Bread, together with the custom of redeeming every firstborn, were to remind Israel of this awful cost (12:14-20, 24-27, 42-49; 13:1-16). In this symbolic way God revealed a bit more of His mysterious plan to provide salvation for mankind through the voluntary death of the perfect "Passover Lamb," Jesus the Messiah. His death and resurrection during the Passover celebration fulfilled this plan for all who believe. *"Christ our Passover is sacrificed for us"* (1 Cor. 5:7).

The terrible blow falls and the land of Egypt echoes with wails of anguish. A son lies dead in every unbelieving Egyptian household. Pharaoh calls Moses, *"Then he called for Moses and Aaron by night, and said, Rise, go out from among my people, both you and the children of Israel. And go, serve the Lord as you have said"* (12:31). The Egyptian people also urged them to hurry and leave, *"We shall all be dead!"* That very night the "Exodus" begins. Just as God promised Abraham long before, they go out laden with great plunder and riches given to them by the frantic Egyptians (Gen. 15:14; Ex. 12:35-36).

ACT V—THE LORD AND PHARAOH'S ARMY (13:17–15:21)

Yet Israel's deliverance is not complete. God's redemption of Israel is in two stages. First, He redeemed them from His own judgment through the blood of the Passover Lamb. Now He delivers them from the attack of their enemy through the power of the Red Sea passage.

No sooner have the Israelites escaped from Egypt than Pharaoh comes charging after them with his powerful army of chariots and horsemen. But all is in the Lord's plan. In Act V, He speaks to Moses three times:

1) *"Speak to the children of Israel, that they turn..."* (14:2).

With these words the Lord determines the final conflict with the arrogant Pharaoh, setting it up in order to demonstrate His righteous wrath and awesome power. He says repeatedly, *"I will gain honor over Pharaoh and over all his army, that the Egyptians may know that I am the Lord"* (14:4, 17, 18). God is truly glorified when He judges with complete authority and justice.

With this command He also leads His people straight into a seemingly hopeless situation, caught between Pharaoh's army and the Red Sea, so that they may learn to trust Him alone. Moses tells them, *"Fear not, stand still and see the salvation of the Lord"* (14:13).

2) *"Speak to the children of Israel, that they go forward!"* (14:15).

The Lord moves into action as the "Angel of the Lord" (14:19-20). The pillar of cloud which lead them out of Egypt (13:21-22) now moves between them and Pharaoh's army, a source of light to them but of darkness to the Egyptians (14:20). The Lord opens a thoroughfare through the middle of the sea. By faith the Israelites step between the towering walls of water and cross over into freedom.

3) *"Stretch out your hand over the sea, that the waters may come back"* (14:26).

Pharaoh's army makes a fatal mistake and tries to follow the Israelites. God's wrath falls on them, finally crushing Pharaoh's rebellion against his Creator. Their corpses litter the coast of the sea, a dreadful testimony to the fact that God is the judge of the ungodly. Thus Israel begins to learn the *"fear of the Lord"* (14:31).

In chapter 15, a great song celebrates the Lord's mighty victory. The Lord is the "Man of War," who fights wonderfully for the one who belongs to Him, but terribly against the one who resists Him. In the midst of this song a key verse looks ahead to the taking of the promised land, *"You will*

*bring them in and plant them in the mountain of Your inheritance, in the place,
O Lord"* (15:17). No enemy can stop Him. He will not rest until all His
loved ones are with Him.

ACT VI—THE LORD AND HIS PEOPLE (15:22–18)

The final act finds Israel beginning their journey to Canaan
(Palestine). The Lord also begins the long process of training the grumbling, rebellious people He has redeemed. He promises to be their
"Healer," keeping them from the diseases of the nations, if they will only
listen to Him (15:26). He provides "bread from heaven" (manna) for their
hunger (ch. 16) and water from the rock for their thirst (17:1-7). He gives
them their first taste of battle, in a victory over the Amalekites, declaring
Himself as *"The Lord my Banner"* (17:8-16). And finally, through Moses'
father-in-law Jethro, He provides them with wisdom for government
(ch. 18).

The curtain falls as Israel, grumbling yet sustained by the Lord's
grace, reaches Mount Sinai (19:1-2). They are a free but ignorant people,
redeemed by the Lord their God.

CONCLUSION

Hundreds of years before Moses, God made a mysterious covenant
with Abraham and told him,

> *Know certainly that your descendants will be strangers in a land that is not
> theirs, and will serve them, and they will afflict them four hundred years.
> And also the nation whom they serve I will judge; afterward they shall come
> out with great possessions* (Gen. 15:13-14).

God has now demonstrated beyond all shadow of doubt that what He
has promised He is also able to perform. He delivered His people and
judged their enemy in such a way as will never be forgotten.

Nothing can stop Him from carrying out His promises. We should
sing for joy with ancient Israel (Ex. 15:2),

> *The Lord is my strength and song,*
> *And He has become my salvation:*
> *He is my God, and I will praise Him;*
> *My father's God, and I will exalt Him.*

ENDNOTES

1 Walter Kaiser, *The Expositor's Bible Commentary,* Exodus, p. 292

2 Note how the book of Exodus begins. The prominent fact is the fulfillment by God of His repeated promise to multiply the seed of the patriarchs. Kaiser says, "Verses 1-7 are a virtual commentary on the ancient promise made to Abraham, Isaac, and Jacob that their seed would be as numerous as the stars of heaven and the sands of the sea (e.g. Gen. 15:5; 22:17). In fact, as if to underscore this connection with Genesis,

> vv. 1-4 virtually repeat Genesis 35:22-26;
> v. 5 is a reiteration of Genesis 46:27;
> v. 6 of Genesis 50:26; and
> v. 7 of Genesis 1:28   (Ibid., p. 302).

3 Ibid., p. 348

4

Pharaoh hardens his heart:	God hardens Pharaoh's heart:
3:19	4:21; 7:3 (prophetic)
7:13 (NASB), 14, 22; 8:15, 19, 32; 9:7	9:12
9:34, 35	10:1, 20, 27; 11:10; 14:4, 8, 17

5 This is demonstrated in part by the nature of the plagues which destroyed or used those very things that the Egyptians worshiped as gods. The following plagues were clearly judgments directed at certain Egyptian gods.

> #1 Nile turned to blood—The Nile River was worshiped as the supreme good god of Egypt, *Osiris.* Blood was the symbol of the evil god *Typhon.*

> #2 Frogs—the goddess *Hekt*

> #4 Insects/beetles—the Egyptian sun-god *Ra* had the head of a beetle

> #8 Locusts—the god *Serapis* was supposed to protect from locusts

> #9 Darkness—the sun-god *Ra* was thus shown to be utterly impotent

6 Gaebelein's *Concise Commentary on the Bible,* p. 63.

1. Under what kind of conditions were the Israelites living in Exodus 1–2, and how did the Lord respond to their distress (2:24)?

2. In Exodus 3 God reveals His name? What does this name mean?

3. In Exodus 6:6-8, God commands Moses to declare His purpose to the Israelites. On the seven lines below, write out the seven things God promises to do with the words "I will...".
   1)
   2)
   3)
   4)
   5)
   6)
   7)

4. What was God's purpose in bringing plagues on the land of Egypt, according to Exodus 7:5, 17; 8:22 and 9:14?

5. What was the reason God gave Pharaoh originally to let Israel go (Ex. 4:22-23)? What connection had God made between Israel and Pharaoh's firstborn son?

6. Through the central events of the Passover in Exodus 12, what principles of God's plan to redeem mankind were established?

What was God's promise to obedient Israelites in 12:13?

How does this promise apply to those who believe in Christ as the Lamb of God (1 Cor. 5:7)?

7. The lesson notes refer to two stages of God's redemption. What are they?
    1)

    2)

8. What did the Lord want Israel to learn as He deliberately allowed them to be trapped by Pharaoh's army after escaping Egypt (Ex. 14:13-14, 30-31)? How can we apply this to our own struggles?

9. According to Exodus 14:4 and 14:17-18, what did God want the Egyptians to learn through the Red Sea events?

10. Read the song of Moses in Exodus 15. What is the source of the Israelites' joy in verses 1-3? What has the Lord done for you that gives you cause to celebrate?

11. In chapters 16–18, the Israelites begin their new life with the Lord. How does the Lord provide for their needs? What kind of attitude do they display toward the Lord and Moses?

12. How can you apply this lesson to your own relationship with the Lord?

PEOPLE OF THE PROMISE
Moses' Second Era

Recommended Readings: Exodus 19; 25–31; 40; Leviticus 1; 8–10; 16

In the book of Genesis, God promised Abraham, *"In you all the families of the earth will be blessed."* Four hundred years later, Abraham's descendants, the Israelites, have finally been delivered from bondage in Egypt through unforgettable displays of God's power and faithfulness. Our last lesson ended with Israel arriving as a redeemed people at Mount Sinai, where they were to camp for more than a year. There at the holy mountain God revealed Himself to His servant Moses as never before to any man. The sacred record of the Lord's words to Moses at Sinai fill most of the chapters from Exodus 19 to Numbers 10.

The Lord had redeemed His people for a unique relationship with Himself. When they arrived at Mt. Sinai, He told them of His great plan:

You have seen what I did to the Egyptians, and how I bore you on eagles' wings and brought you to Myself…you shall be a special treasure to Me above all people; for all the earth is Mine. And you shall be to Me a kingdom of priests and a holy nation (Ex. 19:4-6).

Why did God choose Israel? How can a truly just God favor one people above others? At least part of the answer lies in these verses. Israel was to be a channel of blessing to all nations, a "priestly nation." As a true, biblical priest represents man to God and God to man, so the Israelites were to be God's representatives to the idolatrous nations around them. Through them, as through Abraham, Isaac, Jacob, and Joseph before, all the peoples of the world were to be blessed by God. But a massive transformation was necessary to fit Israel for this task.

If Israel was to be a blessing to all the other nations, then Israel must

for this purpose be separated from all the other nations. This separation was to be effected by a revelation to her of the holiness of God."[1]

Above all, Israel was to be distinguished by holiness: *"You shall be holy
to Me: for I the Lord am holy, and have separated you from other people, that you
should be Mine"* (Lev. 20:26; see also Lev. 11:44-45; 19:2; 20:7).

God had referred to Israel as *"My son, My firstborn"* (Ex. 4:22-23). By
bringing the nation into being, God was, metaphorically speaking,
"Fathering" them. Moses reminded them later, *"Is He not your Father, who
bought you? Has He not made you and established you?"* (Deut. 32:6). Thus
there was to be a family relationship, not merely an ethnic, political, or
social unity, and a family likeness—a restoring of the God-like holiness
lost in the Fall.

Sadly, throughout their history, Israel failed in this calling and became
as wicked as the other nations. Nevertheless, the unchanging principles
found in Exodus 19–40 and Leviticus still teach us (Part I) what is necessary for God to dwell with us, and (Part II) what is necessary for us to
dwell with God.

PART I—GOD DRAWS NEAR TO HIS PEOPLE (EX. 19-40)

"Let them construct a sanctuary for Me that I may dwell among them."
In the most awe-inspiring event of the Old Testament, the Lord
Himself descended upon Mount Sinai in blazing fire. Moses was repeatedly commanded to warn the people to stay away from the mountain,
"lest many of them perish" (Ex. 19:10-13, 21-22, 24). Mount Sinai was all in
smoke, and the whole mountain quaked violently. There was thunder and
lightning flashes and a long trumpet blast. When the trembling people
saw and heard all this, they begged Moses to mediate for them, *"Let not
God speak with us, lest we die!"* (20:19). Moses told them, *"Fear not: for God
is come to prove you, and that his fear may be before your faces, that ye sin not"*
(20:20, KJV).

To train Israel for this special relationship with Himself, the Lord gave
them His Law (chs. 20–23), beginning with the Ten Commandments (20:1-
17). It was not given so they could become His people. They were already
His purchased possession by grace, by "the free loving act of deliverance
from Egypt."[2] But because they were His, God's holy character became
Israel's standard: *"Be holy, for I am holy"* (Lev. 11:45).

"The single most important fact in the experience of this new nation
of Israel was that God had come to 'tabernacle' or 'dwell' in her midst."[3]
In amazing condescension the Lord of Heaven spoke to Moses, *"Let them
make Me a sanctuary; that I may dwell among them"* (Ex. 25:8). This confirmed
His ancient promise to *"dwell in the tents of Shem"* (Gen. 9:27, see p. 34-35).

THE TABERNACLE

God's intention for the tabernacle is stated clearly in Exodus 29:43-46:

> *I will meet with the children of Israel, and the tabernacle shall be sanctified by My glory. So I will consecrate the tabernacle of meeting and the altar...I will dwell among the children of Israel and will be their God. And they shall know that I am the Lord their God, who brought them up out of the land of Egypt, that I may dwell among them. I am the Lord their God.*

For the infinitely holy God to dwell among sinful mortals, He Himself must prepare the way. In Exodus chapters 25–28, the Lord gives Moses detailed instructions in how to build the special tent of worship called the "tabernacle," warning him, *"See to it that you make them according to the pattern which was shown you on the mountain"* (Ex. 25:40). In this tabernacle and its furniture God was teaching His people the basic lessons of His conditions for dwelling among men. Notice three key points:

A) ***God desires to dwell in fellowship with men.*** The very existence of this tabernacle tells us much about the heart of the gracious God who is willing to come down and be with His creatures. He loves the men and women He has created, and in spite of their stubborn sinfulness, desires true friendship with them. True, He is *"the High and Lofty One who inhabits eternity, whose name is Holy."* But He adds, *"I dwell in the high and holy place, with him who has a contrite and humble spirit"* (Isa. 57:15; see also Isa. 66:1-2).

Amazing as it is, He teaches us that His eternal purpose is to dwell among men. The Bible's closing chapters tell us of the ultimate fulfillment of this grand plan:

> *Behold, the tabernacle of God is with men, and He will dwell with them, and they shall be His people. God Himself will be with them and be their God.* (Rev. 21:3).

B) ***God dwells in unapproachable holiness.*** We also learn from the tabernacle that God dwells in unapproachable holiness and light. He is so holy and glorious that man cannot approach Him and live. In the language of the New Testament, He is *"the blessed and only Potentate, the King of kings and Lord of lords, who alone has immortality, dwelling in unapproachable light, whom no man has seen or can see* (1 Tim. 6:15-16).

Therefore, as can be seen in the diagram on the following page, a high linen curtain with one entry surrounded the courtyard walls (Ex. 27:9-18). A heavy screen separated the sanctuary itself from the courtyard (26:36-37). Another veil separated the *"Holy Place"* from the *"Holy of Holies"* where the glory of God appeared above the ark of the covenant (26:31-33). This ark represented the throne of Almighty God (Isa. 6:1). One who entered the holy place wrongly, died instantly. One who touched the holy furniture wrongly, died instantly. Any who performed the tabernacle service wrongly, died instantly. Every detail of the tabernacle shouted the solemn lesson that *"No man can see Me and live!"* (Ex. 33:20). Sinful man cannot approach the holiness of God, a *"consuming fire"* (Deut. 4:24).

C) God has prepared the means to reconcile men to Himself and allow them to approach Him. To bridge the awful chasm between sinful man and Himself, the Lord established a single, unchanging way. He revealed this way of approach in the five articles of furniture on the path from the courtyard door to the most holy place (see the sketch below):

- The Altar of Burnt Offering
- The Laver for Cleansing
- The Table with the Bread of the Presence
- The Seven-fold Lampstand
- The Altar of Incense

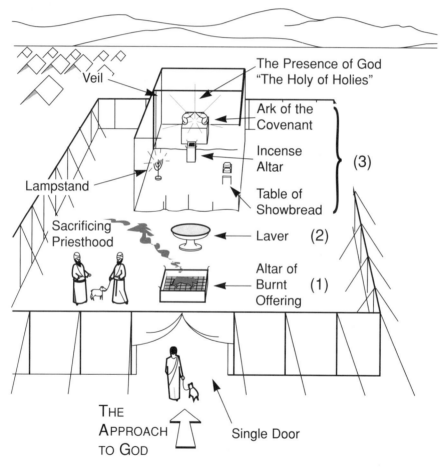

Through these pieces of furniture, the Lord was laying down the principles by which He saves man from his sin and maintains him in His own presence. For sinful man to approach God, the following three things are essential:

1) His sins must be forgiven. Like a welcome mat at the front door of a house, the altar at the door of God's house was the place where the black guilt of sins was removed. Only by the blood of an innocent, spotless sacrifice could sins be forgiven. The reason is that sin's penalty is death. Death must take place for sin to be justly forgiven under God's law, and so the sacrificial animal died in the place of the sinning human, thereby paying the death penalty and atoning for the sin.

This altar symbolized the cross upon which Christ would die centuries later. The sacrificial animals symbolized Christ Himself, the Lamb of God. He was perfectly sinless, but on the cross took upon Himself our sins. His death paid the penalty for the sins of the world.

2) He must be washed. The priest, who represented the people, must be washed with the water from the "laver" or special basin before entering the Holy Place. This represented the removing of the defilement or dirt of sin. To stand in the Holy Place one must have *"clean hands, and a pure heart* (Ps. 24:4). One must have that inner *"holiness, without which no man shall see the Lord"* (Heb. 12:14). Sinful man is not only *guilty,* but also *defiled* as a result of sin. Germs and viruses which are invisible to the naked eye can kill us from within. Likewise inner hatred, bitterness, immorality, lying, etc., defiles and kills our spirit. Not only must man's guilt be removed by the blood of a sacrifice, but also he must be washed from the defilement of his sins. God later provided both forgiveness and cleansing through Christ.

Jesus rose from the dead on the third day. Through the power of His resurrection He gives new life to all who believe in Him. Forty days later, He ascended into heaven and sat down on the throne of God as Lord and Saviour. Another week later, He sent the promised Spirit to dwell within His disciples. The Holy Spirit, taking up residence in their hearts, washed and renewed them completely (see Titus 3:5). While many religions give hope of divine forgiveness, only in the gospel of Christ is divine regeneration offered.

3) He must have intercession. The third necessity for sinful man to approach the holy God was continual intercession. God appointed the sons of Moses' brother, Aaron, for this service in the Holy Place. Regularly they entered the first section of the tabernacle and maintained the three articles of furniture which symbolized this intercession for the people. These pieces of furniture were the Lampstand, the Table, and the Incense Altar. In the Holy Place the priests performed the following service:

- They filled the seven lamps with pure olive oil, keeping them burning night and day. Through His priestly work as *"the Light of the World"* (Jn. 8:12), Christ enables His people to walk in light.
- Each Sabbath day they replaced the twelve loaves of bread on the table which symbolized the people's fellowship with God. Jesus

Christ declared, *"I am the bread of life. He who comes to Me shall never hunger, and he who believes in Me shall never thirst"* (Jn. 6:35). Through His priestly mediation we are able to live in that wonderful fellowship with the Living God for which we were created.

• Just in front of the inner veil stood a second altar called the golden altar. On this altar the priest would burn incense with fire taken from the bronze altar of burnt offering, symbolizing divine worship, intercession, and prayer on the basis of a completed sacrifice. The sweet smelling odor filled the Holy Place. In the same way Christ always lives to make intercession for His people as both their Advocate and their High Priest, who offered up Himself for their sin. *"We have an Advocate with the Father, Jesus Christ the righteous. And He Himself is the propitiation for our sins, and not for ours only but also for the whole world"* (1 Jn. 2:1-2; see Heb. 7:25-27).

We can summarize the beautiful symbolism of the tabernacle and its furniture in the following diagram:

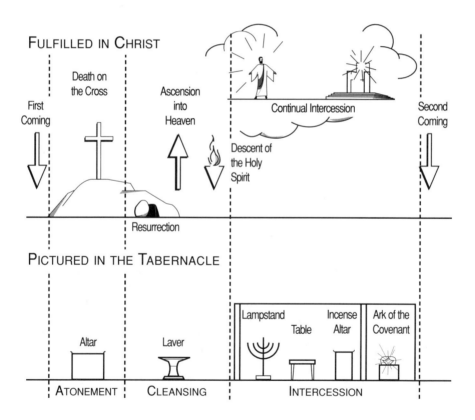

THE PRIESTHOOD

As mentioned above, God appointed the sons of Aaron to serve Him in the tabernacle as priests. They were to offer the sacrifices and maintain the worship within the sanctuary. He ordered special symbolic garments to be made for them (Ex. 28), and had them anointed with oil to signify their consecration to this holy service. There could be no dwelling of God among men without a mediating, sacrificing priesthood.

We can hardly overestimate the importance of this tabernacle and sacerdotal (sacrificing) priesthood. It clearly established the necessity of mediation between God and sinful men. God's holiness demands corresponding holiness in those who approach Him. Sinful, lawbreaking, fallen people, such as we all naturally are, need a mediator offering the blood of a sacrifice. The unchanging divine principle is *"without shedding of blood is no remission"* (Heb. 9:22). There can be no relationship with God and no acceptable worship except on this basis.

CONTINUAL SERVICE IN THE HOUSE

We should notice services that the Lord commanded Israel to perform before Him "continually." The major priestly functions are highlighted by this word, referring to service performed at both altars, the lampstand, and the table, as well as to the breastplate worn by the high priest.[4]

> *You shall set the showbread on the table before Me always* (Ex. 25:30).
> *Bring…pure oil of pressed olives for the light, to cause the lamp to burn continually…from evening until morning before the Lord* (Ex. 27:20-21).
> *Aaron shall bear the names of the sons of Israel…over his heart, when he goes into the holy place, as a memorial before the Lord continually* (Ex. 28:29).
> *You shall offer on the altar: two lambs of the first year, day by day continually…in the morning, and…at twilight…a continual burnt offering…at the door of the tabernacle of meeting before the Lord* (see Ex. 29:38-42).
> *And when Aaron lights the lamps at twilight, he shall burn incense on it, a perpetual incense before the Lord throughout your generations* (Ex. 30:8).

These priestly ministries have a very personal application for believers in Christ today. The believer's body has been made a temple or tabernacle of God the Holy Spirit (1 Cor. 6:19-20). The "holy place" of the tabernacle pictures the "inner man," which God desires to maintain continually as His dwelling place. Christ is for us the Living Bread, the Light of Life, the Great High Priest, and the Sacrificial Lamb. As priests (see 1 Pet. 2:5) we should continuously, daily, open our spirits to Him, allowing Him to cleanse us with a fresh appreciation of His blood, to carry us into God's presence, to fill our lamp and replenish our table.

Anne Grannis has taught us the way to do this in her beautiful poem:

> "I want my life so cleared of self
> That my dear Lord may come
> And set up His own furnishings
> And make my heart His home.
> And since I know what this requires,
> Each morning while it's still,
> I slip into that secret room
> And *leave with Him my will.*
>
> He always takes it graciously,
> Presenting me with His;
> I'm ready then to meet the day,
> And any task there is.
> And this is how my Lord controls
> My interests, my ills,
> Because we meet at break of day
> For *an exchange of wills."*

In response to these continual preparations, the Lord graciously came and lived continuously among His people. *"The cloud of the Lord was above the tabernacle by day, and fire was over it by night, in the sight of all the house of Israel, throughout all their journeys"* (Ex. 40:38).

"THE GLORY OF GOD"

When all the work had been finished and the tabernacle erected according to God's commandments, *"the cloud covered the tabernacle of meeting, and the glory of the Lord filled the tabernacle* (Ex. 40:34). Thus God's *drawing near* to His people is a central theme in the book of Exodus. In the early chapters, aware of their sufferings, He *"came down"* to deliver them from the power of the Egyptians (3:8). In 19:20, He *"came down"* on Mount Sinai to establish His covenant with His people. And in 40:34, He *comes down* to dwell among His people. These events form one account of God's drawing near to take personal responsibility for His people.

PART II—GOD'S PEOPLE DRAW NEAR (LEVITICUS)

"Sanctify yourselves therefore, and be ye holy: for I am the Lord your God."

As the book of Leviticus opens, the Lord addresses Moses again, this time not from the mountain, but *"from the tent of meeting"* (1:1). Now that God has provided all that is necessary for His presence in their midst and has drawn near to them, He calls the Israelites to draw near to Him. All is ready, but to enjoy fellowship with God we must use the means He has provided.

His central demand is that His people consecrate themselves, or cleanse themselves from defiling practices: *"Sanctify yourselves therefore and be ye holy, for I am the Lord your God"* (Lev. 20:7). Israel must separate themselves from the idolatrous practices of the neighboring nations, bring the sacrifices God commanded, participate in the appointed festivals, and practice holiness as described by God's law.

Every major area of life was governed by the Law: food, family life, sexual relations, health and sickness, housing, use of the land, etc. Essentially the book of Leviticus is a book of laws; laws concerning offerings (chs. 1–7), laws concerning priesthood (chs. 8–10), laws concerning ceremonial purity and cleanliness (chs. 11–15) and various laws concerning practical holiness (chs. 17–27). These laws enabled God's people to dwell in fellowship with Him. The Seven Feasts of the Lord in Leviticus 23 also present a symbolic overview of God's prophetic program for Israel (see p. 199).

The central provision of God's Law was the sacrificial system. A sinning person who humbled himself before God, confessing his sin, would bring one of the offerings as prescribed in chapters 1–5. He would lay his hand on the head of the animal and it would be slaughtered and offered to the Lord in fire as an "atonement" on the man's behalf, *"and it shall be accepted for him"* (Lev. 1:3-4), and *"it shall be forgiven him"* (Lev. 4:26).

All the laws of cleanliness, diet, feasts, etc., taught the people to *"make a distinction between the unclean and the clean,"* and to live in fellowship with the holy God who had redeemed them. Yet in spite of these detailed guidelines, the sad reality of man's sinful nature made acts of sin inevitable. Thus the priests not only interceded for the people and taught them God's law, but offered various sacrifices to deal with inner and outer defilement in their lives. God who loved them made provision for the atonement of their sins. He promised them that if they would trust in Him and take sin seriously, they would live in His presence. *"Therefore, having these promises, beloved, let us cleanse ourselves from all filthiness of the flesh and spirit, perfecting holiness in the fear of God"* (2 Cor. 7:1).

THE DAY OF ATONEMENT

This fascinating ceremony detailed in Leviticus 16 was deeply significant in the overall plan of God. Other than one time each year, the High Priest never entered the Holy of Holies behind the inner veil, *"before the mercy seat, which is upon the ark; that he die not: for I will appear in the cloud upon the mercy seat"* (Lev. 16:2). But on that one holy day ("the Day of Atonement") he was to enter only with the blood of sacrificed bulls and goats, offered for his sins and for those of the congregation. He was to bring the blood behind the veil into the "Holy of Holies" and sprinkle it on the "mercy seat," the "atonement cover" or lid of the ark, which hid the stone tablets on which the Ten Commandments were inscribed. The Lord described the purpose of the ritual this way:

He shall make atonement for the Holy Place, because of the uncleanness of the children of Israel, and because of their transgressions, for all their sins; and so he shall do for the tabernacle of meeting which remains among them in the midst of their uncleanness…to make an atonement for the children of Israel for all their sins once a year" (Lev. 16:16, 34).

The New Testament teaches us that Christ, as God's true "High Priest," offered Himself to God as the final, perfect sacrifice for sins. Just as He died on the cross He cried out "It is finished," and at that very moment *"the veil of the temple was torn in two from top to bottom"* (Jn. 19:30; Mt. 27:51).

The way into the presence of God was finally opened once and for all by the death of Christ. When Christ rose from the dead and returned to heaven, He was in fact performing His high priestly ministry, entering in by the value of His own blood to the very throne of God to make atonement for our sins forever.

Christ is not entered into the holy places made with hands, which are the figures of the true; but into heaven itself, now to appear in the presence of God for us…not with the blood of goats and calves, but with His own blood He entered the Most Holy Place once for all, having obtained eternal redemption…now once in the end of the world hath He appeared to put away sin by the sacrifice of Himself (Heb. 9:24 KJV, 12, 26).

It is wonderful to learn that over the ark was a "mercy seat" where atoning blood was sprinkled. God's throne is *"the throne of grace"* to which we are invited to *"come boldly"* (Heb. 4:16).

CONCLUSION

God came down, revealed Himself, redeemed and took possession of His own chosen ones, the people of the Promise. He provided the means by which He could dwell with them and they could draw near to Him. His word to believers in the Lord Jesus is full of welcoming assurance as He calls us to draw near:

Therefore, brethren, having boldness to enter the Holiest by the blood of Jesus, by a new and living way which He consecrated for us, through the veil, that is, His flesh, and having a High Priest over the house of God, let us draw near with a true heart in full assurance of faith, having our hearts sprinkled from an evil conscience and our bodies washed with pure water (Heb. 10:19-22).

ENDNOTES

1 James M. Gray, D. D., *Commentary on the Whole Bible,* p. 99.

2 Walter C. Kaiser, *Towards an Old Testament Theology,* p. 114.

3 Kaiser, p. 119.

4 A full list of the occurrences of this word *"continual"* in the Tabernacle directions adds detail to this picture:

In the Holy Place
- Bread of the Presence set (Ex. 25:30; Lev. 24:8; Num. 4:7)
- Lamps burning (Ex. 27:20; Lev. 24:2, 3, 4)
- Incense burning (Ex. 30:8)
- Names, Urim and Thummim on the breastplate (28:29-30)
- Miter—"Holy to the Lord" (28:36-38)

At the bronze altar
- fire burning (Lev. 6:13)
- burnt and grain offerings (Ex. 29:38, 42; Lev. 6:20; Num. 4:16; 28:3, 6, 10, 15, 23, 24, 31; 29:11, 16, 19, 22, 25, 28, 31, 34, 38)

1. In the space below write out Exodus 19:5-6. Then in your own words explain God's purpose in choosing Israel.

2. What was to be the distinguishing characteristic of God's people (Lev. 11:44-45; 20:26)? How did this relate to God's original purpose in creating man as expressed in Genesis 1:26-27?

3. Why did God order the people of Israel to make a sanctuary (Ex. 25:8)?

4. Using the plan below, locate the various pieces of furniture in the tabernacle and its courtyard. Then fill in below the three essential requirements for man to approach God.

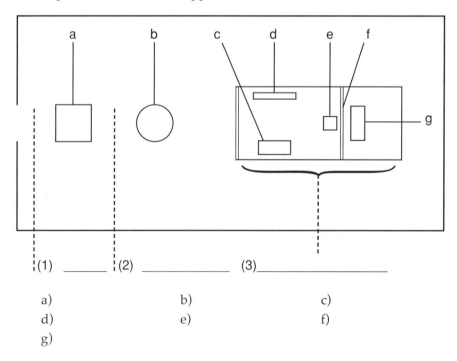

(1) _____ (2) _____ (3)_____

a)   b)   c)

d)   e)   f)

g)

5. Summarize the way in which the three requirements were fulfilled in Christ. Explain the past and present aspects of salvation which He has obtained for His people.

    1)

    2)

    3)

6. Why was a priesthood necessary? What was God's original intention for His people in Exodus 19:6? How does the principle expressed in Hebrews 9:22 apply to this question?

7. How would the sanctuary and the priests be "sanctified" according to Exodus 29:42-46?

8. How did the Lord show that He had come to dwell among His people when the tabernacle was finished (Ex. 40:34)?

    When and why had He "come down" prior to this?

9. What priestly service done on the annual Day of Atonement was forbidden throughout the rest of the year (Lev. 16)?

10. When Christ died on the Cross, the veil of the temple was torn in two from top to bottom (Mt. 27:51). What did this mean? Consider Hebrews 10:19-22 in your answer.

11. How can you apply this lesson to your own relationship with the Lord?

THE LAW AND THE PROMISE
MOSES' THIRD ERA

Recommended Readings: Exodus 19–20; 24; 32–34; Numbers 11–14; 16–17; 22–24; Deuteronomy 4–11; 27–34

In our last study we spoke of the Lord's descent upon Mount Sinai as the most awe-inspiring event of the Old Testament. We can go still further; the year spent at the foot of the mountain was also the most important event in Israel's history. The very name "Old Testament" or "Old Covenant" derives from this time. At Sinai God established His covenant with the people of Israel. There He gave them His holy Law. Their identity was formed there. All that follows, until the coming of Messiah Himself, is shaped by and grounded in this critical revelation. These events, more than any others, distinguished Israel from all other nations on earth. Moses summarized Israel's privilege in two weighty questions:

> *What great nation is there that has God so near to it, as the Lord our God is to us, for whatever reason we may call upon Him? And what great nation is there that has such statutes and righteous judgments as are in all this law which I set before you this day?* (Deut. 4:7-8).

In these two questions Moses pointed out the two great facts of Mount Sinai:

1) God's drawing near to dwell among His people in His sanctuary. We looked at the implications of this fact in Study 5.

2) The revealing of the Law of God, with its foundation in the Ten Commandments. The implications of God's giving this holy, righteous, and good standard will be explored in Study 6.

Israel had not merely been redeemed from the enemy's power, but had also been brought into a relationship with God by His love. It is the same for us. We are redeemed not just *from* sin, but *to* God, in order to belong to Him and serve Him obediently in love. Israel's relationship with God was a binding "covenant," which again is the central idea of Old Testament history.

A covenant is a formal, solemn agreement, reconciling two people or groups, often confirmed with an oath. In particular, mutual responsibility is pledged. A brief search for the word "covenant" in the books of Moses reveals three clear groupings of references because God made three covenants during this period of time:

1)   *The covenant with Noah* (Gen. 6:18; 9:9, 17) was an *"Everlasting Covenant"* between God and every living creature on the earth (9:16). God promised never again to destroy the earth by flood nor to curse it again on man's account (8:21). The sign of this covenant was the rainbow (9:12-17).

2)   *The covenant with Abraham* (Gen. 15, 17, 22), as we saw in Study 3, was a covenant or promise to bless all mankind through Abraham's seed, culminating in the Messiah. The sign of this covenant was the rite of circumcision (Gen. 17:11).

3)   Now through Moses' mediation *a covenant is made with Israel,* centered in the Ten Commandments. God promises to make them His special people if they will obey Him (Ex. 19:5-6). The sign of this covenant was the Sabbath (Ex. 31:13-17; Ezek. 20:12), and it's permanent reminder was the *"Ark of the Covenant"* in which were kept the two stone tablets upon which the Ten Commandments were written by the finger of God.

We shall see in this lesson that God's people fail utterly to keep His law. But God does not forsake them, because of His previous promise to Abraham and the patriarchs. Thus the *conditional* covenant at Sinai is doomed to break down because of man's failure, but God's unconditional covenant to Abraham will certainly be fulfilled because it depends on God's own faithfulness and power. Let's consider this in more detail.

I. THE MOUNT SINAI COVENANT (EXODUS 19–24, 32–34)

In Exodus 19–24 and 32–34 we see this covenant given by God, broken by Israel, and renewed by God's mercy.

THE COVENANT GIVEN (EXODUS 19–24)

When the Lord spoke to Israel from the midst of the fire on Mount Sinai, He was establishing the terms of a covenant with them: *"The Lord spoke to you out of the midst of the fire. You heard the sound of the words, but saw no form; you only heard a voice. So He declared to you His covenant which He commanded you to perform, the Ten Commandments; and He wrote them on two tablets of stone"* (Deut. 4:12-13). He then called Moses up the mountain again and commanded him to teach His *"statutes and judgments"* in detail to the Israelites (Deut. 4:14).

When He had finished speaking with Moses, God Himself wrote the *"Ten Words"* on two stone tablets, which He called the *"Tables of Testimony"* (Ex. 31:18; 32:15; 34:29). A "testimony" is a formal, solemn statement of what is true. In the Ten Commandments God was testifying to His own character, as if to say, "My people, this is the way I am; My standard for you is based on My own unchanging attributes." He warns them that this is the true standard, which conforms to His holiness. The two stone tablets were a permanent witness to their Author and to the fact that He had spoken. This covenant bound Israel to obedience and declared in no uncertain terms the penalty of disobedience. At least eight of the ten commandments carried the death penalty.[1]

This covenant was ratified with the blood of sacrifice (Ex. 24:1-8). Moses read them the *"Book of the Covenant"* and the people gave their word, *"All that the Lord has said will we do, and be obedient"* (24:7). Moses then took the blood and sprinkled it on the people and said, *"This is the blood of the covenant which the Lord has made with you according to all these words"* (24:8).

THE COVENANT BROKEN AND GIVEN AGAIN (EXODUS 32-34)

No sooner had they ratified this covenant, while Moses was still on the mountain receiving from the Lord the detailed plans for the tabernacle, than Israel broke the first two articles of the Covenant. They had Moses' brother, Aaron, make a golden calf and began to worship it, calling out, *"This is your god, O Israel, that brought you out of the land of Egypt!"* (Ex. 32:4). An idolatrous orgy followed.

The Lord declared His intention to destroy them completely and start a new nation with Moses. But Moses interceded, pleading the value of the promise God had made to Abraham, Isaac, and Israel (32:7-13), and God *"repented,"* consistent with His own faithfulness. Moses descended the mountain, broke the two stone tablets, and rebuked the people, *"You have committed a great sin. So now I will go up to the Lord; perhaps I can make atonement for your sin"* (32:30).

An amazing interchange followed, in which Moses poured out his desire to see God's glory. The Lord determined to pardon Israel and again made a covenant with them to perform great things for them. He repeated the essential terms of the covenant (Ex. 33-34) and re-wrote the Ten Commandments on two new tablets which He had Moses cut out (34:1). At the end of forty days Moses came down the mountain with the skin of his face shining from the glory of God (Ex. 34:27-29).

THE LAW AND THE PROMISE

In this narrative we see Israel's failure to keep the Law from the very time it was given, but we also gain new insight into the unchangeableness of God's unconditional promise to Abraham. "Any successful agreement between God and man must really be a divine 'grant,' and never a mere contract between two parties—God and man—each with equal rights."[2] It must depend on God's faithfulness, for man will always fail.

This inescapable fact is clearly presented in Leviticus 26 (and repeated in Deuteronomy 29). There God presented Israel with a list of blessing for obedience and curses for disobedience. Enjoyment of the blessings of the covenant relationship depended on this: *"Walk in My statutes, and keep My commandments"* (26:3). But breaking the Law would result in disaster. God said, *"I will...avenge the quarrel of My covenant"* (Lev. 26:25). The basis for punishment was disobedience to God's holy Law. But when they failed, began to be punished and then repented, the Lord said He would remember His covenant with the patriarchs (26:42—three times). The Lord will not break His covenant with them by utterly destroying Israel. As Paul says in Romans 11:28-29, Israel was *"beloved for the fathers' sakes. For the gifts and calling of God are without repentance."* The source of all blessing is not the Law, but this Abrahamic Covenant or "Promise."

What then was the purpose of the Law? It was imposed by God in order to expose sin and reveal man's sinful nature for what it is in God's eyes—exceedingly wicked and deserving death. The full weight of God's righteous Law reveals man's deep need to take refuge in God's unconditional promise. Centuries later, the New Testament expressed this truth this way:

- *"The law...was added because of transgressions"* (Gal. 3:19).
- *"By the law is the knowledge of sin"* (Rom. 3:20).
- *"I would not have known sin, except through the law...sin through the commandment might become exceeding sinful"* (Rom. 7:7-13).
- *"The law was our tutor to bring us to Christ"* (Gal. 3:24).

II. "THE DEATH OF THE OLD and THE BIRTH OF THE NEW" (NUMBERS)

Perhaps nowhere is the rebellious nature of man more clearly illustrated than in the book of Numbers. Nor is God's holy wrath against sin more clearly revealed anywhere else.

The fourth book of Moses presents a sobering, chilling reality. The God who had entered into covenant with Abraham (Gen. 12), who had delivered His people from bondage in the Exodus (Ex. 14–15), who had revealed His holiness and the means to approach His grace through celebrative and sacrificial worship (Lev. 1–7)—this same Yahweh was also a God of wrath and a consuming fire. His wrath extends to His errant children as well as to the enemy nations of Egypt and Canaan...This association of the Lord's wrath and mercy, His anger and His love—no matter how strange it may seem to us—is a marked feature of the teaching of the Torah and the Prophets.[3]

The book of Numbers is marked by two census-takings (in chapters 1 and 26), separated by a time span of around thirty-eight years. Two generations are introduced and their stories told. Chapters 1–25 give us the disastrous experience of the first generation in the desert ("the death of the old"); chapters 26–36 present the prospects for the second generation to enter the promised land ("the birth of the new").[4]

"THE DEATH OF THE OLD" (NUMBERS 1–21, 25)

As the book begins, the Lord tells Moses, *"Take ye the sum of all the congregation of the children of Israel"* (Num. 1:2). The time has finally come to leave Mount Sinai. Preparation is made for the march to the promised land, with detailed instructions for the priests and Levites, for making and breaking camp, carrying the tabernacle and its furniture, etc. (2:1–10:10). The Lord Himself was to go with them. He appeared during the day in a cloud covering the tabernacle and at night in a pillar of fire. When the cloud rose from above the tabernacle, Israel would journey, and when the cloud settled they would pitch their tents (9:15-23).

Finally the journey began. *"They first took their journey according to the commandment of the Lord"* (10:11-13). Yet in spite of all the preparations God made for His people, the record of Israel's journey is tragic. No sooner had they begun than the people begin to complain and the Lord's judgment began to fall on them (11:1). The people complained about food and water (ch. 11, 15, 17). Aaron and Miriam complained about their brother Moses' leadership (ch. 12). The spies sent into the land brought back a fearful report and the people refused to enter, rebelling against the Lord's promises, turned back into the desert to wander for 38 extra years (chs. 13–14). Korah and his clan rebel against Moses and Aaron's leadership (16–17). The people became impatient on the way (21:4-9), and finally fell into gross idolatry and immorality with the pagan people of Moab (ch. 25). Only the zealous action of Phinehas stemmed the wrath of God at that time, and limited the number who died to twenty-four thousand (25:6-18).

The result of all this rebellion was death. Over and over again multitudes of Israelites fell under God's judgment. So heavy was the death toll that when the second census was taken in chapter 26, among those who were numbered in preparation for entering the land,

> But among these there was not a man of those who were numbered by Moses and Aaron…in the Wilderness of Sinai. For the Lord had said of them, "They shall surely die in the wilderness." So there was not left a man of them, except Caleb…and Joshua (26:64-65).

The map on the following page summarizes the long years and various stages of Israel's journey through the wilderness. Moses reviews this journey in Deuteronomy 1:19–3:29.

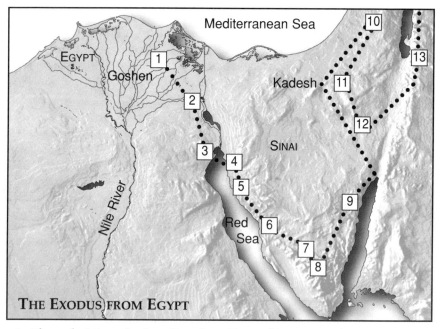

THE EXODUS FROM EGYPT

1 Pharaoh drives the Israelites from Egypt (Ex. 12:29-36).

2 The people journey from Rameses to Succoth (Ex. 12:37-39).

3 Pharaoh changes his mind and pursues Israel, catching up to them at the Red Sea (Ex. 14:5-12).

4 Israel passes through the sea on dry ground, but the waters return, drowning the Egyptians (Ex. 14:13-31).

5 Three days later they reach Marah and are unable to drink its bitter waters (Ex. 15:22-26).

6 God provides them with bread and quail from heaven (Ex. 16).

7 God brings water from the rock. The Amalekites attack Israel but are defeated. Moses' father-in-law advises him (Ex. 17–18).

8 Israel receives God's Law at Mt. Sinai (Ex. 19–32).

9 Miriam becomes leprous for her jealousy and rebellion against Moses (Num. 12:1-16).

10 Eleven days after leaving Sinai, Moses sends twelve spies into the land of Canaan (Num. 13:1-24).

11 The returning spies bring a bad report, causing the Israelites to rebel and demand a new leader to take them back to Egypt (Num. 13:25–14:10).

12 Israel is condemned to wander in desert for 40 years (Num. 14:11-38).

13 God finally orders Israel to move north through Edom and Moab, then enables them to destroy Heshbon (kingdom of Sihon) and Bashan (kingdom of Og). They camp in the plains of Moab beyond the Jordan, opposite Jericho (Num. 21).

"A STAR SHALL COME OUT OF JACOB" (NUMBERS 22–24)

If Israel's hopes were tied to their ability to keep the Law, they were finished. Perhaps they wondered, "Has God finished with us? Have we any hope?" But God's purposes were bound to His promise to Abraham, not to Israel's faithfulness.

In one of the most remarkable sections of the Bible, the Lord worked providentially and directly to proclaim His continued faithfulness to His people, despite their unfaithfulness. This section is the comic account of Balaam, the pagan diviner (Num. 22–24). Here the God of laughter brings a smile to His people to encourage them in the prospects of their new hope, even as the older persons among them were still dying: God's promises will still be realized…in us![5]

Balaam was an internationally known diviner.[6] Balak, the king of Moab, afraid of the approaching Israelite army, hired him to curse Israel. Instead, the Lord brings from his mouth blessings on Israel and curses on their enemies (chs. 23–24). In response to the furious king, Balaam says, *"I have received commandment to bless: and he hath blessed; and I cannot reverse it"* (23:20).

God's blessing on Israel rests on His sovereign will. The immediate enjoyment of God's blessing will ever be dependent on the faithfulness of His people. But the ultimate realization of God's blessing is sure—because of the character of God, which is incapable of change:

> *God is not a man, that He should lie;*
> *Nor the Son of man, that He should repent;*
> *Has He said, and will He not do it?*
> *Or has He spoken, and will He not make it good?* (Num. 23:19).

Most remarkably, this untoward, alien man, Balaam—who stands at enmity with Israel and is no friend of God—was given a vision of the coming of a Victor-King, a Deliverer who is the Promised One, even the Messiah Yeshua [Jesus]:

> *I shall see Him, but not now:*
> *I shall behold Him, but not nigh:*
> *There shall come a Star out of Jacob,*
> *And a Scepter shall rise out of Israel* (Num. 24:17 KJV).[7]

"THE BIRTH OF THE NEW" (NUMBERS 26-36)

So we see that Israel's sin does not negate God's purposes in grace.

The Lord punishes Israel severely for their sins, but He remains in their midst. Over and over He disciplines and restores them because of His promises to the fathers. The new generation whose census is taken in chapter 26 is then prepared anew for the entrance into the promised land (chs. 27-36). Hope is still alive because of the Lord's faithfulness.

III. "LIFE OR DEATH" (DEUTERONOMY)

After nearly forty years of wandering in the desert, Israel is once again ready to enter Palestine. The whole generation that had refused to enter the first time has died. Now across the Jordan River in the land of Moab, just outside the promised land, Moses repeats and expounds the Law of God to the people of Israel. The book of Deuteronomy is largely concerned with Moses' second giving of the Law to this new generation. "Deuteronomy" means "second law." Before they entered the land they must hear the Word of God again.

The main part of the book of Deuteronomy is made up of four discourses of Moses:

1. (chs. 1–4) Recounting the exodus and wanderings of the past forty years.

2. (chs. 5–26) Repeating, expounding, and applying the Ten Commandments.

3. (chs. 27–28) Giving a list of curses and blessings upon their response.

4. (chs. 29–30) Summarizing the covenant made in Moab.

After recounting the history of the preceding forty years (1–4), "Moses summoned all Israel" to hear the ordinances of God (5:1). He took them back to Mount Sinai and the covenant the Lord God had made with them there, emphasizing that God had made it with them, not just with their fathers. He then repeated the Ten Commandments that the Lord had spoken "out of the midst of the fire" (5:4-21; see Ex. 20). The importance of these Commandments cannot be exaggerated. When rightly examined, we will find that God's standards for mankind are exceedingly high. He demands inward and outward holiness. He requires the love of our whole being toward Himself first and also toward our fellow men and women.

The laws of Deuteronomy 6–25 are an expansion of the Ten Commandments.[8] Let's examine how these foundational principles of God-given moral absolutes apply to our lives. The Ten Commandments, or the Decalogue, are usually divided into two sections or "tables."

THE TEN COMMANDMENTS
"The Two Tables of the Testimony"

GODWARD COMMANDMENTS	MANWARD COMMANDMENTS
1. Thou shalt have no other gods before Me.	5. Honor thy father and thy mother.
2. Thou shalt not make unto thee any graven image.	6. Thou shalt not kill.
3. Thou shalt not take the name of the Lord thy God in vain.	7. Thou shalt not commit adultery.
4. Remember the sabbath day, to keep it holy.	8. Thou shalt not steal.
	9. Thou shalt not bear false witness.
	10. Thou shalt not covet.
SUMMARY: Thou shalt love the Lord thy God with all thy heart, and with all thy soul, and with all thy strength.	SUMMARY: Thou shalt love thy neighbor as thyself.

THE GODWARD COMMANDMENTS

The first four commandments were summarized by Jesus this way: *"You shall love the Lord your God with all your heart, with all your soul, with all your mind, and with all your strength"* (Mk. 12:30—quoting Deut. 6:5). These commandments deal with our responsibilities toward God.

FIRST AND SECOND COMMANDMENTS (5:6-10; 6:1–12:32)
"You shall have no other gods."

Moses begins to develop the Law, urging the people to listen and be careful to do it. This great statement is the foundation: *"Hear, O Israel: The Lord our God, the Lord is one! You shall love the Lord your God with all your heart, with all your soul, and with all your strength"* (6:4-5). He is a jealous God (5:9; 6:15), demanding exclusive devotion from those He has redeemed. No rivals will be tolerated. They cannot be—they are all false. Drastic action must be taken to eliminate all idols (7:5, 25-26; 12:2-3) so that they would not be a temptation, turning them from the Lord.

Idolatry refers not only to physical idols, but to anything that comes between us and God. He must have our full love and service. No possession, no job, no relationship, or any other thing may be permitted to separate us from the great and awesome God who loves us perfectly and disciplines us as His own "sons" (8:5). This standard is very high: to love and serve Him with our whole being all the hours and days of our entire life!

THIRD COMMANDMENT (5:11; 13:1-14:27)
"You shall not take the name of the Lord your God in vain."

Using the name of God in vain is forbidden. For example, use of His holy name to express our surprise or anger is sinful. Needless confirming of our word or meaningless repetition of His name, whether for religious purposes or simply absent-mindedly, also violates this law. Israel is strictly warned to reject any prophet or dreamer, any family member, or any other person who tries to turn them against their God, whose name is Yahweh, "the Lord" (13:1-18). The holiness of His name is to characterize every aspect of the lives of His people (14:1-27).

FOURTH COMMANDMENT (5:12-15; 14:28–16:17)
"Keep the Sabbath day."

The command to remember the seventh day concerns right relations with work. Israel was required to set time aside from work for rest and for the worship and service of God. One day in seven belonged to the Lord ceremonially in order to emphasize the priority of God's claim on our whole life. At the end of every three years a tithe of all their produce was to go to the Lord (14:28-29). Every seventh year all debts were to be canceled and Hebrew slaves released (ch. 15). Annual feasts where the people were to *"appear before the Lord"* (16:1-17) emphasized the point: God's interests must take priority over material pursuits!

THE MANWARD COMMANDMENTS

The Lord summed up the second group of six commandments in these words from Leviticus 19:18: *"You shall love your neighbor as yourself"* (Mk. 12:31). Thus as Paul says in his epistle to the Romans, *"Love does no harm to a neighbor; therefore love is the fulfillment of the law"* (13:10).

FIFTH COMMANDMENT (5:16; 16:18–18:22)
"Honor your father and your mother."

Respect for parents is expanded in these chapters to include other God-ordained authority: the judges (17:2-13); the king (17:14-20); the priests (18:1-8); and the prophets (18:9-22). Authority and submission to that authority is a basic principle of God's order. Man must learn that disobedience has severe consequences in every realm.

SIXTH COMMANDMENT (5:17; 19:1–22:8)
"You shall not murder."

Because human beings were made in the image of God, murder required the death penalty (Gen. 9:5-6). "So sacred was life, that all violent forms of snatching it away caused guilt to fall on the land...and must lead to the yielding up of another life...that murderer's life was owed to God; not to society; not to the grieving loved ones, and not even as a preventative measure."[9] Even the killing of an unborn fetus brought death to the "murderer" (Ex. 21:22-25).[10]

SEVENTH COMMANDMENT (5:18; 22:9–23:18)
"You shall not commit adultery."

Marriage between one man and one woman was clearly established in the first chapters of the Bible: *"They shall be one flesh"* (Gen. 2:24). Polygamy arose after the Fall because of man's sin and willfulness (Gen. 4:19). Although examples of polygamy include such men as the patriarchs (Gen. 16:1-2; 29–30), the plan of God from the beginning was monogamy (see Jesus' words in Mt. 19:3-9).

Moral excellence and sexual purity are essential to holiness in the sight of God, so we find detailed legislation in these chapters (22:13–23:1). No matter what our culture tells us, according to the living God, sexual relations are limited strictly to monogamous marriage. Premarital sex is sin, despite society's claim that it is "natural." So is use of prostitutes, even if legalized by man. Anything else is condemned by God and will be punished. Suggestions that men "need" sexual relations or cannot abstain are an attempt to excuse the breaking of God's law.

EIGHTH COMMANDMENT (5:19; 23:20–24:7)
"You shall not steal."

All property comes from God. We are simply stewards. Therefore, "every form of stealing or withholding property that rightfully belongs to someone else is condemned…23:20-21 deal with the theft of property and…[24:1-7] with the theft of 'life'."[11] Even common activities such as cheating on taxes or delaying the payment of debts are not excusable.

NINTH COMMANDMENT (5:20; 24:8–25:4)
"You shall not bear false witness against your neighbor."

Although men tend toward falsehood, the Lord is characterized by truth: *"God is not a man, that He should lie…has He said, and will He not do it?"* (Num. 23:19). Therefore honesty and integrity are not optional for His people—they are essential. All forms of mocking, slander, belittling and lying are forbidden. Even fairness to animals was required (25:4).

TENTH COMMANDMENT (5:21; 25:5–26:15)
"You shall not covet…"

The final commandment is inward in focus. It addresses the motives behind our acts, thoughts, and words. To covet is to desire that which is not rightly ours. The responsibility to one's brother's wife after his death was a legitimate exception (25:4-10). False weights in selling goods were evidence of a mind looking for ways to take more than rightly his (25:13-16). Conversely, an Israelite's willing offering of the first fruits of his produce to God (26:1-15) showed that inner contentment which God desires in His people.

Thus the Law governed Israel's responsibilities both to their God and to their fellow-man. Much morality today is based on the principle, "it's OK as long as you don't hurt anyone." But not only does this actually fall far short of the standard of the manward commandments, but it also utterly fails to consider the Godward responsibility of man to his Creator. To us as well, the Lord says, *"Set your hearts on all the words which I testify among you today...because it is your life"* (Deut. 32:46-47).

This was the foundation of their life. In order to enjoy God's blessing in their new land, they must know and obey God's Law, and more than that, take refuge in God's promise to the patriarchs. Failure to take seriously God's perfect hatred of sin and the unswerving standard of holiness leads us to a hope that we're not so bad. We begin to think God would be wrong to send us to hell as due punishment for our sins. But in the white light of God's law, *"Every mouth may be stopped, and all the world may become guilty before God...For all have sinned, and fall short of the glory of God"* (Rom. 3:19-23). God's salvation is based solely on His mercy and His grace in the promised Messiah. It leaves man no ground for pride or boasting.

CONCLUSION

The final chapters of Deuteronomy (31–34) give us the four momentous events of the last days of Moses' life:

1. Moses *commissions* Joshua as Israel's new leader (ch. 31).
2. Moses teaches the *Song* of testimony to Israel (ch. 32).
3. Moses *blesses* each of the 12 tribes (ch. 33).
4. Moses *dies* and is buried by the Lord (ch. 34).

Moses was handing over the leadership of Israel to Joshua, just as the Lord had commanded him. He was fully aware of Israel's past and future failures. The Lord told him clearly that *"This people will rise and play the harlot with the gods of the foreigners of the land, where they go to be among them, and they will forsake Me and break My covenant which I have made with them"* (31:16).

But even as he did so, Moses was looking beyond the days of Joshua into the distant future to the time when God would raise up another *"Prophet"* like himself (Deut. 18:15)—Israel's final leader and Saviour to whom the Law was ultimately leading them—Jesus the Messiah (See Acts 3:22-26). Let us join Moses in singing praise to the God who has planned and carried out such a gracious and just salvation for us (Deut. 32:3-4):

Ascribe greatness to our God.
He is the Rock, His work is perfect:
For all His ways are justice:
A God of truth and without injustice; righteous and upright is He.

ENDNOTES

1 1st: No other god (Ex. 22:20; Deut. 13; 17:1-5)

   2nd: No idols (Num. 25:2-5)

   3rd: Not taking the Lord's Name in vain (Lev. 24:10-16, 23)

   4th: Keeping the Sabbath Day holy (Num. 15:32-36)

   5th: Honoring father and mother (Ex. 21:15, 17; Lev. 20:9; Deut. 21:18-21)

   6th: Shall not murder (Ex. 21:12-14; Lev. 24:17, 21; Deut. 19:11-13)

   7th: Shall not commit adultery (Lev. 20:10; Deut. 22:22)

   9th: Shall not bear false witness   (Deut. 19:16-21, if for murder).

2 William Hendriksen, *New Testament Commentary*, Eph., p. 130.

3 Ronald B. Allen, *Expositor's Bible Commentary*, Vol. 2, Numbers, pp. 675-676.

4 See Allen's excellent discussion of the structure of Numbers in the *Expositor's Bible Commentary*.

5 Allen, p. 677.

6 Ibid.

7 Ibid.

8 The structure which follows is found in Walter Kaiser, *Toward Old Testament Ethics*, Zondervan, 1983, p. 129:

Deut. 5	Commandment	Deuteronomy	Description
5:6-10	1-2	6:1–12:32	Worship
5:11	3	13:1–14:27	Name of God
5:12-15	4	14:28–16:17	Sabbath
5:16	5	16:18–18:22	Authority
5:17	6	19:1–22:8	Homicide
5:18	7	22:9–23:19	Adultery
5:19	8	23:20–24:7	Theft
5:20	9	24:8–25:4	False Charges
5:21	10	25:5–26:15	Coveting

9 Ibid., p. 91.

10 "On the basis of Job 10:8-12, Ps. 51:5-6; and 139:13-16, we conclude that the child in the womb was regarded and valued as a human person and under the protection of his or her Creator." Ibid.

11 Ibid., p. 136.

1. What is a covenant?

   With whom did the Lord make covenants in the following passages?
   Gen. 6:18; 9:9, 17
   Gen. 15; 17; 22
   Exodus 19–20

2. Why did the Lord refer to the two stone tablets as the *"Tablets of the Testimony"* (Ex. 31:18; 32:15; 34:29)? To what was God "testifying" when He gave the Ten Commandments?

3. Was Israel able to keep their promise to the Lord (Ex. 24:7)? What was God's purpose in giving the Law? Consider Galatians 3:19; Romans 3:20; 7:7-13 in your answer.

   What is the relationship between the Law and the Promise? Note Galatians 3:16-19.

4. Why did the Lord say in Numbers 14:23, *"They certainly shall not see the land of which I swore to their fathers"?* How many of those who were counted in Numbers 1 were still alive when the second census was taken in Numbers 26?

5. Write out Numbers 23:19 below and give your thoughts regarding God's character as expressed there.

For questions 6-9, choose four of the Ten Commandments, two from the "Godward" group, and two from the "manward" group (see notes). On the left write out the key sentence of that commandment, and on the right consider how one might break this commandment in his or her own life. Include inward sins as well as outward.

Commandment   **Present-day application**

6. (No.   )

7. (No.   )

8. (No.   )

9. (No.   )

10. What do you learn about the promised Messiah from these two passages spoken by Balaam and Moses?
    Num. 24:17-19

    Deut. 18:15

11. How can you apply this lesson to your own relationship with the Lord?

ENTERING THE PROMISED REST
Pre-Monarchical Era

7

Recommended Readings: Deuteronomy 1:8; 6:1-18; 8:7-10; 30:15-20;
Joshua 1–8; 23–24; Judges 2:1-19; Ruth 1–4

The book of Exodus records how God led His people out of Egypt, the book of Joshua how they entered Canaan, a sort of "In-odus." *"He brought us out from there, that He might bring us in, to give us the land of which He swore to our fathers"* (Deut. 6:23). God had sworn to Abraham centuries earlier, *"Unto thy seed will I give this land"* (Gen. 12:7; see also 13:14-15; 15:7). The fulfillment of that promise is the central focus of the book of Joshua.

The name of Joshua means Saviour:

> "The people of Israel had to be settled in the Promised Land to prepare for the coming of another Joshua, Jesus Christ, who was to live and die in that same land as Saviour, not only of Israel, but of the entire human race."[1]

The era from Joshua to Saul, the first king of Israel, covers a period of approximately 350 years (1400-1050 BC),[2] and is known as the "Pre-Monarchical Era." Following the conquest and possession of the Promised Land as chronicled in Joshua, Israel was loosely governed by a series of "judges." The "ups" and (more frequently) "downs" of that depressing era are recorded in the book of Judges. The small book of Ruth is an example of faith in a discouraging era. These books provide us with a wealth of both positive and negative examples for living a victorious life of faith in the Lord even today. But the background for this period is found in Deuteronomy.

INHERITANCE AND REST IN THE LAND

Nearly seventy times in Deuteronomy it was pledged that Israel would one day *"inherit"* or *"possess"* the land promised to *"the fathers"* (Deut. 1:8; 6:10, 18; 7:8; 34:4). The land belonged to the Lord (Lev. 25:23), as does the whole earth (Ex. 9:29; Job 41:11; Ps. 24:1; 89:11). But now He was openly declaring His ownership by giving it to His people and by *"[putting] His name there, even unto His habitation shall ye seek, and thither thou shalt come"* (Deut. 12:5, 11, 18; 16:2, 6, 15-16; etc.).

It was a delightful gift, *"a land flowing with milk and honey"* (Deut. 26:9). *"A good land,"* like God's creation in Genesis 1–2, *"...a land of brooks of water, of fountains and springs, that flow out of valleys and hills;...in which you will lack nothing"* (Deut. 8:7-10). God wanted His people to live in a place of *"blessing"* (Deut. 15:4; 28:8).

A new provision to the ancient promise was God's *"rest."* A share in the "rest of God" was to be given to His people. Canaan was *"...the rest and the inheritance which the Lord your God is giving you...He gives you rest from all your enemies"* (Deut. 12:9-10). The results of Israel's military campaigns were summed up years later with these words: *"The Lord gave them rest all around, according to all that He had sworn to their fathers"* (Josh. 21:44). Thus God was fulfilling His promise.

But although Joshua led Israel to their promised rest, and *"not a word failed of any good thing which the Lord had spoken to the house of Israel. All came to pass"* (v. 45), we read later of "rest" received by David in 2 Samuel 7:1, 11, by Asa in 2 Chronicles 14:6-7, and of a still-future rest to come (Ps. 95; Heb. 4:4-6). The complete fulfillment of God's promises is often more complex than might be expected at first. We still look forward to the final fulfillment of the promised "rest."

> In the Old Testament view of fulfillment...specifically named generations received their share of the completion of the single plan of God...that ancient offer of rest was ultimately tied up with the events of the second advent [when the Messiah would reign over all peoples and lands (Ps. 95)]. Every other rest was only an 'earnest' or down payment, on the final Sabbath rest yet to come.[3]

JOSHUA—CONQUEST AND POSSESSION OF THE LAND

In the carrying out of His unchangeable purpose, God uses human instruments. In fact, the Lord often seems more concerned with the development of the character of the people He is using than in the work He is accomplishing through them. Many chapters of Holy Scripture record the lives of various people of God. Ultimately God's purpose in history is the redemption of individual people, and He takes delight in working patiently with each one to transform them into His own perfect image. If we want God to use us, we must gladly submit to His personal discipline in our lives, and seek to know Him and His will for us.

THE MAN JOSHUA

Who was Joshua? What kind of a man was he? He first enters the scene in Exodus 17:8-11, where as a young man he leads the Israelites in a victorious battle over the Amalekite army which had attacked them in the wilderness. In Exodus 24:12-18, we see Joshua accompanying Moses up Mt. Sinai and spending forty days and nights there as the Lord reveals the plans for His sanctuary to Moses. He comes down the mountain with Moses, carrying the tablets with the ten commandments, to find the Israelites fallen into idolatry (Ex. 32:15-20). Thus he witnesses some of the most crucial events in Israel's early history.

But the passage that tells us the most about Joshua's early years is Exodus 33:7-11, where Moses is seen going outside the camp to a special tent which he called the *"tent of meeting."* There the pillar of cloud which symbolized God's presence would descend, and *"the Lord spoke to Moses."* Exodus 33:11 is an extraordinary summary telling us not only of Moses' relationship with the Lord, but giving us insight into Joshua's heart as well:

> So the Lord spoke to Moses face to face, as a man speaks to his friend. And he would return to the camp, but his servant Joshua the son of Nun, a young man, did not depart from the tabernacle.

Joshua was a man who longed to know God, and to hear His voice as Moses did. He was willing to spend long hours away from family and friends for that purpose. Are you this kind of person?

One last event in Joshua's earlier career is worth noting here. When the twelve Israelites, who had been sent to spy out Canaan, returned with their report, ten of them said it was impossible to conquer the powerful inhabitants of the land, thus leading the people to dismay. But Joshua and Caleb tried—unsuccessfully—to persuade the people to boldly trust in the Lord:

> Only do not rebel against the Lord, nor fear the people of the land, for they are our bread; their protection has departed from them, and the Lord is with us. Do not fear them (Num. 14:9).

So we see Joshua as a man of faith. The Lord described him to Moses as *"a man in whom is the spirit"* (Num. 27.18), who *"wholly followed the Lord"* (Num. 32:12).

In Deuteronomy 31, we read of the transition of leadership from Moses to Joshua. The result is summarized in the last chapter of the book:

> Joshua the son of Nun was full of the spirit of wisdom, for Moses had laid his hands on him; so the children of Israel heeded him (Deut. 34:9).

Yet in spite of all his years of preparation, to follow in Moses' footsteps was a massive challenge, and Joshua was understandably afraid. So the Lord spoke to him directly, encouraging him in four specific ways in Joshua chapter 1:

1) He gave him a clear promise:

Every place that the sole of your foot will tread upon I have given you...No man shall be able to stand before you all the days of your life; as I was with Moses, so I will be with you. I will not leave you nor forsake you...to this people you shall divide as an inheritance the land which I swore to their fathers to give them (1:3-6).

2) He urged him three times to *"be strong and of good courage"* because of the presence of God with him (1:6, 7, 9).

3) He commanded him to carefully follow the Law given to Moses. The result: *"you may prosper wherever you go. This Book of the Law shall not depart from your mouth, but you shall meditate in it day and night, that you may observe to do according to all that is written in it"* (1:7-8).

PREPARATION FOR ENTERING THE LAND OF PROMISE

Following the story of Rahab and the Israelite spies, Joshua 3–5 details the remarkable steps of preparation for entering the land and for the battle of Jericho.

1) To show Israel that His power had not changed since the Red Sea crossing, the Lord miraculously stopped the flow of the Jordan River so they could cross into the Promised Land (chs. 3–4). While the priests, who carried the ark of the covenant, stood in the middle of the Jordan River bed, Joshua set up 12 stones there as a memorial. He also had men take twelve stones from the river to their first camping ground, Gilgal, where he set them up as another memorial. In later years, when their children asked about these stones, they were to tell them the following:

Israel crossed over this Jordan on dry land; for the Lord your God dried up the waters of the Jordan before you...as the Lord your God did to the Red Sea...that all the peoples of the earth may know the hand of the Lord, that it is mighty, that you may fear the Lord your God forever (Josh. 4:22-24).

We need to refresh our minds, actively remembering the Lord's mighty acts of deliverance, and realizing that He who was mighty for His people in the past is mighty for us today. If crossing the Red Sea is a picture of salvation, then crossing the Jordan River may be a picture of identification with Christ.[4]

When their enemies heard of this miracle of God, *"their heart melted; and there was no spirit in them any longer because of the children of Israel"* (5:1). They grasped the hopelessness of their situation, perhaps more clearly than the Israelites.

2) Then the men of Israel were circumcised for the first time since leav-

ing Egypt (5:2-9). This was the sign of God's covenant with Abraham (Gen. 17:11) and should remind Abraham's descendants of His eternal faithfulness to His promises.

Circumcision also meant that past bondage had been "cut off" and that as children of promise, Israel should stand firm in the freedom God had delivered them into. The Lord declared to Joshua, *"This day I have rolled away the reproach of Egypt from you"* (Josh. 5:9). No more slavery—God wanted them to master their enemies in His power.

This lesson is just as crucial for God's people today, who are spiritually "circumcised" when they receive Christ.

> *In Him you were also circumcised with the circumcision made without hands, by putting off the body of the sins of the flesh, by the circumcision of Christ, buried with Him in baptism, in which you also were raised with Him through faith in the working of God, who raised Him from the dead. And you, being dead in your trespasses and the uncircumcision of your flesh, He has made alive together with Him, having forgiven you all trespasses, having wiped out the handwriting of requirements that was against us, which was contrary to us. And He has taken it out of the way, having nailed it to the cross* (Col. 2:11-14).

> *It was for freedom that Christ set us free; therefore keep standing firm and do not be subject again to a yoke of slavery.* (Gal. 5:1 NASB).

3) Finally, Israel celebrated the Passover on the east bank of the Jordan River. They had been redeemed to God by the blood of the lamb, and were never to forget it. On the day after the Passover a new era began: *"The manna ceased on the morrow after they had eaten of the old corn of the land"* (Josh. 5:12).

CONQUEST AND INHERITANCE OF THE LAND

From chapter 6 onward, the book of Joshua records the conquest and possession of the Promised Land. The central point of the book is found in Joshua 11:23:

> *So Joshua took the whole land, according to all that the Lord said unto Moses; and Joshua gave it for an inheritance unto Israel according to their divisions by their tribes. And the land rested from war.*

Chapters 6–11 tell of the taking of the land, and chapters 12–24 tell of the dividing of the land among the tribes. The land was God's generous *"gift"* to His people (Deut. 1:20, 25; 2:29; 4:40), but Israel still had to *"possess"* it militarily in order to receive it. Divine sovereignty (given) and human responsibility (possessing) are side by side: *"the land which the Lord God of your fathers is giving you to possess"* (Deut. 12:1). Christians must battle in the *"heavenlies"* in order to take possession or *"lay hold"* of all the blessings which have been freely granted to us there in Christ (compare

Eph. 1:3 and 6:12). *"I press on in order that I may lay hold of that for which also I was laid hold of by Christ Jesus"* (Phil. 3:12).

The Lord is *"a Man of War"* (Ex. 15:3) and *"the battle is the Lord's"* (1 Sam. 17:47). One of the great names of God in the Bible is *"The Lord of Hosts"* (or armies). He had given specific laws for battle which Israel must follow.[5] In a very significant event *"the Angel of the Lord,"* who was actually the Lord Himself, came to Joshua before the first battle as the *"Captain of the host of the Lord"* (Josh. 5:13-15; see Appendix 8 for a fuller discussion of the appearances of God's appearances as the Angel). This was to teach Joshua that the Lord "does not come merely to help us, but to take full control"[6] as the Captain.

For a correct view of our world today, we must understand that there is a war in progress. Although invisible to our eyes, it is a real war in the spiritual realm, the *"heavenly places."* The New Testament describes it this way: *"Be strong in the Lord...For we do not wrestle against flesh and blood, but against principalities, against powers, against the rulers of the darkness of this age, against spiritual hosts of wickedness in the heavenly places"* (Eph. 6:10-12).

Throughout the Scriptures we catch glimpses of this war and these spirit armies (Gen. 32:1-2; Josh. 5:13-15; 2 Ki. 6:8-18; Dan. 10:12-21). In the garden of Eden the Lord said to Satan, *"I will put enmity between you and the woman, and between your seed and her Seed"* (Gen. 3:15). The spiritual and physical realms are interconnected in this war between the Lord's people and the enemy. Faith, obedience, and prayer are mighty weapons which make a real difference. The battles for the land of promise recorded in the book of Joshua, particularly the two battles recorded in chapters 6–8, teach us key lessons for doing battle against the enemy to enter into or "possess" our inheritance in Christ. In fact the whole book of Joshua can be seen as a sort of "spiritual warfare manual."

God told Abraham long before, that when the sin of the wicked Canaanite people was complete, those nations would be utterly destroyed in punishment for their depravity. Israel was now to be God's instrument of punishment (see Gen. 15:16). Further discussion of the often troublesome issue of holy war and God's dreadful order to totally destroy every person in these nations can be found in Appendix 7, pages 238-239.

By faith the people of Israel were able to conquer the powerful city of Jericho without lifting a weapon. As the Lord commanded them, they marched around the city silently once each day for six consecutive days led by seven priests carrying the ark of the Lord (6:1-14). On the seventh day He sent them around the city seven times and told them after the seventh time, *"Shout; for the Lord has given you the city"* (6:15-16). The great city wall fell down flat and the encircling Israelites went straight ahead and took the city, destroying everything in it as the Lord had commanded (6:20-21). The Lord fought for Israel when they obeyed and believed Him.

By disobedience Israel was defeated by the little city of Ai. The Lord had sternly warned the Israelites to take nothing at all from Jericho for themselves, lest they *"make the camp of Israel a curse, and trouble it"* (6:18). But one man named Achan from the tribe of Judah took a beautiful mantle, some gold and silver, and hid them under the ground of his tent. As the men of Ai defeated Israel, Joshua fell to his face before the Lord in dismay. But the Lord said to him,

> *Get up! Why do you lie thus on your face? Israel has sinned, and they have also transgressed My covenant which I commanded them. For they have even taken some of the accursed things, and have both stolen and deceived; and they have also put it among their own stuff. Therefore the children of Israel could not stand before their enemies* (Josh. 7:10-12).

Joshua investigated and uncovered Achan's sin. Achan and all that belonged to him were stoned to death and burned (7:15-26). Then the Lord sent the people out again, with the assurance, *"Do not be afraid, nor be dismayed;…I have given into your hand the king of Ai"* (8:1). This time Israel won a great victory and Ai was totally destroyed.

It is crucial to see the way the Lord deals with His people. One man sinned, but God said to Joshua, *"Israel has sinned,"* and all Israel was defeated because of the one sin! The sin of one Israelite was seen by God as the congregation's sin: "The Divine Presence imparted a unity to the whole assembly; it bound them all together in such a manner as to involve all in the sin of the one."[7] The same principle is still in effect today in churches of God's people: *"Do you not know that a little leaven leavens the whole lump?"* (1 Cor. 5:6). We need to be extremely careful about sin, as our sin involves and affects the whole family of God.

When Israel obeyed the Lord's rules for war (Deut. 12:1-4; 20:1-20; 21:10-14; 23:9-14), *"the Lord fought for Israel"* (Josh. 10:14). These successful campaigns are recorded in Joshua 6, 8, 10 and 11. God's people were to trust and not fear, knowing that the Lord had delivered the enemy into their hands" (see Josh. 6:2, 16; 8:1; 10:8; 11:6).

But when Israel disobeyed, they were easily defeated or deceived. Israel's failures due to disobedience are illustrated in Joshua 7 and 9 and throughout the book of Judges. The Lord said to Joshua after Israel had been humiliated by the people of Ai, *"neither will I be with you anymore, unless you destroy the accursed from among you"* (Josh. 7:12). Only after the sin was dealt with could they continue with the Lord.

Israel got into trouble not only through sins of commission like Achan's, but also through sins of omission. In Joshua 9 we see how representatives of one of the condemned nations, the Gibeonites, craftily deceived Joshua and Israel's leaders into making a peace treaty with them rather than destroying them completely as commanded. Their guile succeeded because Israel's leaders *"did not ask counsel of the Lord"* (Josh. 9:14). We are all too prone to forget the warning of the Lord Jesus to His disciples, *"for without Me you can do nothing"* (Jn. 15:5).

We dare not underestimate our enemy. His schemes to get us to compromise with sin and make peace with him are very subtle. *"He is a liar, and the father of it"* (Jn. 8:44), and his demons are called *"seducing spirits"* (1 Tim. 4:1). We are also confronted continually by *"the sleight of men, and cunning craftiness"* (Eph. 4:14). Only by the active guidance of God can we overcome. We must discipline ourselves to pray and listen to the Lord, *"Lest Satan should take advantage of us: for we are not ignorant of his devices"* (2 Cor. 2:11).

These principles are seen in operation throughout Joshua's lifetime. In a memorable farewell message, he addressed the nation's leaders after *"the Lord had given rest to Israel from all their enemies round about"* (Josh. 23:1). He urged them, *"Hold fast to the Lord your God,"* and warned them that if they ever turned back the Lord would not fight for them and they would ultimately be *"destroyed...from this good land which the Lord your God has given you"* (23:7-13). They must choose whom they would serve. The people vowed to serve the Lord (24:14-18). But he warned them that they would not be able to serve Him. *"For He is an holy God; He is a jealous God"* (24:19). For more on the jealousy of God, see Study 12, pp. 167-168.

Nevertheless, the people insisted that they would serve the Lord, and Joshua dismissed them to their inheritance (24:28). Soon afterward Joshua himself died. The map (at left) shows approximately how the land was divided among the twelve tribes.

TERRITORY GIVEN TO THE TWELVE TRIBES

JUDGES—FAILURE, REPENTANCE, AND BLESSING IN THE LAND

How long did the people's good intentions last? Not long. *"The people served the Lord all the days of Joshua,"* but within a single generation they began to do *"evil in the sight of the Lord"* (Judges 2:7, 11). They began to worship the gods of the pagan peoples still living in the land. "Then the children of Israel did evil in the sight of the Lord, and served the Baals; *"and they forsook the Lord God of their fathers, who had brought them out of the land of Egypt; and they followed other gods from among the gods of the people who were all around them, and they bowed down to them; and they provoked the Lord to anger"* (Judges 2:11-12).

The worship of these idols embroiled the Israelites in immoral, occult practices. We need to realize that all idolatry, whether openly participating in pagan religions or simply setting up little idols in our hearts (see Ezek. 14:3), opens the door to involvement in the realm of demons:

> *The things which the Gentiles sacrifice, they sacrifice to demons, and not to God: and I do not want you to have fellowship with demons* (1 Cor. 10:20).

There is no middle ground. We cannot avoid taking sides. If we are not actively for the Lord, we are against Him. Jesus told His disciples plainly: *"He that is not with me is against me: and he that gathereth not with me scattereth"* (Lk. 11:23).

The inevitable result of Israel's apostasy was that the Lord's anger burned against them, and He abandoned them to their own devices:

> *He delivered them into the hands of plunderers who despoiled them; and He sold them into the hands of their enemies all around, so that they could no longer stand before their enemies* (Judges 2:14).

But this was no surprise. In fact, the Lord had deliberately allowed a group of nations to remain in the land at the end of Joshua's era, not driving them out quickly. His purpose in this was two-fold:

1) In order to test Israel by them, *"whether they will keep the way of the Lord to walk in them, as their fathers kept it, or not"* (Judges 2:22; see 3:4).
2) In order that the new generation, who had not experienced the victorious wars of Canaan under Joshua taught them war (see Judges 3:2).

The Lord deals with us the same way today. He has not driven Satan and the spiritual forces of wickedness out of the world yet, although their doom is certain. He allows us to face the enemy both to test us, and to teach us spiritual warfare. Each individual and each generation of believers must do battle themselves to possess and enjoy their God-given inheritance.

The tribes of Israel failed to drive out the inhabitants of the land (Judges 1:19, 21, 27-36). As a result, for the next few hundred years a sad cycle was repeated over and over in the Promised Land:

Sin ⇨ Punishment ⇨ Repentance ⇨ God's compassion
⇩   ⇧
A period of Rest in the land ⇦ A Deliverer (the judges)

The primary purpose of the Book of Judges is to show that Israel's *spiritual condition* determined their political and material situation. When Israel turned to God in obedience, God graciously sent deliverers to rescue the people from oppression. When they disregarded Joshua's warning and worshiped the gods of Canaan, the nation came under the control of tyrants and invaders.[8]

The key "that made this history more than just a dreary report of constant failure was the doctrine of repentance,"[9] just as promised in Deuteronomy 30:1-10. Whenever Israel *"cried to the Lord"* He *"raised up a deliverer"* to restore them (Judges 3:9, 15; 4:3; etc.). "Repentance was the basis for any new work of God after a time of failure. And the result of that repentance was the *'good'* (blessing) God would do to them."[10] The lesson for us is clear: If we have been disobedient and have abandoned God's way, we should immediately forsake our wrongdoing and turn to the Lord. He will abundantly pardon.

The flow of the book of Judges is downhill, recording a moral decline in the lives of the judges themselves. Compare the first judge Othniel (3:9-11) with the last judge Samson (16:20). Othniel fought to win a section of the land for Caleb. He desired to marry Caleb's daughter Achsah, who is presented as a woman desiring God's blessing (Jud. 1:11-15; also Josh. 15:13-19). In strong contrast, Samson fought to avenge his personal offenses (14:12–15:8). He desired a Philistine woman to satisfy his own taste in women, telling his parents, *"Get her for me, for she pleases me well"* (14:1-3). His sad demise was caused by his affair with a prostitute (16:1-21).

As the book progresses, Israel's plight worsens. The stunning victories of Deborah and Barak and of Gideon (chs. 4-8), are followed by the less decisive efforts of Jephthah (11) and Samson (13-16). Jephthah's victory over Ammon failed to prevent civil war. Samson's personal heroics did not throw off the Philistine yoke. By the end of the book, the stories of sin and all-out civil war depict the nation's desperate need for unity and order. The repeated references to a time when Israel "had no king and everyone did what was right in his own eyes" (17:6; 18:1; 19:1; 21:25) open the way for the carrying out of God's purpose in the next era through the "kingdom" He would establish. We see the tribe of Judah taking the leadership role (Judges 1:1-2; 20:18), and therefore it is no surprise that God's chosen king, David, comes from Judah, even as God promised centuries before (Gen. 49:10).[11]

RUTH—ENTERING THE PROMISED RACE

The little book of Ruth stands in contrast with Judges, reminding us that God was quietly working out His plan through the discouraging *"days when the judges governed"* (1:1). "While most of Israel was wandering away from the Lord, there was a Gentile maiden named Ruth whose faith shone out with brilliance."[12] God graciously brought her into the *"seed"* of Abraham through her marriage to Naomi's relative or *"kinsman redeemer,"* Boaz.[13] Their child, Obed, would be the grandfather of the famous shepherd-king David (4:16-22).

From the line of David would come Messiah, the ultimate King of the promise. By taking on Himself human nature, He would become the true "kinsman redeemer," and redeem His fallen "kinsmen."

RAHAB AND RUTH

The record of the Pre-monarchical era is bracketed by the narratives of two Gentile women: *Rahab*, the Canaanite prostitute (Josh. 2), and *Ruth* the Moabite. While their former moral lives are complete opposites, both women are shining examples of faith in action. Both came from idolatry to believe in the Lord as the true God and took refuge *"under His wings"* (Ruth 2:12).

Rahab is cited in the New Testament as an example of true faith which is demonstrated by actions (Jas. 2:25). Her bold words, *"I know that the Lord has given you the land,"* shows understanding of God's promise to Abraham's seed. She accepted this as truth, and she feared God, confessing Him as *"God in heaven above and in earth beneath"* (Josh. 2:9-11). She put her life on the line by hiding the Israelite spies from her own countrymen and entrusted herself to God's people for protection (Josh. 2:12-14).

But these two women have even deeper significance in God's plan as Gentile women brought into the kingly tribe of Judah and the lineage of David. The names of both are found in the genealogy of Jesus Christ that opens the New Testament, where Rahab appears as Boaz's mother and Ruth's mother-in-law (Mt. 1:5).[14] Each is included as a direct exception to the law of the Lord concerning their nation:

Rahab—A Canaanite, whose people were to be utterly destroyed without mercy as God's judgment (Deut. 7:2; 20:16-18).

Ruth—A Moabite, whose people were never to enter the assembly of the Lord (Deut. 23:3).

They were both examples of God's grace. Though their people were under God's judgment, they took refuge in Him and were saved from His wrath. All of us who come from non-Jewish backgrounds to Christ are like these two women.

Remember that you, once Gentiles in the flesh—who are called Uncircumcision by what is called the Circumcision made in the flesh by hands—that at that time you were without Christ, being aliens from the commonwealth of Israel and strangers from the covenants of promise, having no hope and without God in the world. But now in Christ Jesus you who once were far off have been brought near by the blood of Christ (Eph. 2:11-13).

CONCLUSION

In spite of repeated failure by His people, the God of Abraham, Isaac, and Jacob was true to His promise. His words were fulfilled in history: *"Not a word failed of any good thing which the Lord had spoken to the house of Israel. All came to pass"* (Josh. 21:45; 23:14). God's word is not an "empty" word. What He says comes to pass.

Yet in order to personally share in the promised "rest" and joy of life in the Lord, we must obey His word. By His power we must drive the enemy from every part of our life. We must give ourselves to knowing God and walking closely with Him in our spiritual warfare. Let us take our stand with Joshua and declare,

"As for me and my house, we will serve the Lord!" (Josh. 24:15).

ENDNOTES

1 Donald H. Madvig, *Expositor's Bible Commentary,* Joshua, p. 239.

2 For a discussion of the issues involved in dating this period, see the *Expositor's Bible Commentary,* Vol. 3, pp. 240-241, 376-377, 555.

3 Kaiser, *Towards an Old Testament Theology,* p. 130.

4 Christ's death *for* us delivers us from bondage to sin, and our crucifixion *with* Christ delivers us from the self-life. Viewing the Christian life in this way, we need to get out of the "wilderness" and into the "land." We must "cross the Jordan," reckoning ourselves as having died with Christ to sin and having risen with Him to new life in God. We can then yield ourselves to Him as instruments of righteousness. See, for example, Charles R. Solomon, *Handbook to Happiness, A Guide to Victorious Living and Effective Counseling,* Living Studies, Tyndale House Publishers, Wheaton, IL, pp. 91-103.

5 Deuteronomy 12:1-4; 20; 21:10-14; 23:9-14; 25:17-19.

6 William MacDonald, *Old Testament Digest,* Walterick Publishers.

7 C. H. Mackintosh; *The Treasury of C. H. Mackintosh,* p. 829.

8 Herbert Wolf, *Expositor's Bible Commentary,* Vol. 3, Judges, p. 378.

9 Kaiser, p. 137.

10 Ibid., p. 138.

11 Wolf, p. 378.

12 MacDonald, *Old Testament Digest,* Walterick Publishers, Vol. 2, Introduction to Ruth.

13 The Hebrew word *"goel"* or *"ga'al"* indicates redeeming through a sacrifice. This word appears in Ruth at least 20 times in various forms, referring to the near relative charged with redeeming the inheritance of his dead relative (Ruth 2:20; 3:9, 12-13; 4:1, 3, 4, 6, 8, 14). See also Gen. 38; Deut. 25:5-10; Lev. 25:25, 35, 47-49; Jer. 32:6-25 for examples of this practice. This same word is used of God Himself as the Redeemer (Ps. 19:14; 78:35; Isa. 41:14; 44:6, 24; 47:4; 48:17; 49:7, 26; 54:5, 8; 59:20; 60:16; 63:16. The coming Messiah is called the *"goel"* or Kinsman-Redeemer in Job 19:25 and Isaiah 59:20.

14 Like many biblical family trees, "this genealogy is not intended to be complete. Salmon lived at the beginning of the period of the judges, a span of almost 400 years. Names are often deliberately omitted in biblical genealogies." (Wm. MacDonald, *Believer's Bible Commentary,* Old Testament, Nelson, p. 293).

1. What was God's purpose in bringing His people out of Egyptian slavery according to Deuteronomy 6:23?

2. List some of the characteristics of the Promised Land in Deuteronomy 8:7-10; 12:9-10, 15:4 and 26:9.

3. What qualities did the Lord find in Joshua in the following verses that made Him speak so highly of him, and choose him as Moses successor? Does He find these in you?

    Ex. 33:11

    Num. 14:9

    Num. 27:18

    Num. 32:12

    Deut. 34:9

4. Read Joshua 1:1-9 and write out Joshua 1:8 below.

    What promises are given to Joshua if he obeys these words (1:8)?

    How does this principle apply to your life? What practical steps can you take to improve your obedience to Joshua 1:8?

5. In chapter 5:13-15 Joshua encounters an awesome Being who calls himself the *"Captain of the host of the Lord."* Compare with the following verses: Gen. 16:7-14; 22:11-18; 31:11-13; Ex. 13:21; 14:19; Judges 2:1-4; 6:11-24; 13:2-23. Who was this Being? Give verses to support your conclusion.

6. Joshua 6 records Israel's victory over the city of Jericho. What did the Israelites have to do to succeed in this battle (5:13–6:21)?

    What principles do you see for believers in our "spiritual warfare" today?

7. Joshua 7–8 records Israel's battles with the tiny town of Ai. What caused their initial defeat (7:10-13)?

    What caused their victory in chapter 8?

    What principles do you see for believers in our "spiritual warfare" today (note 1 Cor. 5:6)?

8. Read Joshua's farewell message to Israel in Joshua chapter 23. What specific advice does he give them in verses 6-11?

9. How can you apply the principles of Joshua and Judges to your own relationship with the Lord and the church? How are you using the weapons of spiritual warfare?

10. The book of Ruth is a beautiful story of a Gentile woman's faith and God's faithfulness to His people. But it has a greater significance. Read Ruth 4:13-22 along with Genesis 46:12 and 49:10. Why is the story of Ruth important?

KING OF THE PROMISE
DAVID'S ERA

Recommended Readings: 1 Samuel 16:1-13; 2 Samuel 7; Psalm 2; 45; 89:1-4, 19-37; 110; 132

The final verses of the book of Ruth prepared us to look for the arrival of David, *"the man raised up on high, the anointed of the God of Jacob, and the sweet psalmist of Israel"* (2 Sam. 23:1). He was Israel's model king, to whom all future kings would be compared. He was also their greatest psalmist, writing some of the most beloved songs of worship ever penned. David's forty-year reign is among the most import-ant segments in divine history, primarily because of the greatness of the promises he received from God.

A PROMISED KING

The Lord Himself was Israel's King, who would *"reign for ever and ever"* (Ex. 15:18). Yet clearly a human king, as God's representative, was also foreseen in God's plan (Num. 24:17). From Genesis 49:10 we know that Israel's promised king was to come from the tribe of Judah. He knew that Israel would reject His sole kingship and want to be like the rest of the nations. Therefore in Deuteronomy 17:14-20 He gave specific guidelines for the future king.

But there were at least two premature starts during the era of the judges:

1) Abimelech

When the men of Israel offered Gideon the throne after his victory over Midian, he refused, saying, *"The Lord shall rule over you"* (Judges 8:22-23). However, Gideon's son Abimelech usurped the kingly office, murdering his brothers in the process. Judges 9 tells the tragic results of that false "kingdom."

2) Saul

The last of the judges of Israel was Samuel. He was also the first (other than Moses and the unnamed prophet in Judges 6:8) of a long line of prophets (Acts 3:24). His mother Hannah had been barren for many years, a pattern seen in the mothers of many of God's chosen men:

- Isaac's mother Sarah (Gen. 11:30; 16:1)
- Jacob's mother Rebekah (Gen. 25:21)
- Joseph's mother Rachel (Gen. 29:31; 30:1-2)
- Samson's mother, wife of Manoah (Judges 13:2-3)
- John the Baptist's mother Elisabeth (Lk. 1:7, 36)

The Lord frequently arranges the circumstances of His greatest works to highlight the barrenness of all human effort, and to show that *"with God nothing will be impossible"* (Lk. 1:37). Hannah's impassioned prayer for a child was answered, and she dedicated her baby boy Samuel to God's service in the tabernacle at Shiloh (1 Sam. 1–2). God called him to a special work as a young boy. Before long *"all Israel from Dan to Beersheba knew that Samuel had been established as a prophet of the Lord"* (3:20). Samuel judged Israel faithfully all the days of his life (1 Sam. 4–7).

When Samuel grew old the people demanded a king to fight their battles for them so they would be *"like all the nations"* (1 Sam. 8:5, 20). In doing so they were in fact rejecting the Lord as king. Samuel's warnings were ignored and God gave them what they asked for: Saul (8:10–10:1). As God's *"chosen"* one (10:1, 24) Saul accomplished the task appointed him and was a victorious leader (9:16; 14:47-48). But after disobeying the Lord twice (13:8-14; 15:1-26), showing his inner *"rebellion"* (15:23), Saul was told twice, *"Because you have rejected the word of the Lord, He also has rejected you from being king"* (15:23, see also v. 26).

When Saul was rejected, the Lord *"sought for Himself a man after His own heart"* (1 Sam. 13:14) and sent Samuel to anoint one of Jesse's sons to be king. Jesse made seven of his fine sons pass in front of the old prophet, but not until young, insignificant David was called from tending the sheep did Samuel hear God's word, *"Arise, anoint him; for this is he!"* (16:1-13). The oil poured on his head symbolized God's enabling or anointing for ruling His people: *"the Spirit of the Lord came upon David from that day forward"* (16:13). This Hebrew word *mashiyach*, meaning "the anointed," gradually became a title for God's coming Saviour-King: *"Messiah"* (Ps. 2:2; Isa. 61:1; Dan. 9:25-26).

"A Man After My Heart, Who Will Do All My Will"

Even so great a prophet as Samuel, who grew up in the temple serving the Lord and *"judged Israel all the days of his life"* (7:15), had to learn that *"the Lord does not see as man sees; for man looks at the outward appearance, but the Lord looks at the heart"* (1 Sam. 16:6-7; note also 10:23-24). We also find this a difficult lesson to learn. We are impressed by appearance, wealth, or education rather than by the inner character traits that God values. What in fact did the Lord see in the shepherd boy's heart?

- A deep love and delight in God Himself (Ps. 23; 34; 63; 145).
- A longing to know and obey God's Word (1 Ki. 14:8; 15:5; Ps. 17:4; 19:7-14; 37:31; Acts 13:22).
- Confident, courageous faith in the Living God (1 Sam. 17:41-50; Ps. 3:3-6; 27:1-3).
- A sensitive spirit, quick to confess his sin, and aware of the deceitfulness of his heart (2 Sam. 12:1-13; Ps. 19:12-13; 32; 40:12; 51).
- Humility and patient self-restraint when wronged (1 Sam. 24:1-15; 26; 2 Sam. 16:5-13; Ps. 37).
- Determination to worship the Lord and to lead others to praise Him as well (2 Sam. 6:12-22; 1 Chron. 16; Ps. 34:1-3; 103:1-3; 108:1-5; 138).

This *"heart"* is what God's kingdom is all about (Mt. 5–7). What does God see when He looks at our hearts? Do we have the courage to say with David, *"Search me, O God, and know my heart…see if there is any wicked way in me"* (Ps. 139:23-24).

The second half of 1 Samuel tells of David's long years as a fugitive, running from King Saul's jealousy and hatred (18–30). During these years of deep personal struggle, David wrote some of his most moving psalms of trust in the Lord (e.g., 31, 34, 56, 57, 63, 142). But at last in God's time Saul was killed in battle along with his son Jonathan (1 Sam. 31–2 Sam. 1), and after a victorious struggle against Saul's sons, David was crowned king of all Israel (2 Sam. 5:1-5).

THE JOURNEYS OF THE ARK OF THE LORD

The books of Samuel include a history of the sad travels of the golden *"ark of the covenant of the Lord,"* which should have remained in the Holy of Holies in the tabernacle at Shiloh. Finding themselves defeated by the Philistines, rather than repenting and seeking God as Joshua did when Israel was defeated by the little city of Ai (Josh. 7:6-9), elders of Israel get the bright idea of bringing the ark to the battlefield, hoping that *"when it comes among us, it may save us from the hand of our enemies"* (1 Sam. 4:1-3).

But God will not be used or taken lightly. The remainder of 1 Samuel 4 records the tragic story of how *"the glory departed from Israel"* (4:22). The Philistines capture the ark in battle and take it to their capital, but find to their dismay that the God of Israel begins to fight against them. When they set the ark alongside the idol of their god Dagon in their temple, they soon find Dagon face down on the ground before the ark, with his stone head and hands broken off on the threshold. God's curse brings such plagues on the idol-worshipping Philistines that they soon send the ark back to Israel (1 Sam. 5–6), where it remains for twenty years in the house of a man named Abinadab (1 Sam. 7:1-2).

During this period many Israelites also die as a result of carelessly handling the holy vessel which symbolized God's throne (1 Sam. 6:19-20; 2 Sam. 6:1-11). But finally David succeeds in bringing the ark of God into Jerusalem and ends the tragic years of spiritual neglect (2 Sam. 6:12–18). The presence of *"the Lord of hosts who dwells between the cherubim"* (2 Sam. 6:2) will be with the throne of the new kingdom. The stage is now set for the key event of David's life.

A PROMISED DYNASTY (2 SAMUEL 7)

God's promise to David in 2 Samuel 7 has to be among the most brilliant moments in the history of salvation. It is matched in importance and prestige only by the promise made to Abraham in Genesis 12 and later to all Israel and Judah in Jeremiah's New Covenant (Jer. 31).[1]

The chapter is the account of David's proposal to build a *"house"* for the Lord (7:1-3) and God's counter-proposal to make a *"house"* (a dynasty or line of descendants) for David instead (v. 11). It was God's project, part of the ever-expanding purpose of God. He promised David, *"I will set up thy seed after thee...I will be his Father and he shall be My son"* (vv. 12-14), and, *"thine house and thy kingdom shall be established for ever before thee"* (v. 16).

In this great unilateral transaction God's blessing of Abraham is developed further in a closely related blessing of David. A comparison of common elements reveals this close relationship:

- *"a great name"* (v. 9 with Gen. 12:2).
- *"a place"* (v. 10 with Gen. 15:7; Deut. 11:24-25; Josh. 1:4-5).
- *"set up your seed after you"* (v. 12 with Gen. 17:7-10, 19).
- *"He shall be My son"* (v. 14 with Ex. 4:22).
- *"Thou hast confirmed to Thyself Thy people Israel to be a people unto thee for ever: and thou, Lord, art become their God."* (v. 24 KJV, with Gen. 17:7-8; Ex. 6:7; Lev. 26:12; Deut. 29:13).
- *"There is none like Thee"* (v. 22 with Ex. 8:10; 9:14; 15:11; Deut. 33:26)
- *"What one nation...is like Thy people"* (v. 23 with Deut. 4:7-8; 5:26)
- *"Adonai Yahweh,"* a rarely used name (vv. 18-22, 28, 29 with Gen. 15:2, 8)

"A Charter for Mankind"

David's response to God was, *"Who am I, O Lord God? And what is my house, that You have brought me this far? And yet this was a small thing in Your sight, O Lord God; and You have also spoken of Your servant's house for a great while to come. Is this the manner of man, O Lord God?"* (7:18-19).

What God had now spoken to him…was the divine 'torah' or pre-scription…for poor human creatures…With the realization that he had just been granted an everlasting dynasty, dominion, and king-dom, David blurted out in uncontainable joy: *'And this is the Charter of man, O Lord God!'* (19b NASB). Thus the ancient plan of God would con-tinue, only now it would involve a king and a kingdom…and the future of all mankind.[2]

God's promise to Abraham that through his "seed" all nations would be blessed was now centered in King David and his descendants. Through this eternal kingdom of David all nations would be blessed.

THE PSALMS OF THE KING

"Although all scripture breatheth the grace of God, yet sweet beyond all others is the book of Psalms."[3] The psalms have always been one of the best-loved parts of the Word of God for believers. Here every experience and emotion of the believer's life is given expression. Here songs of wor-ship and praise, frustration and loneliness, rejection and suffering, confes-sion and hope, joy and trust, are all poured out freely to the psalmist's faithful, heavenly Shepherd (Ps. 23).

Nearly half of the 150 psalms in Scripture were composed by David. While stirring and strengthening the hearts of His people through the cen-turies, God also used these songs to reveal many deep truths relating to His promise. Especially rich and wonderful are the "Messianic" psalms. Jesus Christ told His disciples to look for Him there, saying, *"all things must be fulfilled, which were written…in the psalms, concerning me* (Lk. 24:44).

Of those [psalms] which allude to the life of David, there are none in which the Son of David is not the principle subject. David's com-plaints are Messiah's complaints. David's afflictions are Messiah's suf-ferings. David's penitential supplications are Messiah's under the bur-den of the imputed guilt of man. David's songs of triumph and thanksgiving are Messiah's, for His victory over sin, and death, and hell. In a word, there is not a page of the book of Psalms in which the pious reader will not find his Saviour, if he reads with a view to find-ing Him.[4]

While all of David's Psalms draw us to Christ, some are called Messianic because they clearly and primarily refer to One far beyond David and his own experiences. These Messianic Psalms can be gathered into two major groups:

I. PSALMS OF MESSIAH'S PERSONAL SUFFERING AND GLORY
    (2, 8, 16, 22, 31, 40, 41, 45, 68, 69, 109, 110, 118)

These psalms are all confirmed as Messianic by the Spirit of God in the

New Testament (see Appendix 2). They are portraits painted in both the deep-toned shades of the sufferings of Messiah and the bright radiance of His glories to follow (1 Pet. 1:11). We are allowed to feel the inner emotions of His anguish, indignation, and joy through the outworking of God's plan. In these psalms, aspects of His character, His deity and humanity, His obedience, betrayal, sufferings, crucifixion, and resurrection are detailed as in no other part of the Old Testament. Nowhere can we draw nearer to the heart of the Master than here.

It is also amazing to realize how Christ made these ancient psalms part of His heart and soul during His life on the earth. "Here are His own prayers pre-written by the Spirit of God."[5] Even on the cross they filled His mind (Ps. 22:1; 31:5).

> It appears to have been the manual of the Son of God; He who had not the Spirit by measure, in whom were hidden all the treasures of wisdom and knowledge, who spake as never man spake, yet chose to conclude His life, to solace Himself in His greatest agony, and at last to breathe out His soul, in the psalmist's words rather than His own.[6]

How much should this tell us about the value of the psalms for our own spiritual lives! Perhaps our weakness in prayer would be greatly strengthened if we learned to appropriate for ourselves the words of the psalms more regularly.

II. Psalms of Messiah's Davidic Kingdom (2, 18, 20, 21, 24, 45, 72, 89, 101, 110, 132, 144)

While not referring so directly to Messiah as the first group (except for 2, 45, and 110, which must be included in both groups) these "royal psalms are steeped in the ideology of the Davidic dynasty and presupposes the promise and oath made to him. They form a unity centering on the Davidic king who, as Yahweh's son, resided in Jerusalem, ruled over Yahweh's people, and was heir to the promise."[7] We'll notice five of the most remarkable of these:

Psalm 2
The fulfillment of God's purposes centers in the kingly line that is set *"upon My holy hill of Zion"* (v. 6). "Man's laughable conspiracy against Christ is met by God's decree that His Son shall be given universal dominion."[8]

Psalm 45
The mystery of this passage is that the Davidic king (Messiah) is addressed as "God" by the psalmist (v. 6), and yet is Himself anointed by God (v. 7)! The grace, majesty, strength and righteousness of God in heaven is to be bound up in this amazing One who is *"fairer than the children of men"* (vv. 2-4).

PSALM 89

Psalm 89 is the OT exposition of the faithfulness of God. It is also God's commentary on 2 Samuel 7. "After commenting at length on the Davidic covenant in verses 3-4 and 19-37; verses 38-51 lamented the downfall of the monarchy and pleaded that God would be faithful to His promise to David."[9] God declared that He had sworn an oath of faithfulness, saying *"I will not lie to David."*

PSALM 110

In this, the most quoted psalm in the New Testament (see Appendix 2), the psalmist brings together both the royal dominion and the priesthood of Messiah whom he calls his "Lord": *"The Lord said unto My Lord, sit Thou at My right hand, until I make Thine enemies Thy footstool"* (v. 1). *"The Lord hath sworn, and will not repent, Thou art a priest for ever after the order of Melchizedek"* (v. 4).

PSALM 132

The ark of God and the Davidic kingdom are the main topics of this psalm, which celebrates the *"oath"* sworn to David by God (v. 11) and the shout of the ark: *"Arise, O Lord, into Thy rest; thou, and the ark of Thy strength...For Thy servant David's sake"* (vv. 8-10; compare with Moses' shout in Num. 10:35-36).

Several additional psalms, which Kaiser calls "eschatological" or "enthronement Psalms" (47, 93-100),[10] present God Himself as taking up the scepter of His kingdom and coming to judge the earth. This further emphasizes the divine/human identity of the Person ultimately to rule on the throne of this kingdom.

Perhaps most important in our study of God's promise is the way in which God deals with His people through their representative:

> ...the fact that what happened to the king happened to the people. Their lives were totally bound up with his. When he acted in faithfulness and righteousness, prosperity and blessing were the result (Ps. 18; 45:6-7; 101). But when the king was rejected, so were they. The king, then, became the channel of God's blessings and judgments. So it would be with the last David or the new David; only His realm would be boundless, and His reign would be righteous, just, and full of every perfection."[11]

CONCLUSION

In spite of his own sins, his rebellious family, and the bloodiness of David's reign (2 Sam. 11–1 Ki. 2), God's guarantee in grace still held. It depended not on David's faithfulness but on God's faithfulness! Centuries later, announcing Messiah's long-awaited birth, the angel Gabriel said, *"He shall be great, and shall be called the Son of the Highest: and the Lord God shall give to him the throne of his father David"* (Lk. 1:32).

When God raised the Lord Jesus from the dead and exalted Him to His right hand as a Prince and a Saviour, it was according to the *"everlasting covenant with you, even the sure mercies of David"* (Acts 13:34; Isa. 55:3; also Heb. 13:20 where Christ is the "Great Shepherd" brought up from the dead), and we who belong to Him are exhorted to stand firm in faith and *"remember that Jesus Christ of the seed of David was raised from the dead according to my gospel"* (2 Tim. 2:8).

The Lord Jesus testifies, *"I am the root and the offspring of David, and the Bright and Morning Star,"* and says *"Surely I come quickly"* (Rev. 22:16, 20). The King of the Promise will reign for ever and ever. To Him be all the glory and honor.

ENDNOTES

1 Kaiser, TOTT, p. 143.

2 Ibid., p. 155.

3 *Henry and Scott's Commentary on the Psalms,* Introduction.

4 Ibid.

5 Ibid.

6 Ibid.

7 Kaiser, p. 159.

8 Source unknown.

9 Kaiser, p. 161.

10 Ibid., p. 162.

11 Ibid.

1. Why was Saul rejected from being king of Israel after being chosen by the Lord (1 Sam. 13:13-14; 15:23, 26)?

    What principle do you see in 1 Samuel 15:22 for pleasing God? How does He view disobedience to His word (1 Sam. 15:23)?

2. What action did the Lord command Samuel to perform to show that David was His choice to be king (1 Sam. 16:12-13)? What title for God's chosen Saviour and King grew out of this action (p. 114; also see Ps. 2:2; Dan. 9:25-26)?

    What divine action accompanied this symbolic act (1 Sam. 16:13; Isa. 61:1)?

3. *"The Lord looks at the heart"* (1 Sam. 16:7). List some of the qualities of David's heart that pleased the Lord.

    Which of these qualities do you find or not find in your own heart?

4. Why did people die while approaching or carrying the ark of the Covenant (1 Sam. 6:19-20; 1 Chron. 13 and 15). What important principle do you see in this sobering record?

5. Read all of 2 Samuel 7 carefully. What action by David prompted this great revelation by God (2 Sam. 7:1-2)?

In your own words summarize God's promise to David in verses 9-16.

What similarities can you find between this promise and the promise to Abraham recorded in Genesis 12:1-3; 15:6; 17:7-10, 19?

6. Read Matthew 1:1. Why do you suppose the New Testament starts with Jesus' genealogy?

7. Read Psalm 2. How is the Messiah referred to in the following verses:
    v. 2   v. 6
    v. 7   v. 12

8. Read Psalm 45. Describe and identify the King to whom the psalm is written (vv. 2-7).

9. Read Psalm 110, which was written by David. In verse 1 who is "the Lord" speaking to? Who is David's "Lord"?

10. Summarize in your own words David's role in God's plan.

11. How can you apply this lesson to your own relationship with the Lord?

LIFE IN THE PROMISE
SOLOMON'S ERA

Recommended Readings: Job 1–2; 19:23-26; 28:28; 38–42; Psalm 1; 25; 112; Proverbs 1:7; 9:10; 15:33; Ecclesiastes 5:1-7; 12:13-14

The era of King David's son Solomon was the high point of Israel's national glory. 1 Kings 1–11 records the history of his splendid kingdom, with the construction of the temple in Jerusalem as the centerpiece (chs. 5–8). After the ark of the covenant was brought in, *"the glory of the Lord had filled the house of the Lord,"* and Solomon eloquently dedicated the temple to the Lord as the center of Israel's worship and the symbol of dependence on Him (ch. 8).

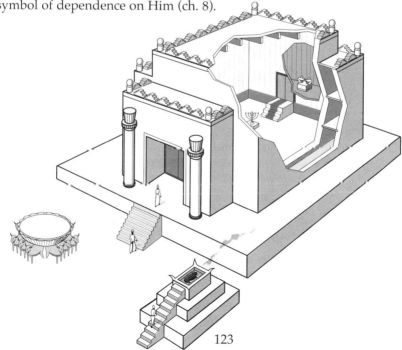

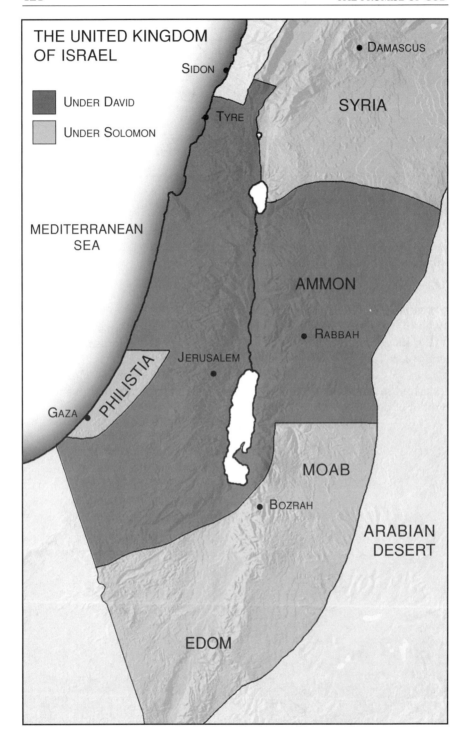

THE UNITED KINGDOM
OF ISRAEL

UNDER DAVID

UNDER SOLOMON

SIDON

DAMASCUS

SYRIA

TYRE

MEDITERRANEAN
SEA

AMMON

RABBAH

JERUSALEM

PHILISTIA

GAZA

MOAB

BOZRAH

ARABIAN
DESERT

EDOM

This great kingdom under Solomon's rule probably extended from the Gulf of Aqaba in the south to the Euphrates River in the north (see map on the previous page).

Yet in spite of his vast wealth and great political achievements, it is the wisdom of Solomon that has become legendary. When God told him to ask for whatever he desired, Solomon requested *"an understanding heart to judge Thy people."* Because he hadn't asked for long life, riches, or victory for himself, the Lord responded, *"I have given you a wise and understanding heart, so that there has not been anyone like you before you, nor shall any like you arise after you. And I have also given you what you have not asked: both riches and honor, so that there shall not be anyone like you among the kings all your days"* (3:12-13).

God kept His promise: *"King Solomon surpassed all the kings of the earth in riches and wisdom. Now all the earth sought the presence of Solomon to hear his wisdom, which God had put in his heart"* (10:23-24).

THE WISDOM BOOKS

In our first lesson we considered the general structure of the Old Testament as we have it today. The foundation of God's plan is laid in the Pentateuch, as God creates man in His own image and then redeems from among fallen men a particular people for Himself. Upon this foundation the on-going history of God's people is recorded in the books from Joshua through Esther. We are now nearly more than halfway through these historical books.

We saw that the third and fourth group of books were written during the eras recorded in the historical books. In the third group we begin to share in the thoughts of God's people as they pour out their deepest feelings to God and one another. We look at the life God gives to His people through their eyes. In the last study we saw how the psalms of David became the Holy Spirit's vehicle for Messianic prophecy, even as they expressed David's heartfelt prayer and praise to the Lord.

Solomon wrote some 3,000 proverbs and more than 1,000 songs (1 Ki. 4:32). He authored most of the book of *Proverbs,* as well as *Ecclesiastes* and the *Song of Solomon.* Together with the book of *Job* and the *Psalms,* these writings make up the five so-called "Wisdom Books" which follow the historical books and precede the writings of the prophets:

Genesis to Esther . . . . Historical Books
Job to Song of Solomon. . . . . Wisdom Books
Isaiah to Malachi . . . . Prophetic Books

In these "Wisdom books" all people are divided into two groups, known variously as the Righteous and the Wicked, the Upright and the Crooked, those with Understanding and those without, and most frequently the Wise and the Foolish (for example, Prov. 14:1-9).

These books deal with real life. Some of the most difficult moral and philosophical issues of mankind are confronted here as nowhere else. The profound questions of why innocent people suffer, why the wicked are permitted to prosper, why God allows injustice to continue, and the meaning of life are not only raised, but substantially answered. Central to these answers is the promise of God to bless all mankind, which we have traced from Genesis onward.

JOB

Job may be the most ancient book in the Bible, probably written during the era of the patriarchs. It addresses the dark riddle of how the world is governed. Why do righteous people suffer as Job did? Why does God allow believers to pass through trials? Where does evil originate? What is the role of Satan?

After boldly claiming that Job only feared God for the blessings he was receiving, Satan twice receives limited permission to test Job (1:8-12; 2:3-6). In less time than it takes to read the chapters, Job is devastated. The main part of this poetic book is organized around several cycles of heated discussion between Job and his friends (chs. 3–37). They have come to "comfort" him after he lost everything but his life and his wife, who actually urged him to *"curse God, and die"* (2:9).

The three friends, Eliphaz, Bildad, and Zophar, charge that Job is suffering because he has sinned in some way, and that he should repent in order for God to restore his fortunes. Job insists (correctly) that this is not the reason for his misery, and blames God (wrongly) for dealing with him unfairly. The book ends with the Lord breaking His silence to challenge Job, bringing him to repentance for his self-righteousness and rash words (38:1–41:6), and rebuking his friends for their ignorant accusations of Job (42:7-9).

The lessons of Job are many. We learn that the general rule of God's blessing on a righteous life has exceptions; Job is greatly afflicted in spite of his righteousness. A long-range view of the conflict between Satan and God is needed to see that God may permit His people to suffer for reasons of deep significance unknown to them. We also see how we should respond to tragedy in our lives: *"The Lord gave, and the Lord has taken away; Blessed be the name of the Lord...shall we receive good at the hand of God, and shall we not receive evil?"* (1:21; 2:10).

Even when we don't understand God's reasons, we must refuse to attribute unfairness or unkindness to Him. *"In all this, Job did not sin by charging God with wrongdoing"* (1:22, NIV). We should also accept the Bible's realistic assessment of our intrinsic sinfulness: *"man, who drinks iniquity like water?"* (15:16).

Most important for our study is the way God's promise provided an ultimate hope in the midst of Job's deepest anguish. *"Though He slay me, yet will I trust in Him,"* he burst out in 13:15. He longed for a mediator to stand between him and God (9:33), and in one of the greatest moments of faith and insight in all of Scripture, declared, "I know that my Redeemer lives, And He shall stand at last on the earth; and after my skin is destroyed, this I know, that in my flesh I shall see God, whom I shall see for myself, and my eyes shall behold, and not another" (19:25-27). God's purpose included a then-living Redeemer who would one day stand on earth.

Job was sure that a day of resurrection was coming. He maintained faith in the unchangeable purpose of God while enduring the deepest physical and spiritual trials. He is an example for all who believe God's promise:

> *Take the prophets, who spoke in the name of the Lord, as an example of suffering and patience. Indeed we count them blessed who endure. You have heard of the perseverance of Job and seen the end intended by the Lord—that the Lord is very compassionate and merciful* (Jas. 5:10-11).

The "Wisdom" Psalms and the Proverbs

Believing God's promise brings the one who believes into a right relationship with God. This relationship is not a religion. It is a miraculous God-given new life, affecting every aspect of human experience. Too often we underestimate the interest God has in us, thinking that He simply wants to make us "better people." In fact His grace is so great that He desires to give us a share in His own glorious, infinite life:

> *As His divine power has given to us all things that pertain to life and godliness, through the knowledge of Him who called us by glory and virtue, by which have been given to us exceedingly great and precious promises, that through these you may be partakers of the divine nature, having escaped the corruption that is in the world through lust* (2 Pet. 1:3-4).

In the book of Job, in certain psalms (specifically 1, 19b, 25, 32, 34, 49, 78, 111, 112, 119, 127, 128, 133), in Proverbs, Ecclesiastes, and the Song of Solomon, this new life is called "wisdom." This is why we call them the Wisdom Books.

Life in the Lord

This wise life includes justice (Prov. 17:15), diligence (Prov. 14:23), honesty (Prov. 12:19, 22), and a gentle, restrained tongue (Prov. 10:19; 11:12; 15:1, 4). One who fears the Lord avoids and even hates evil (Job 1:1, 8; 28:28; Ps. 34:11, 13-14; Prov. 3:7). The wise man's delight is in the law of the Lord (Ps. 1:2), and all pride, arrogance, perverted speech, anger, and envy are to be jettisoned (Prov. 8: 13; 14:2; 22:24; 23:17). The Lord requires life, not religion, from His people.

THE FEAR OF THE LORD

The foundational truth of these wisdom books is that *"the fear of the Lord is the beginning of wisdom"* (Job 28:28; Prov. 1:7; 9:10; 15:33; Eccl. 12:13). It is the first principle of true understanding. Only when rightly related to God are we prepared to understand and enjoy the created realm, one another, and life itself. *"The fear of the Lord is a fountain of life"* (Prov. 14:27).

This *"fear of God"* is not the fear of an awful, unpredictable tyrant who must be pacified at all times. Rather it is to know that God is our all-wise Creator and that He is the holy *"Judge of all the earth"* (Gen. 18:25). One day we will certainly stand before Him! Solomon said,

> *Let us hear the conclusion of the whole matter: fear God and keep His commandments, for this is man's all. For God will bring every work into judgment, including every secret thing, whether good or evil* (Eccl. 12:13-14).

The fear of the Lord was far from a new teaching in Solomon's time. In fact this foundational truth links the Solomonic era with all the preceding eras we have studied:

> In olden days men of faith were said to "walk in the fear of God" and to "serve the Lord with fear." However intimate their communion with God, however bold their prayers, at the base of their religious life was the conception of God as awesome and dreadful. This idea of God transcendent runs through the whole Bible and gives color and tone to the character of the saints. This fear of God was more than a natural apprehension of danger; it was a non-rational dread, an acute feeling of personal insufficiency in the presence of God the Almighty. Whenever God appeared to men in Bible times, the results were the same—a wrenching sensation of sinfulness and guilt.[1]

Believers in God's promise have always shown through their lives that they feared God. This separated them from the rest of mankind. God deals with those who fear Him in a special way:

> *Who is the man that fears the Lord? Him shall He teach in the way He chooses. He himself shall dwell in prosperity, and his descendants shall inherit the earth* (Ps. 25:12-13).

We too must live in the fear of God. It is as crucial today as the day it was written by David. Let's trace the fear of the Lord through the eras we've studied in previous lessons:

Pre-Patriarchal Era

In the Pre-Patriarchal Era this line of God-fearers is first recorded in Genesis chapter 5. Enoch *"walked with God"* (Gen. 5:22, 24) which meant that he lived in light of God's coming judgment (see Jude 14-15). Noah *"found grace in the eyes of the Lord...Noah was a just man, perfect in his gener-*

ations. Noah walked with God" (Gen. 6:8-9). Hebrews adds, *"By faith Noah, being divinely warned of things not yet seen, moved with godly fear, prepared an ark for the saving of his household, by which he condemned the world and became heir of the righteousness which is according to faith"* (11:7).

Patriarchal Era

The patriarchs' fear of God produced obedient trust in His promise. When Abraham offered Isaac, God said, *"Now I know that you fear God"* (Gen. 22:12). To Jacob, the Lord was *"the fear of his father Isaac"* (31:42, 53). Joseph explained his righteous behavior simply: *"I fear God"* (39:8-9; 42:18).

Moses' Era

In the era of Moses, the Law was summarized in these words: *"What does the Lord your God require of you, but to fear the Lord your God, to walk in all His ways and to love Him, to serve the Lord your God with all your heart and with all your soul, and to keep the commandments of the Lord"* (Deut. 10:12-13).

Pre-Monarchical Era

After Israel entered the Land of Promise, and again after they had victoriously possessed it, Joshua continued to drive home the same theme, *"Fear the Lord"* (Josh. 4:24).

David's Era

In David's last words, he concludes that *"He who rules over men must be just, ruling in the fear of God. And he shall be like the light of the morning when the sun rises, a morning without clouds…Although my house is not so with God, yet He has made with me an everlasting covenant, ordered in all things and secure"* (2 Sam. 23:3-5). Thus in every era the fear of the Lord was the essential response of faith to the divine word of promise and blessing. This was the key to the enjoyment of God's gift of life.

ECCLESIASTES

With deep insight into the human dilemma, *"The Preacher, the son of David"* (Solomon) exposes the meaninglessness of life without a God-given hope in something greater than what is found *"under the sun"* (1:3). He tells of his futile search for satisfaction and significance in every realm man can enter: education, pleasure, eating and drinking, wealth, possessions, work, music, sex, prestige, and more. The common fate of **all** men, rich or poor, wise or foolish, is death and the grave: *"All go to one place; all are of the dust, and all turn to dust again"* (3:20). *"As he came from his mother's womb, naked shall he return, to go as he came; and he shall take nothing…"* (5:15). So why bother? Why am I alive? Isn't there anything more?

Everything that the world has to offer, put together, cannot satisfy the heart of man. It was Pascal who said, "There is a God-shaped vacuum in the human heart." And Augustine observed, "You have made us, O Lord, for Yourself, and our heart shall find no rest until it rest in You."[2]

This book reveals the barrenness of secular humanism by exposing the final futility of life without an eternal hope. It raises profound questions only answered by the promise of God in Christ. Without a purpose which lifts us beyond death, our hearts are unsatisfied, because God has set eternity in the heart of man (3:11). Only resurrection and eternal life answer the charge, *"Vanity of vanities, saith the preacher; all is vanity"* (12:8 *"meaningless"* NASB). The promise of God to bless all mankind through a divine Redeemer, and to dwell with His redeemed ones forever in love meets the deepest needs of the human heart. We are called to trust gladly in Him and His wise goodness, and to leave the many unanswered questions of life for Him to answer in His own time.

SONG OF SOLOMON

"The Song of Songs, which is Solomon's" is a fitting answer to Ecclesiastes, which it directly follows. With God all is not "meaningless;" far from it. God's purpose for His people is rich with love, significance and joy. It is nothing less than a holy love relationship with Him. The basic tenet of God's Law is to *"love the Lord your God with all your heart, with all your soul, and with all your strength"* (Deut. 6:5). Satan has said that God's purpose can never work, man will never love God freely for who He is, but only for what he can get from God (Job 1:9-11; 2:4-5). Indeed true love is one thing that can never be purchased by favors or obtained by power. Yet the Lord intends to take a people for Himself to be His beloved, His spiritual bride! He is wooing a people who will love Him eternally in spirit and in truth.

With the Lord, all His gifts of life are full of pleasure; and the greatest of these is love: "If a man would give for love all the wealth of his house, it would be utterly despised" (8:7). The Song of Solomon celebrates the gift of monogamous marital love, which was a *"flame from the Lord"* (Song 8:6-7 NASB; also Prov. 5:18-21). The two main characters are the Shulamite woman and her "beloved." But this song contains a deeper significance as well. The love relationship in the song pictures the relationship between the Lord and His people. Its movements seem even to symbolically outline the whole history of His dealings with His beloved ones.[3]

Love is very powerful, and no love is as long-suffering as the Lord's. The tragic centuries which follow Solomon's reign will show this beyond all doubt. In fact the perfect marriage love found in his Song was sadly lacking in Solomon's own marital life (1 Ki. 11:1-13). As a result of Solomon's gross polygamy and his turning to the gods of his wives, the spiritual love between God and His people began to grow cold. In this way the Song provides a deep contrast and fitting introduction to the prophetic books (Isaiah–Malachi), which condemn Israel for their spiritual adultery. Nevertheless, the zealous covenant love of God, which began with His choice of Abraham, will not be vanquished, even by the disobedience of His people.

SEEKING WISDOM FROM THE LORD

A personal knowledge of the Living God must originate with God: *"The Almighty—we cannot find Him out"* (Job 37:23). But because He has determined to bless us, we can come and seek Him.

> Wisdom is to be found with God, and nowhere else; unless the quest of wisdom brings a man to his knees in awe and reverence, knowing his own helplessness to make himself wise, wisdom remains for him a closed book.[4]

We must eagerly and diligently seek wisdom from God, or we will not be wise. "Wisdom" says, *"I love them that love Me; and those that seek Me early shall find Me"* (Prov. 8:17). The blessed man's *"delight is in the law of the Lord; and in His law does he meditate day and night"* (Ps. 1:2). God's promise to him is rich and full: *"Blessed is the man that fears the Lord, that delights greatly in His commands…His righteousness endures forever…he shall not be moved"* (Ps. 112:1-6).

Much time must be spent in the Word of God, where God's wisdom is found. Early morning hours or late nights may be required in order to find this time. The Bible must be read, studied, meditated on, and put into daily life. The wisdom we find may seem like foolishness to the majority of people around us, but it will be God's wisdom, not majority wisdom (1 Cor. 1:18–2:16; Jas. 3:17-18). There we will find Messiah, *"in whom are hid all the treasures of wisdom and knowledge"* (Col. 2:3). It will cost us a lot to seek wisdom, but there is no other way, and her *"fruit is better than gold, yes than fine gold"* (Prov. 8:19).

CONCLUSION

True wisdom is insight into the ways and heart of God Himself. It is the knowledge of the Holy One. Living faith in the unchangeable purpose of God gives significance to every aspect of our daily life. This is the greatest wisdom. *"The secret of the Lord is with those that fear Him; and He will show them His covenant"* (Ps. 25:14).

ENDNOTES

1 A.W. Tozer, *The Knowledge of the Holy,* Harper & Row, 1961, p. 71.

2 William MacDonald, *Believer's Bible Commentary,* Nelson, p. 878.

3 See C. E. Hocking, *Rise Up My Love,* Precious Seed Publications, 1988, for an excellent treatment of various ways the Song has been interpreted.

4 Lawrence E. Toombs, quoted in Kaiser, p. 175.

1. The book of Job records a fascinating encounter between God, Satan, and a believer named Job. What facts can you list about Satan and his activities from Job 1–2?

   Why do you think God allowed Satan to test Job as He did (1:8-12; 2:3-6)?

2. What key biblical truths are expressed in Job 19:25-27?

3. Why did Solomon's request in 1 Kings 3:5-13 please the Lord?

   What did the Lord promise Solomon as a result?

4. What one important spiritual principle is found in all of the following verses: Job 28:28; Prov. 1:7; 9:10; 19:23; Eccl. 12:13? Why is this principle true?

   What practical effects come from this principle (Prov. 8:13; 14:2; 28:17)?

5. List the characteristics of a "wise" life found in these verses:
   Prov. 17:15   Ps. 1:2
   Prov. 14:23   Prov. 22:24
   Prov. 12:19, 22
   Prov. 10:19; 11:12; 15:1, 4

6. On page 128 of the notes, there is a quote from A. W. Tozer explaining the fear of the Lord. Read the paragraph again. How does this description of the patriarchs' reverence for the Lord compare with your own relationship with God?

Do you fear God? If so, in what practical way does this affect your life?

7. What promise is given to those who fear the Lord in Psalm 25:12-14?

8. How was the fear of the Lord demonstrated in the lives of these two patriarchs?

   Abraham (Gen. 22:12)

   Joseph (Gen. 39:6-12; 42:18)

9. In what two ways does Solomon sum up his conclusions after searching every area of life for meaning and purpose?

   Eccl. 1:2

   Eccl. 12:13-14

   How do you harmonize these verses? In what way is life meaningless?

10. The Song of Solomon is a magnificent love poem. How is love described in Song of Solomon 8:6-8?

    What can you say about God's pattern for marriage as described in Proverbs 5:15-21? If you are married, how well does this picture describe your own marriage?

    If the Song of Solomon pictures the love relationship between the Lord and His own people, what does that tell you about God's attitude toward unfaithfulness in His people?

11. How does your life now or in the past resemble either Job's or Solomon's? In what specific areas would you like to see change or growth?

PROPHETS OF THE PROMISE
FIRST PRE-EXILIC ERA

Recommended Readings: Hosea 4:1-6; 6:1-7; 14; Joel 2:1-2, 28-32; 3:18; Amos 9:11-15; Obadiah 15-18

God's purpose is unchanging. Yet, as we have seen, He has chosen to reveal and carry out that purpose progressively, era by era, rather than all at once. Let's review the ground we have covered thus far:

Pre-Patriarchal Era (*Genesis 1–11*): Following creation, each of three disastrous judgments on mankind was followed by a far-reaching word of promise. God stated and restated His plan to bless mankind, first to Adam, then to Noah and then to Abraham.

Patriarchal Era (*Genesis 12–50*): God chose one family by whom He would bless *"all the families of the earth."* God promised Abraham, Isaac, and Jacob an heir, an inheritance, and a world-wide heritage of blessing.

Mosaic Era (*Exodus–Deuteronomy*): By Moses' time the "seed" had grown into *a people*. God entered into a covenant relationship with Israel, with the awesome privilege and heavy responsibility of His personal dwelling among them.

Pre-Monarchical Era (*Joshua–Ruth*): The transition from Moses to Joshua brought a new focus for the promise. God's people received *rest in the land* by obedience and faith, yet repeatedly lost it through sin and unbelief.

Davidic Era (*1–2 Samuel; Psalms*): The plan of a seed, worldwide blessing, and "rest" was now focused in *a king*, the son of David. To this anointed One God promised to grant an everlasting kingdom involving the future of all mankind.

Solomonic Era (*1 Kings 1–11; Job–Song of Songs*): The glory of God's presence now filled the temple which David's son had built in Jerusalem. Solomon's reign was a period of unparalleled blessing, the grandest point in Israel's history. The wealthy queen of Sheba came to see for herself whether the glowing reports she had received were true or not. Her conclusion is found in 1 Kings 10:6-9:

> *Then she said to the king: "It was a true report which I heard in my own land about your words and your wisdom. However...the half was not told me. Your wisdom and prosperity exceed the fame of which I heard. Happy are your men and happy are these your servants, who stand continually before you and hear your wisdom! Blessed be the Lord your God, who delighted in you, setting you on the throne of Israel! Because the Lord has loved Israel forever, therefore He made you king, to do justice and righteousness.*

THE DOWNWARD ROAD TO EXILE

Tragically, Solomon did not continue in the fear of the Lord. The seeds of the fall of his kingdom were sown by himself. In disobedience to the law regarding kings in Deuteronomy 17:16-17, he multiplied horses and wives for himself. His pagan wives eventually turned him to idolatry and the Lord determined to tear away part of the kingdom from David's line (1 Ki. 10:26 –11:13).

Humanly speaking, Solomon's son Rehoboam had every opportunity to continue his father's reign. But he foolishly rejected the wise counsel of older men, listening instead to the advice of the young men who had grown up with him. This led to a revolt of ten tribes under the idolatrous leadership of Jeroboam (1 Ki. 12). This division of the kingdom was God's promised judgment on Solomon's sinful neglect of His law: *"For the turn of events was from the Lord, that he might fulfill His word"* (1 Ki. 12:15). Only the tribes of Judah and Benjamin remained loyal to the Davidic king. From then on the kingdom was divided into the Northern Kingdom of Israel and the Southern Kingdom of Judah:

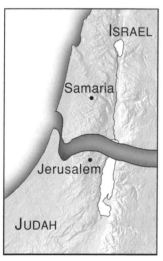

NORTHERN KINGDOM
        ("Israel," "Ephraim" or "Joseph")
Capital: Samaria

        Jeroboam ⇨ Nebat ⇨ Baasha ⇨

                    ↑

THE KINGDOM SPLITS (931 BC)

                    ⬇

        Rehoboam ⇨ Abijah ⇨ Asa ⇨

SOUTHERN KINGDOM
        ("Judah" or "Benjamin")
Capital: Jerusalem

We have called the period following this division the first "Pre-Exilic" era, because after Solomon's death the nation began a 345-year downhill slide which did not end until the Israeli people were carried into exile by the Babylonians (2 Ki. 25).

THE PROPHETS

God did not simply leave the two kingdoms to drift to destruction. He repeatedly sent spokesmen or prophets to warn them of the consequences of the path they were choosing, and to lovingly plead with them to repent.

What is a "prophet"? Often the first idea that comes to mind is one who predicts the future. This is not incorrect, but it is quite incomplete. In fact, prediction was not the main feature of prophecy. Rather, "the prophets were proclaimers of righteousness who preached both law and promise to motivate the people to repentance and holy living…seeing that the future belonged to their God and to His righteous reign."[1] They were God's spokesmen and penmen who "appeared at times of crisis in their nation's history as…the moral conscience of their age."[2]

First the **miracle-working prophets** Elijah and Elisha entered the scene in the northern kingdom (1 Ki. 17–2 Ki. 9). Elijah's stern confrontation of king Ahab revealed God's judgment against His proud, sinful people, while Elisha's ministry of healing and miracles balanced this with His merciful blessing on the repentant, even Gentiles (note Lk. 4:24-28).

Soon the **writing prophets**, beginning with *Joel* and *Obadiah* in the 9th century BC, began to warn of a coming *"Day of the Lord,"* a day when God's judgment would fall on idolatry and sin. Then came *Hosea*, *Amos*, *Jonah* and *Micah* in the 8th century BC to warn the northern kingdom of soon-coming destruction if she didn't repent. Israel was trying to cover her idolatry, immorality, self-indulgence, injustice and other sins with religious practices, but because God was the Holy One, judgment had to come. Except for a few brief responses, the northern tribes plunged headlong into catastrophe. Their capital, Samaria, fell to the Assyrians in 722 BC, and the remainder of the prophets were sent to Judah.

THE WRITINGS OF THE PROPHETS

The writings of the prophets follow the Song of Solomon in the Old Testament. They are called the Prophetic Books or "The Latter Prophets" (See Appendix 1). There are seventeen books in this section. Each carries the name of a different prophet, except for *Lamentations*, which was written by Jeremiah. They are generally divided into two groups, based on the size of the books:

1) The 4 Major Prophets (*Isaiah—Daniel*) are placed first, with the Lamentations of Jeremiah included.

2) The 12 Minor Prophets (*Hosea—Malachi*) which follow, were frequently grouped together as one work.

Eleven of the prophets wrote before the destruction of Jerusalem in 586 BC, during the period of time recorded in 2 Kings. Two wrote during the Exile which followed Jerusalem's fall, and the last three wrote after the return from the Exile. This chronology can be seen with greater detail in Appendix 3. We will look at these books in five chronological eras related to the destruction of Jerusalem and the exile to Babylon:

STUDY 10

FIRST PRE-EXILIC ERA (930–760 BC)
Hosea, Joel, Amos, Obadiah, and Jonah

STUDY 11

SECOND PRE-EXILIC ERA (760–722 BC)
Micah and Isaiah

STUDY 12

THIRD PRE-EXILIC ERA (720–600 BC)
Nahum, Habakkuk, Zephaniah, and Jeremiah

FALL OF JERUSALEM, EXILE BEGINS (586 BC)

STUDY 13

EXILIC ERA (593–537 BC)
Lamentations, Ezekiel, and Daniel

EXILE ENDS, RETURN TO JERUSALEM (420-450 BC)

STUDY 14

POST-EXILIC ERA (538–430 BC)
Haggai, Zechariah, and Malachi

THE PLACE OF THE PROPHETIC WRITINGS IN SCRIPTURE

In our last study we mentioned that in the wisdom books (Job–Song of Songs) God's people record their deep musings, prayers, and anguished crying as they speak from their heart to God and to each other. But when we turn the page between the Song of Solomon and Isaiah, we are conscious of a great change. Now we find not man, but God, speaking directly, in the first person. His own heart is openly revealed as He addresses His people to warn and encourage them. The first verses of Isaiah are a striking example of this.

> *I have nourished and brought up children,*
> *And they have rebelled against Me;*
> *The ox knows its owner and the donkey its master's crib;*
> *But Israel does not know, My people do not consider.*
> *Alas, sinful nation, a people laden with iniquity,*
> *A brood of evildoers, children who are corrupters!*
> *They have forsaken the Lord,*
> *They have provoked to anger the Holy One of Israel,*
> *They have turned away backward* (Isa. 1:2-4).

The prophets relay God's own reflections, His urgent warnings and even His deep anguish over His disobedient children. If the Psalms record the saint's innermost longings for his God, the prophetic writings reflect the *"deep things of God"* (1 Cor. 2:10-11). This type of holy Scripture is particularly characteristic of periods when God's people have strayed away from Him. In these moving writings we hear Him calling them back through His spokesmen, yearning over His people, though too often with very little effect:

> *I taught Ephraim to walk,*
> *Taking them by their arms;*
> *But they did not know that I healed them.*
> *I drew them with gentle cords, with bands of love,*
> *And I was to them as those who take the yoke from their neck.*
> *I stooped and fed them…*
> *My people are bent on backsliding from Me…*
> *How can I give you up, Ephraim?*
> *How can I hand you over, Israel?…*
> *My heart churns within Me; My sympathy is stirred* (Hosea 11:2-8).

How tragic! How vital that we learn from Israel's mistakes to listen when God speaks to us!

THE TWO-FOLD MESSAGE OF THE PROPHETS

OT prophecy bridges the chasm between the failed Old Covenant and the promised New Covenant. These prophecies illuminate the reason for the failure of the first (Israel's sinfulness), and the basis for the certain fulfillment of the second (God's faithfulness).

We can visualize the prophets as a series of messengers trying to hold back the downhill slide to destruction by warning God's people of His judgment, while at the same time looking ahead to future eras when God's promises would be fulfilled:

THE MESSAGE OF THE
PROPHETS:

1) God will inevitably judge and destroy the kingdoms of this world.
2) God will ultimately establish His glorious Kingdom.

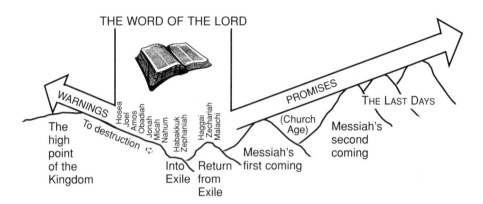

THE WORD OF THE LORD

WARNINGS
To destruction

Hosea
Joel
Amos
Obadiah
Jonah
Micah
Nahum

Habakkuk
Zephaniah

Haggai
Zechariah
Malachi

PROMISES

THE LAST DAYS

The high point of the Kingdom

Into Exile

Return from Exile

Messiah's first coming

(Church Age)

Messiah's second coming

The prophets were men of very different backgrounds and circumstances who wrote over a 400-year span of history. Yet their messages have a powerful, authoritative unity. Two primary themes run through the prophetic writings:

1) GOD'S CERTAIN JUDGMENT ON THE KINGDOMS OF MAN

Why is God silent? Why do wicked nations go unpunished? Is there no ultimate justice? The answer of the prophets is direct and clear. A time of final judgment upon the earth will come. It is called the *"Day of the Lord,"* the time when the God of heaven will openly intervene to settle the score for the wickedness of the nations (Obad. 15; Joel 3:1-21). This Day of the Lord will be awful, a day of *"destruction from the Almighty,"* *"a day of darkness and gloom…cloud and thick darkness,"* *"great and very terrible;"* *"who can bear it?"* (Joel 1:15-16; 2:2,11; Amos 5:18-20).

The Lord insists on true righteousness, not religious activities (Joel 2:13; Amos 5:22-27). God does not want to punish. Instead He pleads for repentance with great compassion even as He warns of coming wrath (Joel 2:12-17; Hos. 6:1-3; 11:1-11; 14:1-3; Jonah 3-4). His judgments are designed to get their attention, and He is grieved that *"yet you have not returned to Me"* (Amos 4:6-12), and that *"My people are determined to turn from Me!"* (Hos. 11:7). Nevertheless, because He is holy, final judgment is inescapable.

2) THE ULTIMATE ESTABLISHMENT OF THE KINGDOM OF GOD

"Israel's sin required most of the prophets' attention. Nevertheless, mingled with these words of judgment were the bright prospects of

God's everlasting kingdom as announced so long ago in the promise."[3]

Although inevitable, judgment will not have the final word. Grace will triumph and God's promise will be fulfilled. There will be a repentant *"remnant"* of Israel that survive the judgment (Obad. 17; Hos. 6:2; 11:11; 14:4-6; Amos 9:8). God would restore and bless them with His kingdom.

"PROPHETIC FORESHORTENING"

To correctly interpret the fulfillment of OT predictive prophecy, we need to understand that the prophets frequently view the two separate comings of Messiah as aspects of a single event. As a painting has only two dimensions, lacking depth, the prophetic perspective generally has no time dimension. This is sometimes called "prophetic foreshortening." Another illustration of this phenomenon is looking at stars or galaxies through a powerful telescope. Stars actually light years apart appear side by side. We can think of Messiah's two comings as two mountain peaks. From a distance, the great valley separating the peaks is lost from view and the two peaks merge into one.

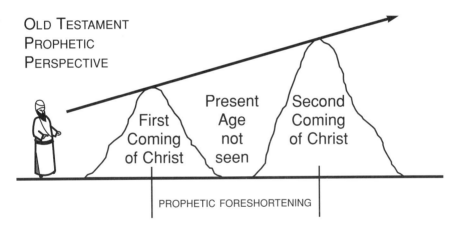

OLD TESTAMENT PROPHETIC PERSPECTIVE

First Coming of Christ

Present Age not seen

Second Coming of Christ

PROPHETIC FORESHORTENING

Therefore only with the additional knowledge that has come through Christ's first coming and the New Testament writings can we rightly interpret these remarkable predictions.

Now let's begin our study of the prophets by looking at the specific contribution of the first five minor prophetic books to the ongoing plan of God.

HOSEA

The book opens with the Lord's shocking command to Hosea, *"Go, take yourself a wife of harlotry and children of harlotry, For the land has committed great harlotry by departing from the Lord"* (1:2). These words fix the special theme of the book: the breaking and restoring of the covenant relationship God has made with Israel. He has "married" them, and loves them as His own "wife," as illustrated in the Song of Solomon. No book expresses the determined love of God more powerfully than Hosea.

Israel has acted like a beloved wife turned prostitute. Because of this unfaithfulness, God must put away His people, making them *Lo-ruhamah*: *"not pitied,"* and *Lo-ammi: "not My people"* (1:6-9). Years later the Lord refers to this putting away of the northern kingdom as a "divorce":[4]

> *I saw that for all the causes for which backsliding Israel had committed adultery, I had put her away and given her a certificate of divorce; yet her treacherous sister Judah did not fear, but went and played the harlot also* (Jer. 3:8).

But Hosea is told to buy his wife back from the prostitution she has fallen into: *"Go again, love a woman (Gomer) who is loved by a lover and is committing adultery, just like the love of the Lord for the children of Israel, who look to other gods."* The Lord will also bring His unfaithful "wife" back to Himself (3:1-5). *"I will betroth you to Me forever…in righteousness and justice, in lovingkindness and mercy"* (2:14-23). This bringing back of defiled Israel is another demonstration that what is impossible through the Law (Deut. 24:1-4) is possible through God's grace.

In 4:1 the Lord summarizes the three-fold charge against Israel: *"The Lord has a case against the inhabitants of the land, because there is no 1)* **truth** *or 2)* **loyal love** *or 3)* **knowledge of God."** (NASB) Then He expands these charges in turn (in reverse order), ending each with a touching appeal and promise to restore Israel:

ACCUSATION AND PUNISHMENT	APPEAL AND PROMISE
1. No knowledge of God (4:2–5:15) "My people are destroyed for lack of knowledge" (4:6).	"Let us return…He will raise us up…let us press on to know the Lord" (6:1-3).
2. No loyal love (6:4–10:15) "Your loyalty is like a morning cloud which goes away" (6:4).	"How can I give you up, O Ephraim? How can I surrender you? I will not…" (11:1-11).
3. No truth (11:12–13:16) "Ephraim surrounds Me with lies…Israel with deceit" (11:12).	"Return, O Israel, to the Lord… 'I will heal their apostasy, I will love them freely'" (14:1-9).

In Hosea we must learn that the infidelity of God's people hurts Him deeply! He will discipline severely because of the nearness of the relationship. Yet God's faithful love is greater than all their sin.

> *Afterward the children of Israel shall return, and seek the Lord their God and David their king. They shall fear the Lord and His goodness in the latter days* (Hos. 3:5).

JOEL

A terrible plague of locusts had left Israel devastated. In his short, forceful message, Joel called on the leaders of Israel to repent of the drunkenness and self-indulgence which were the cause of this judgment and warned that a more terrible time was ahead (1:13–2:17; 3:1-17). Nevertheless, deliverance for Israel will come (2:18-27; 3:18-21). An event of great significance for all humanity is promised in 2:28-32:

> *It shall come to pass afterward that I will pour out My Spirit on all flesh…I will pour out My Spirit in those days…whoever calls on the name of the Lord shall be saved.*

God's plan for salvation would involve the coming of His own Spirit to the world in a way unparalleled in the past. The New Testament makes it clear that the Holy Spirit was poured out by the risen, glorified Messiah on the day of "Pentecost," fifty days after Jesus was crucified and raised from the dead (Acts 2:16-21, 32-33; Rom. 10:12-13).

Other aspects of this prophecy of the Day of the Lord, such as the cosmic disturbances in verses 30-31, await Messiah's second coming to judge the nations (see Mt. 25:31-32), as the continuation of the prediction makes very clear:

> *For behold, in those days and at that time,*
> *When I bring back the captives of Judah and Jerusalem,*
> *I will also gather all nations,*
> *And bring them down to the Valley of Jehoshaphat;*
> *And I will enter into judgment with them there*
> *On account of My people, My heritage Israel,*
> *Whom they have scattered among the nations;*
> *They have also divided up My land* (3:1-2).

AMOS

Privilege brings responsibility. In three distinct sections Amos first "thundered against Israel and her neighbors for their lack of righteousness"[5] (chs. 1–2), then urged Israel to repent or *"prepare to meet thy God!"* (chs. 3–6) and finally in a series of five visions left them no hope except the distant fulfillment of God's promise following certain judgment (chs. 7–9).

God is the Ruler of all history by right of creation (4:13; 5:8-9; 9:5-6).

He knows and judges all nations, including Judah and Israel, and He states His charges in specific terms (chs. 1–2). Through repeated famine, drought, plagues, and fire the Lord warned them (4:6-12). He also warned them through the prophets, *"Surely the Lord God does nothing, unless He reveals His secret to His servants the prophets"* (3:7).

God's people should not think that their privileges will keep them from His discipline. Precisely the opposite is true: *"You only have I known of all the families of the earth: therefore I will punish you for all your iniquities"* (3:2). The Lord tells them in no uncertain terms that their religious worship is unacceptable to Him:

> *I hate, I despise your feast days,*
> *And I do not savor your sacred assemblies.*
> *Though you offer Me burnt offerings and your grain offerings,*
> *I will not accept them,*
> *Nor will I regard your fattened peace offerings.*
> *Take away from Me the noise of your songs,*
> *For I will not hear the melody of your stringed instruments.*
> *But let justice run down like water,*
> *And righteousness like a mighty stream* (5:21-24).

He reminds them that He has endured their idolatry for centuries, even in the wilderness during the exodus from Egypt: *"Did you offer Me sacrifices and offerings In the wilderness forty years, O house of Israel? You also carried Sikkuth your king And Chiun, your idols, The star of your gods, Which you made for yourselves"* (5:25-26).

When the first Christian martyr Stephen quoted these scathing words to the Jewish Sanhedrin (Acts 7:42-43), they became so enraged that they stoned him to death.

Nevertheless restoration is promised once again. God will *"raise up the tabernacle of David"* in David's Promised Seed, the Messiah (9:11). Not only Israel, but all nations will be affected by that restoration: *"In that day"* there will be a *"remnant of Edom and all the Gentiles who are called by My name"* (9:12).

OBADIAH

Although most of Obadiah's brief book concerned the destruction of the nation of Edom, the descendants of Jacob's brother Esau (Gen. 36), his vision looked into the distant future. There he saw *"the day of the Lord"* drawing near on all nations, bringing retribution for their wickedness (v. 15). Edom seems to represent the nations of the earth in these prophecies of final judgment (vv. 15-16; see also Isa. 34:5-6 and Ezek. 36:5).

But beyond that dark day the glorious purpose of God would be fulfilled: *"The kingdom shall be the Lord's!"* (v. 21). It would be centered in Palestine, from Mount Zion itself. No other government can provide this righteous reign. It can only come after a restoration of Jewish exiles to their land and God's terrifying judgment in the last days (vv. 17-21). All other claims to establishing the kingdom of God on earth are clearly false. Christ told His disciples, *"When you see these things happening, know that the kingdom of God is near"* (Lk. 21:31).

CONCLUSION

No sooner had His people begun the downhill course of division and idolatry than *"the word of the Lord"* began to come. The Lord never abandons us to our own ways without clearly warning and calling us back. We can be certain that He will judge and discipline us for our sins, but His promises never fail.

The prophets preach the reality of two facts: 1) God's terrible judgment is still to come on our world; 2) In His time, His Anointed will reign in righteousness, peace, and great blessing for all creation. *"The kingdom shall be the Lord's!"* The final, complete fulfillment of both awaits the second coming of Messiah, the Lord Jesus Christ. In view of these two great realities, we should gladly invest our lives for His kingdom.

ENDNOTES

1 Kaiser, p. 183.

2 Scroggie, *Know Your Bible,* Pickering and Inglis, Ltd., 1972, p. 152.

3 Kaiser, p. 182.

4 MacDonald comments, "Note in [Jer. 3] verse 8 that God divorced Israel and that it was because of adultery. The Saviour's words in Matthew 19:9 are consistent with this. He taught that divorce is permissible for an innocent partner when the spouse has been guilty of immorality." *Believer's Bible Commentary,* p. 1000.

5 Kaiser, p. 193.

1. In your opinion, what is a prophet? Compare this with the definition on page 137.

   Who were the "Major prophets"?

   Who were the "Minor prophets"?

2. How do the prophets' writings fit into the overall scheme of Scripture?

   What change do we observe when we move from the poetic to the prophetic books? (Who is primarily speaking in each?)

3. Describe the "Day of the Lord," according to the following passages: Joel 1:15-16; 2:2, 11; 3:1-21; Amos 5:18-20; Obadiah 15.

4. What does God want from His people in these two passages?
   Joel 2:12-13
   Amos 5:21-24

5. (HOSEA) Why did the Lord tell Hosea to take an adulterous wife (1:2)?

   Why did He later tell Hosea to be reconciled with his adulterous wife (3:1)?

6. What do you learn of the heart of God toward His people in Hosea 11:1-11? Why is He so deeply affected?

   What does He promise to do after Israel's punishment if they repent (2:14-23; 14:4)?

7. (JOEL) A great promise is made in Joel 2:28-29. Write the key elements of this promise in your own words.

8. (AMOS) List some of the sins of which the Lord accuses Israel:
   3:13–4:5
   5:7–13
   5:21–6:7

   After threatening judgment for their sins, the Lord makes a promise to Israel in Amos 9:11-15. Summarize and explain this promise.

9. (OBADIAH) What was the sin of Edom (Obad. 2-4)?

   What does the Lord promise to Israel (17-21)?

10. What do you say? In view of the two great facts preached by the prophets and listed in the Conclusion of the notes, how should we then live?

11. How does this lesson apply to your own priorities in life? Are there any that need to change? How?

'SERVANT' OF THE PROMISE
SECOND PRE-EXILIC ERA

Recommended Readings: Micah 4:1–5:5; Isaiah 4:2-6; 6; 7:14; 9:1-7; 11:1-10; 24–25; 28:16; 35; 37:30-35; 42:1-7; 49; 50:4-9; 52:12–53:12

I n spite of the repeated warnings the prophets sent to them, Israel's wicked kings continued to lead the way to destruction, doing *"evil in the sight of the Lord"* (2 Ki. 15:8-31). Finally in 722 BC the ten tribes of Israel were swept away into captivity by the Assyrian horde. 2 Kings 17:7-18 summarizes the reasons why Israel fell:

> *For so it was that the children of Israel had sinned against the Lord their God...and they had feared other gods, and had walked in the statutes of the nations whom the Lord had cast out from before the children of Israel, and of the kings of Israel.*
> *Yet the Lord testified against Israel and against Judah, by all of His prophets, every seer...Nevertheless they would not hear, but...practiced witchcraft and soothsaying, and sold themselves to do evil...*
> *Therefore the Lord was very angry with Israel, and removed them from His sight; there was none left but the tribe of Judah alone.*

Micah and Isaiah began their prophetic ministries about thirty years before Samaria fell, and continued for sixty years or so (Mic. 1:1; Isa. 1:1; see Appendix 3). Together they were channels for some of the greatest revelation in Scripture. God's promise stood out brilliantly against the dark days in which they prophesied. The promise of Messiah gained new clarity. These prophecies show that He was the Lord of eternity, yet would become a virgin-born infant. He would be both God's humble Servant and His chosen Ruler. He would both suffer and be exalted.

MICAH—THE PROMISED "RULER"

Micah's book is made up of three messages, each beginning with the command to *"Hear..."* (1:2; 3:1; 6:1). The Lord's charges against Israel were clearly stated: idolatry and harlotry (1:7), greed (2:1-2), unjust government (3:1-3), false prophecy and occult practices (3:5-7), profiting from the Lord's name (3:9-11), deception, lies, and violence (6:10-12). What God requires is righteousness, not religious activities (6:6-8).

In spite of threatened doom, each of the book's three sections closed with a note of bright hope (2:12-13; 4–5; 7:7-20). Like Hosea, who prophesied slightly earlier, Micah predicted a repentant *"remnant"* of Israel who would survive the judgment (4:6-7; 5:7; 7:18-20). The Lord (Yahweh) would be their King, leading them through the gate of Jerusalem (2:13). Although the Holy City would soon be *"a heap of ruins"* (3:12), restoration would finally come: *"in the last days, it shall come to pass, that the mountain of the Lord shall be established in the top of the mountains"* (4:1). The Lord will rule from Jerusalem through restored Israelites (4:2-8). Micah rejoiced in God's future pardon of their sins for the sake of the patriarchs with whom He had made His covenant: *"You will give truth to Jacob and mercy to Abraham, which You have sworn to our fathers from days of old"* (7:20).

But his most famous passage is 5:2-5. The promised Messiah's origin in past eternity as well as his birthplace in Palestine were declared in these beautiful words:

> *But you, Bethlehem Ephrathah,*
> *Though you are little among the thousands of Judah,*
> *Yet out of you shall come forth to Me*
> *The One to be Ruler in Israel,*
> *Whose goings forth are from of old, from everlasting...*
> *And He shall stand and feed His flock*
> *In the strength of the Lord,*
> *In the majesty of the name of the Lord His God...*
> *And this One shall be peace.*

God's purpose had not changed. Here we learn it was to be carried out by one born in David's humble village of Bethlehem. He alone would establish the long-awaited Kingdom of God. As God's ruler He would bring in righteousness and peace for all mankind. No political, social, or even religious system is the real answer to earth's vast problems. God's solution is a Person: Jesus the Messiah.

ISAIAH—THE PROMISED "SERVANT"

Isaiah may be the greatest of all the Old Testament prophets. He has been called "the evangelical prophet" and the "Promise theologian." His revelation covers a tremendous range of subjects and often soars to great heights of expression.

Isaiah calls us to consider God, *"the Holy One of Israel."* He calls us to believe and exult in the ancient promise to Abraham and David. God's unfolding plan is again expanded and clarified, and His Messiah is marvelously introduced as the *"Servant of the Lord."* In Isaiah's book we come to the very heart of God's salvation. In fact, the Hebrew name "Isaiah" (Yesh-ah-yaw) means "The Lord is salvation" or "The Lord has saved."

The book can be divided into two main parts. Chapters 1–35 are devoted largely to judgment, and chapters 40–66 to comfort. Linking these two parts is a historical parenthesis (chs. 36–39). The following diagram should help us to visualize this structure, which is remarkably similar to the 66-book structure of the Bible (39 OT books and 27 NT books).

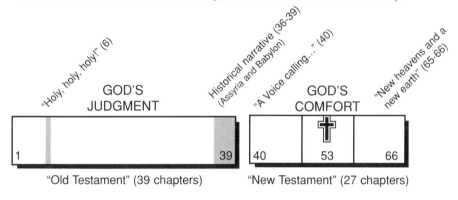

"Old Testament" (39 chapters)   "New Testament" (27 chapters)

THE 'BIBLE' OF ISAIAH

We will examine these two parts of the book of Isaiah in turn and add a few more comments about its fascinating structure in the introduction to the second part.

PART 1 (CHAPTERS 1–35)

"THE HOLY ONE OF ISRAEL" (1–6)

The heart of Isaiah's message is found in his "call" in chapter 6. In this awesome encounter with the Lord in the temple, two realities stand out: God's holiness and His glory! The angelic seraphim who encircle God's throne continually call out, *"Holy, Holy, Holy, is the Lord of Hosts, the whole earth is full of His glory!"* (6:3). In front of God, the prophet Isaiah suddenly knew how sinful he was and how unclean his mouth was (6:5). Only cleansing by virtue of an atoning sacrifice could fit Isaiah to speak for God, so the seraph flew to him with a burning coal from the altar and touched his lips,

> *Lo, this hath touched thy lips; and thine iniquity is taken away, and thy sin purged* (6:7).

God's holiness stands in stark contrast to Israel's unholiness (chs. 1–5;

6:5). His holiness demands judgment (6:11-12), but His glory requires the fulfillment of His promise. After the tree of Israel is felled, there will be a "stump" left, *"a very small remnant"* (1:9). The Lord told Isaiah that *"the holy seed is its stump"* (6:13 NASB). God's promise regarding the seed of Eve, Abraham, and David will be kept just as surely as His people's wickedness must be punished.

Many glimpses are given of the time when *"the Branch of the Lord shall be beautiful and glorious"* (4:2). The Branch became another name for God's anointed Saviour, who would spring up from the *"holy seed."* He would be the living source of God's blessings. These included a fruitful land, lasting holiness, cleansing from the filth of their sin, and the radiant presence of the Lord in their midst (4:2-6). This title *"the Branch"* reappears in 11:1, in Jeremiah 23:5-6; 33:15-16 and Zechariah 3:8; 6:12. (See page 194 for further comments on this title.)

"EMMANUEL" (7–12)

Three sons are born in these chapters. All were signs to Israel. Each is first introduced briefly and then considered in greater detail as follows:

1. **Shear-Jashub**—"the remnant shall return"
(7:3 ⇨ 10:20-22; 11:11, 16) He represented the promise of restoration and blessing following judgment.

2. **Emmanuel**—"God with us"
(7:14 ⇨ 8:8, 10; 9:6-7) This prophecy apparently had a partial fulfillment through a birth in King Ahaz's day (7:15-16). It was intended as a sign of God's personal presence working out His plan through David's seed in spite of Ahaz's arrogance.

But the promise of a child born to a virgin was ultimately fulfilled in Jesus the Messiah's birth (Mt. 1:23). The angel Gabriel announced this glorious event to the chosen woman with these profound words: *"The Holy Spirit will come upon you, and the power of the Highest will overshadow you; therefore, also, that Holy One who is to be born will be called the Son of God"* (Lk. 1:35).

3. **Maher-shalal-hash-baz**—"haste spoil, hurry prey"
(8:1, 3, 4 ⇨ 10:2, 6) This child's name warned of the destruction coming on God's people in Israel. He may be the child referred to in 7:15-16.[1]

Emmanuel's birth and majesty were foretold again in 9:6-7. His "name," which represented His glory, attributes, character, and all that He is,[2] would be *"Wonderful Counselor, Mighty God, Everlasting Father, Prince of Peace."* He would reign forever with justice and righteousness on the throne of David. The Spirit of the Lord would rest on the *"Stem of Jesse...the Branch"* as the blessings of His kingdom and *"the earth shall be full of the knowledge of the Lord as the waters cover the sea"* (chs. 11–12).

THE LORD OF HISTORY (13–27)

"Yahweh's purpose and plan embraced the whole earth with all its nations. Nations rose and fell in accordance with that plan (Isa. 14:24-27)."[3] Judgments on ten nations are pronounced in chapters 13–23, beginning with Babylon and ending with Tyre. Both of these proud kings were pictures of Satan, the unseen ruler of this world (Isa. 14:12-15; Ezek. 28:12-19). Although God uses these nations as *"the rod of His anger"* to punish His own people, their arrogance and cruelty would also be punished (10:5-19). The Lord will judge and *"shake"* all the nations of the earth, because of their guilt:

> *The earth is also polluted by its inhabitants, for they transgressed laws, violated statutes, broke the everlasting covenant. Therefore, a curse devours the earth, and those who live in it are held guilty"* (24:5-6 NASB).

A remarkably specific outline of various aspects of this coming time of judgment is given in 24:21-23; which corresponds perfectly to the more detailed prophecy of the same events in Revelation 19:20–20:15.

After these judgments will the Lord bring in His glorious day in which "all the earth" will be blessed (chs. 25–27). One of the most beautiful and comprehensive promises in the Bible is given in 25:6-9. Tears will be wiped from "all faces" from "all peoples" and "all nations" for "all time." His ultimate victory over sin, sorrow, and even death is proclaimed with great joy:

> *And in this mountain the Lord of hosts will make for all people a feast of choice pieces, a feast of wines on the lees, of fat things full of marrow, of well-refined wines on the lees. And He will destroy on this mountain the surface of the covering cast over all people, and the veil that is spread over all nations. He will swallow up death forever, and the Lord God will wipe away tears from all faces; the rebuke of His people He will take away from all the earth; for the Lord has spoken. And it will be said in that day: "Behold, this is our God; we have waited for Him, and He will save us. This is the Lord; we have waited for Him; we will be glad and rejoice in His salvation."*

"THE PRECIOUS CORNERSTONE" (28–35)

In chapters 28–33, six *"woes"* fall on Samaria and Jerusalem, like six blows of the Judge's gavel (28:1; 29:1, 15; 30:1; 31:1; 33:1). The Lord declared them guilty of all kinds of sin and wickedness. By ignoring the words of the prophets and hoping in lies, Israel thought their house was secure. In reality it was built on sand, ready to collapse (28:17-18). "Meanwhile, the sovereign Lord was laying in Zion a foundation stone…In contrast to the shaky shelter offered by lies, the stone stood firm and immovable."[4] He said, *"Behold, I lay in Zion for a foundation a stone, a tried stone, a precious corner stone, a sure foundation: he that believeth shall not make haste"* (28:16).

Genesis 49:24 and Deuteronomy 32:4 identify the *"Stone of Israel"* and the *"Rock"* as God Himself. He was to be their foundation. Isaiah 8:14 spoke of a future time when the Lord of hosts would become *"a stone of stumbling and for a rock of offense."* Now the Lord speaks of "laying" this precious cornerstone in Zion (Jerusalem). Israel would be called on to trust in this divine work. Psalm 118:22-23 added further insight; we learn that *"The stone which the builders refused is become the head stone of the corner. This is the Lord's doing."*

These passages all refer to the future rejection and murder of the Lord's Messiah by Israel. He would be put to death by His own people. Yet in this very event God would lay the chief cornerstone of His eternal house. It would be an extremely precious stone, but unexpected and difficult for many to accept, a "stumbling stone." The crucifixion of Jesus has had precisely this effect. All must respond to the Cornerstone of Jesus' death and resurrection. The promise is clear: *"The one who trusts in it will never be dismayed."*

The day of God's *"vengeance"* on all nations is declared again in chapter 34; and beyond that a glorious future for God's people in chapter 35. Israel would *"see the glory of the Lord, the majesty of our God"* who will come personally to save them. He presence will be unmistakable:

Then the eyes of the blind shall be opened,
And the ears of the deaf shall be unstopped.
Then the lame shall leap like a deer,
And the tongue of the dumb sing.
For waters shall burst forth in the wilderness,
And streams in the desert
(35:5-6).

Yet sadly they did not recognize Him when He came.

PARENTHETICAL SECTION (36–39)

This parenthetical historical section is parallel to 2 Kings 18:13–20:21. In 701 BC Sennacherib, king of the Assyrian Empire, came with a massive army against the small "remnant" of Judah. But in answer to King Hezekiah's humble prayer of faith, God powerfully delivered them. The heart of the section is 37:31-35. The Lord declared that:

And the remnant who have escaped…shall again take root downward, and bear fruit upward. For out of Jerusalem shall go a remnant…
The zeal of the Lord of hosts will do this…
I will defend this city, to save it for My own sake
And for My servant David's sake.

This deliverance under Hezekiah, a descendant of David, again confirmed the Lord's determination to bring His promises to fulfillment.

The final chapter of this parenthesis (ch. 39) changes the focus from Assyria to Babylon. Hezekiah receives the representatives of the king of Babylon and foolishly shows them all the treasures of Jerusalem. Isaiah rebukes the king for his pride, " *Behold, the days are coming when all that is in your house, and what your fathers have accumulated until this day, shall be carried to Babylon; nothing shall be left"* (39:6). So we are prepared for the second main part of Isaiah's book, where the Holy Spirit of prophecy addresses the Jews of the future Babylonian captivity.

PART II (CHAPTERS 40-66)

These 27 chapters form one of the most remarkable parts of God's Word. It is also one of the sections most loved by God's people throughout the ages. Full of comfort and hope, it reveals the coming Messiah as no other portion of Scripture does. As shown on page 151, even the structure of these chapters is quite remarkable.

It might well be called...the "New Testament within the Old Testament." Its 27 chapters cover the same scope as the 27 chapters of the New Testament. Chapter 40 begins with the predicted voice of John the Baptist crying in the wilderness as do the Gospels; chapters 65-66 climax with the same picture as...Revelation 21-22 of the new heavens and the new earth. Sandwiched between these two is the midpoint, Isaiah 52:13–53:12, which is the greatest theological statement on the meaning of the atonement in all Scripture.[5]

It is laid out in three sections of nine chapters (40–48, 49–57, 58–66). Each ends in a solemn warning for *"the wicked"* who refuse God's salvation (48:22; 57:20-21; 66:24-25). The backdrop of the messages is the Babylonian captivity. Yet the words are full of comfort and hope and the promise of Messiah is very prominent. For the first time he is called the Servant of the Lord. In five sections, sometimes called the "Servant Songs," we meet the person who will carry out God's deep purposes in history. *"The pleasure of the Lord shall prosper in His hand"* (53:10).

It is important to see that the term *"Servant of the Lord"* sometimes refers to the nation Israel and sometimes to one individual—Messiah.[6] God's purposes for the nations would be worked out through Israel (49:22-23). Yet as with the word *"Seed,"* the promise to God's chosen people is focused on His chosen person. The person represents the group. What He does affects their destiny. This principle of "the one" representing "the many" is God's essential way of dealing with the human race. As Adam's initial sin plunged all mankind into sin, so the Servant's redeeming act would deliver all who trust in Him:

Action of the One:			Result for the Many:
Adam's disobedience	⇨	⇨	his physical descendants ("seed") cursed
Servant's obedience	⇨	⇨	His spiritual descendants ("seed") redeemed

In these "servant songs" the Messiah is beautifully revealed:

(42:1-7) God calls us to look with Him: *"Behold! My Servant whom I uphold, My Elect One in whom My soul delights! I have put My Spirit upon Him."* Though His way was gentle and humble, He would bring justice to all nations.

(49:1-8) God promised that His servant would not only restore Israel, but would be the *"light to the Gentiles, that Thou mayest be My salvation unto the end of the earth!"* (v. 6 KJV). Though He would be "Him whom man despises,…whom the nation [Israel] abhors," His ultimate triumph would bring the rulers of the world to bow at His feet (v. 7).

(50:4-10) The Servant speaks of His daily obedience to the Lord God, which would lead into deep humiliation before His vindication: *"I gave My back to those who struck Me, and My cheeks to those who plucked out the beard; I did not hide My face from shame and spitting"* (v. 6).

(52:13-53:12) This is the greatest of all, and we will return to it a little further on. God speaks of His Servant, and Israel mourns their rejection of Him. Yet He had died as a substitute for their sins, as the atoning sacrifice. We learn here the meaning of His death as Lamb of God: to redeem us from our sins.

(61:1-3) Though not referred to by name, the Servant is clearly speaking. He tells us of His life's goal: *"The Spirit of the Lord God is upon Me, because the Lord has anointed Me to preach good tidings to the poor; He has sent Me to heal the brokenhearted, to proclaim liberty to the captives, and the opening of the prison to those who are bound"* (61:1).

In addition to these specifically Messianic "songs," each of the three main sections reveals the Lord to His people to comfort them in their affliction.

THE SUPREMACY OF THE LORD (40–48)

"Comfort ye, comfort ye My people!" says the Lord (40:1). Isaiah asks, *"What shall I call out?"* He is to tell them, *"Behold your God!"* In Babylonian bondage, they needed to stop and consider the Lord! He is supreme over all things, especially over the false gods of Babylon. Idolatry is pure foolishness (44:9-20; 46:5-7). He asked His people, *"To whom then will you liken Me?"* (40:18, 25). He declares, *"I am the first and I am the last…I am the Lord, and there is none else: there is no God else beside Me!"* (44:6, 8; 45:5, 6, 21).

Israel was to be His witness to this truth (43:10), but had failed. Nevertheless, God planned to use the Persian king Cyrus to deliver them from Babylon's idolatry (see Study 14, pp. 189-191 for more details).

The God of the Scriptures is the only true God, *"a Righteous God and Saviour."* He is utterly just, right, and faithful, especially in His work of salvation. The Lord is unique, separate, and self-sufficient. He is Israel's God, *"the Holy One of Israel"* (41:16, 20). Any other presentation of God must be measured solely against Him. His name is Yahweh, the supreme Creator, the Lord and predictor of all history. Only He discloses the future faultlessly (41:21-26). His salvation plan is the only one and His Servant must be responded to!

THE SALVATION OF THE LORD (49–57)

Two words summarize this second section: servant and salvation. The Servant would ultimately be *"exalted and extolled, and be very high"* (52:13). But He would also suffer greatly. These two aspects of his career, suffering and glory, are so distinctly predicted that some have even suggested that there were to be two "messiahs," a suffering one and a victorious one.[7] Of course there is only one Messiah. But this mystery of His voluntary suffering leading to His glory is the heart of God's salvation.

Isaiah speaks clearly of the sinfulness of all men: *"All we like sheep have gone astray; we have turned every one to his own way"* (53:6). In 64:6 he adds, *"all our righteousnesses are as filthy rags."* Man's religious performance will not make him clean in God's sight. But the Servant's death as a substitute would provide full atonement and complete inner cleansing. The facts of this saving work were predicted with amazing detail in chapter 53:

- His humble, fruitful life in a spiritually barren environment: *"He shall grow up before Him as a tender plant...a root out of a dry ground"* (v. 2).
- His sorrows and rejection by Israel: *"He is despised and rejected of men; a man of sorrows, and acquainted with grief...He was despised, and we esteemed him not"* (v. 3).
- His substitution: *"He was wounded for our transgressions, He was bruised for our iniquities: the chastisement of our peace was upon Him; and with His stripes we are healed"* (v. 5).
- His silent and willing suffering: *"as a lamb to the slaughter, and as a sheep before her shearers is dumb"* (v. 7).
- His death in the place of His people: *"He was cut off out of the land of the living: for the transgression of My people was He stricken"* (v. 8).
- His burial in a rich man's tomb: *"He made his grave with the wicked, and with the rich in his death"* (v. 9).
- His innocence: *"He had done no violence, neither was any deceit in His mouth."* (v. 9).
- His resurrection and reward: *"He shall see His seed, ...and shall be satisfied: by his knowledge shall My righteous servant justify many"* (vv. 10-11).

All was the predetermined plan of God Himself. It was no accident or mistake. It was all carried out by *"the arm of the Lord"* (v. 1). It was God who put our sins on Him (v. 6). We even read the amazing words, *"It pleased the Lord to bruise Him"* (v. 10). The "many" who are justified and reconciled to God are the Servant's deep satisfaction. To have His redeemed people with Him eternally is the joy that was set before Him (Heb. 12:2). Their motivation for serving Him should be: "To win for the Lamb that was slain the reward of His sufferings."[8]

This joyous salvation would not only be for Israel (ch. 54) but would be offered freely to all who would forsake their ways and turn to the Lord in humility (ch. 55). The invitation was based on God's eternal covenant:

Incline your ear, and come unto me:
Hear, and your soul shall live;
And I will make an everlasting covenant with you,
Even the sure mercies of David (Isa. 55:3).

God's plans are greater than we can imagine!

THE SOVEREIGNTY OF THE LORD (58-66)

This final section emphasizes the sovereignty of God. He looked for someone to intercede or help, but found none, so *"His arm brought salvation unto Him!"* (59:16; 63:5). He alone will carry out His purposes, in spite of His people's failure. The promise of God's own Spirit as the channel of blessing appeared earlier (44:3). Now He is seen as the One filling and anointing God's Redeemer for His work (59:19-21; 61). We should notice these and other references which carefully link God, His Servant, and His Spirit in a three-fold unity (42:1; 48:16). This helps prepare the way for further revelation about the triune God of Scripture.

God had said that He would bring an end to *"the former things"* and bring in His *"new thing"* (42:9; 43:18-19; 46:9-13; 48:3). A "new" sincere repentance (58–59), a "new" Jerusalem (60, 62), and greatest of all, a *"new heavens and a new earth"* (65:17-25; 66:10-24) will come through the Redeemer. The promise of God is full of joy and assurance for *"him who is poor and of a contrite spirit, and who trembles at My word"* (66:2).

CONCLUSION: LET US SERVE ONE ANOTHER!

As followers of the great *"Servant of the Lord,"* we are called to humbly serve Him by serving one another.

Have this attitude in yourselves which was also in Christ Jesus, who, although He existed in the form of God, did not regard equality with God a thing to be grasped, but emptied Himself, taking the form of a bond-servant (Phil. 2:5-7 NASB).

Stop and think of the wonder of this truth! Our glorious Master did not please Himself, but devoted Himself to serving undeserving men and women, to perfect them and bring them to glory. *"The Son of Man did not come to be served, but to serve, and to give His life a ransom for many"* (Mk. 10:45). Even now, exalted to high heaven, far above all rule and authority and dominion, He has never stopped serving His people, *"He ever liveth to make intercession for them"* (Heb. 7:25 KJV). Even when He returns as the supreme Master of the house, He will serve those who are found diligently serving Him:

> *Blessed are those servants whom the master, when he comes, will find watching. Assuredly, I say to you that he will gird himself and have them sit down to eat, and will come and serve them* (Lk. 12:37).

He has given great and precious promises to all who walk in His servant footsteps.

> *If anyone serves Me, let him follow Me; and where I am, there My servant will be also. If anyone serves Me, him My Father will honor* (Jn. 12:26).

Of course, it is easier to speak or write about the beauty of servanthood than to be a servant. The apostle Paul painted a striking portrait of a servant of God,[9] which he lived out in real life. We should study it carefully before glibly saying that we want to be servants!

> *In all things we commend ourselves as ministers of God: in much patience, in tribulations, in needs, in distresses, in stripes, in imprisonments, in tumults, in labors, in sleeplessness, in fastings; by purity, by knowledge, by longsuffering, by kindness, by the Holy Spirit, by sincere love, by the word of truth, by the power of God, by the armor of righteousness on the right hand and on the left, by honor and dishonor, by evil report and good report; as deceivers, and yet true; as unknown, and yet well known; as dying, and behold we live; as chastened, and yet not killed; as sorrowful, yet always rejoicing; as poor, yet making many rich; as having nothing, and yet possessing all things* (2 Cor. 6:4-10).

A beautiful modern hymn called "The Servant King" was written by British hymn writer Graham Kendrick. We can adopt these words of worship for ourselves:

> This is our God, the Servant King,
> He calls us now to follow Him,
> To bring our lives as a daily offering,
> Of worship to the Servant King.
>
> So let us learn how to serve,
> And in our lives enthrone Him;
> Each other's needs to prefer,
> For it is Christ we're serving.

ENDNOTES

1 MacDonald, *Believer's Bible Commentary,* pp. 945-946.

2 See Exodus 33:19-20 with 34:5-7, and Deuteronomy 3:3-4 for clear examples of the significance of the Lord's 'name."

3 Kaiser, p. 210.

4 Ibid., p. 211.

5 Ibid., p. 205

6 The Servant of the Lord is...

the nation Israel
in these passages:
41:8-10; 43:8-13; 43:14–44:5;
44:6-8: 44:21-23; 44:24–45:13;
48:1, 7, 10-12, 17

the man Messiah
in these passages:
42:1-7; 49:1-6; 50:4-10;
52:13–53:12

7 Some Jewish Rabbis saw in these two seemingly conflicting groups of prophecies two separate 'Messiahs.' They called the suffering, dying one, 'Messiah son of Joseph,' and the vicarious Messiah who would reign over the nations 'Messiah son of David.' See David Baron's great work, *Commentary on Zechariah,* Kregel Publications, Grand Rapids, MI, p. 76.

8 This phrase is said to have been the motto of the great Moravian Missionary Movement.

9 I owe this insight to a message given by J.B. Nicholson, Jr. at Palos Hills, IL, in 1996.

1. The ten northern tribes of Israel were taken into exile in 722 BC Read 2 Kings 17:7-18 and in your own words summarize the reasons why the Lord brought this to pass.

2. (MICAH) Micah has three sections. Each of them ends with bright promises for Israel's future. What will God do for them according to these passages?
    (2:12-13)

    (4-5)

    (7:7-20)

3. In the space below, write Micah 5:2, 4-5 in your own words:

4. (ISAIAH) In each of the following passages in Isaiah a special title is given to God's promised Messiah. Find the title and briefly explain its meaning as you understand it.

    TITLE: MEANING:
    4:2

    7:14

    9:6
    (choose 2)

    11:1

    28:16

5. In Isaiah's short historical section (chs. 36–39) the Lord answers Hezekiah's prayer for deliverance from the massive Assyrian army. Why is the Lord going to save them?

6. According to Isaiah 40:9-11, who is the One who will come as Saviour and Shepherd?

    Summarize God's promise in Isaiah 40:28-31 in your own words.

7. Read these three "Servant Songs": Isaiah 42:1-7; 49:1-8; 50:4-10. Describe the character of the Servant of the Lord.

8. Carefully read the famous passage in Isaiah 52:13–53:12. For each of its five sections below, write all the facts about the Messiah that you can find.
    (52:13-15)

    (53:1-3)

    (53:4-6)

    (53:7-9)

    (53:10-12)

9. In Isaiah 55:1-3, 59:16, and 61:10 God's salvation is described. According to these passages, how and by whom is this salvation provided?

10. To many the idea of Messiah's atoning death is a "stumbling stone" or just foolishness. Why is this (Isa. 28:16; see also 1 Cor. 1:18-31)?

    How can you apply this lesson to your own relationship with the Lord?

RENEWAL OF THE PROMISE
THIRD PRE-EXILIC ERA

Recommended Readings: Jer. 3:16-17; 23:5-7; 31:31-37; 32:16–33:26; Jonah 1–4; Nahum 1:2-3, 15–2:3; Habakkuk 2:3-4; 3:16-19; Zephaniah 3:8-20

Israel's sin and stubborn refusal to listen to God's prophets ended in inevitable tragedy. In 722 BC Samaria, capital of the northern 10-tribe kingdom, fell to the Assyrian invaders (2 Ki. 17). This should have been a graphic lesson to the southern kingdom of Judah, but they also plunged headlong into disaster.

Once again God sent prophets, this time to Jerusalem to warn Judah. The nation was on the brink of destruction, and the prophets' theme was again wrath and judgment. Yet instead of concluding that the ancient plan had finally failed, God not only renewed His promise but expanded it to such an extent that He called it *"A New Covenant"* (Jer. 31:31).

The final chapters of 2 Kings record the sad history of the years preceding the fall of Jerusalem. With monotonous regularity we read the words used to describe almost all the kings of Israel, now applied to David's descendants, the kings of Judah: *"he did evil in the sight of the Lord"* (21:2, 20; 23:32, 37; 24:9, 19). The only exception to this roll call of idolatrous kings was Josiah, whose repairs on the temple and radical reforms led to a remarkable distinction:

> *Before him there was no king like him, who turned to the Lord with all his heart, with all his soul, and with all his might, according to all the Law of Moses; nor after him did any arise like him* (2 Ki. 23:25).

During the repairing of the temple, the high priest *"found the book of the law in the house of the Lord"* (2 Ki. 22:8). The king read the book and realized that they were in deep trouble as a result of neglecting the word of God for so long. In distress and repentance he led the people to make a covenant before the Lord:

...to follow the Lord and to keep His commandments and His testimonies and His statutes, with all his heart and all his soul, to perform the words of this covenant that were written in this book. And all the people took a stand for the covenant (2 Ki. 23:3).

But these reforms were too late and did not go deep enough. Josiah's brief interlude of righteous leadership lasted only one generation. The guilty verdict had been given by the Judge and it was only a matter of time before the sentence was executed (2 Ki. 23:26-27).

We should learn from this history of the kings of Israel. That's why this long and often repetitive history was recorded in the first place. *"Whatsoever things were written aforetime were written for our learning"* (Rom. 15:4).

Now all these things happened to them as examples, and they were written for our admonition, upon whom the ends of the ages have come. Therefore let him who thinks he stands take heed lest he fall (1 Cor. 10:11-12).

For this reason we need some understanding of the era of the kings. To grasp the overall layout of these books it is useful to see that the transitions between books are also transitions from one key leader to another:

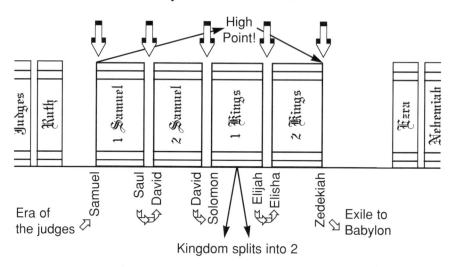

THE HISTORY OF THE KINGDOM
Key Transition Points

The so-called "minor" prophets in this 7th-Century period were *Nahum, Habakkuk,* and *Zephaniah.* We will include *Jonah* in this study because he and Nahum were both prophets to Nineveh. The "major" prophet of the period was *Jeremiah.* Each of these prophets dealt with a particular question relating to the workings of God. Believers today face many of the same perplexing issues.

Jonah—What should be our attitude to cruel regimes which persecute the people of God? Does He really expect us to bring His message to them?

Nahum—Does God's compassion last forever? What of His righteous judgment on the wicked?

Habakkuk—How can the God of justice use wicked regimes to discipline His less wicked people?

Zephaniah—Does God really love us? What is He looking for from us? Look at all we've been through!

Jeremiah—Is there really any hope of restoration? Is the wound curable? Or is this situation too difficult even for God?

The answer to all of these questions is ultimately found in the renewed promise of God to carry out His unchangeable purpose. Even in the darkest of days, when all hope seems to be lost and judgment is inevitable, God's faithfulness can be depended upon. The zeal of the Lord will carry all His purposes of grace and love on to fulfillment.

JONAH AND NAHUM: PROPHETS TO THE GENTILES

A significant part of Old Testament prophecy consists of judgments on the various nations around Israel. Here is a sample:

Isaiah 13–25; 34; 4 . . . . Babylon, Assyria, Philistia, Moab, Damascus, Ethiopia, Egypt, Edom, Arabia, Tyre, all the nations of the world.

Jeremiah 46–51 . . . . Egypt, Philistia, Moab, Ammon, Edom, Damascus, Kedar, Hazor, Elam, Babylon.

Ezekiel 25–32; 35; 38–39 . . . . . . Ammon, Moab, Edom, Philistia, Tyre, Sidon, Egypt, Assyria; Gog and Magog.

Daniel 2, 7. . . . . Babylon, Media-Persia, Greece, Rome.

Amos 1:3–2:3. . . . . Damascus, Philistia, Tyre, Edom, Ammon, Moab.

Zechariah 9:1-7 . . . . Damascus, Tyre, Sidon, Philistia.

Three complete books are focused on Gentile nations:

> *Obadiah* . . . . Edom
> *Jonah.* . . . . Assyria
> *Nahum* . . . . Assyria

This phenomenon reminds us of some important principles:

1) God is interested in and loves all nations. His plan from the call of Abraham onward was to bless all nations (Gen. 12:3).

2) God holds all nations accountable to Himself as *"the Judge of all the earth"* (Gen. 18:25).
3) *"Righteousness exalts a nation: but sin is a reproach to any people"* (Prov. 14:34). What may be called "national sins" are a sobering reality. It is likely that these prophecies were sent to the nations to whom they were addressed (Jer. 27:3-4). It might be worth while to ask what message God might send if He sent a prophet to our own country! What are the national sins of our nation?

Nineveh was capital of the great Assyrian Empire established by the descendants of Nimrod (Gen. 10:8-11). It was one of the crudest and most violent regimes in world history, lasting from 1100-612 BC The Assyrians' cruelty to their captives was legendary, including such barbaric acts as cutting off hands, feet, ears, or noses, and burning children alive.

Two prophets were sent to Nineveh: *Jonah* and *Nahum*. Although their messages were similar ("Judgment is coming on Nineveh!"), the results were very different. The Ninevites responded to Jonah's warning by repenting, and God spared the city. But one hundred years later, Nahum proclaimed that Nineveh's destruction was now irrevocable. We might say that the book of Jonah reveals the "kindness" of God while Nahum shows His "severity" (Rom. 11:22).

JONAH—A VENGEFUL PROPHET

One wide-spread misconception regarding the prophets of God is that they were sinless. But though true servants of God, the biblical prophets were far from sinless. The Bible clearly exposes their shortcomings (see Study 3, pp. 44-46).

Jonah preached effectively to Israel during the reign of Jeroboam II (2 Ki. 14:23). But he is best known as the prophet who was swallowed by a huge fish while trying to escape his assignment from God to warn the wicked Assyrian capital Nineveh of impending judgment (ch. 1). After three days inside the fish, he repented of his disobedience and the fish vomited him out onto dry land (ch. 2).

The prophet then received a second chance to go to Nineveh. This time he went and his preaching was rewarded with a citywide turning to God—a lesson on the importance of obedience. The Ninevites repented and God relented of the judgment He had threatened (ch. 3). But the real lesson of the book comes in chapter 4. Jonah becomes angry with God for sparing the city. He wanted vengeance on Israel's enemies! He complained,

> *Was not this what I said when I was still in my country?...for I know that You are a gracious and merciful God, slow to anger and abundant in lovingkindness, One who relents from doing harm* (4:2).

The book of Jonah clearly shows God's heart of compassion for the misguided and condemned peoples of the earth: *"Should I not pity Nineveh, that great city, in which are more than one hundred and twenty thousand persons who cannot discern between their right hand and their left—and much live- stock?"* (4:11). Lack of love and compassion for the enemies of God's peo- ple reveals a prophet (or any person) who is completely out of tune with the heart of God. If we belong to Him, we must resist the tendency to be like Jonah, and instead be gracious and compassionate toward all men.

Finally, God's progressive revelation shows that Jonah was a picture of One much greater who came centuries later. Jesus the Messiah would be engulfed, not with sea waters, but with the waves of God's judgment on mankind's sin. He would spend three days, not in the belly of a fish, but in the heart of the earth, and then be raised from the dead. This burial and mighty resurrection was called *"the sign of the prophet Jonah"* (Mt. 12:38-41). Jesus would be the source of eternal salvation, which is only *"of the Lord"* (Jonah 2:9).

NAHUM—"A JEALOUS AND AVENGING GOD"

In the hands of men and women, seeking vengeance on one's enemies leads only to escalating hatred and unending war. God's people are strict- ly commanded in the New Testament, *"Do not avenge yourselves, but rather give place to wrath; for it is written, 'Vengeance is Mine, I will repay,' says the Lord"* (Rom. 12:19 and Heb. 10:30, quoting Deut. 32:35). However, the sec- ond part of this verse is as important as the first. God will repay. All evil will be justly avenged by God.

Like Jonah, Nahum is given a message for the people of Nineveh. But unlike Jonah's offer of God's mercy, Nahum declares that time has run out for the cruel, idolatrous Assyrian kingdom. Where Jonah acknowledged, *"You are a gracious and merciful God, slow to anger and abundant in lov- ingkindness, One who relents from doing harm"* (Jon. 4:2), Nahum ominously declared the other side of the balance:

> *God is jealous, and the Lord avenges; the Lord avenges and is furious. The Lord will take vengeance on His adversaries, and He reserves wrath for His enemies; the Lord is slow to anger and great in power, and will not at all acquit the wicked* (Nah. 1:2-3).

After years of affliction, God the Avenger would move to vindicate His people in perfect justice. Using the total destruction of Nineveh as a clear lesson, the book of Nahum announces the awful judgment of God against all sinners world-wide. The proud *"bloody city! it is all full of lies"* (3:1), would be forced to recognize the universal sovereignty of the Lord. Nineveh, *"the well-favored harlot, the mistress of witchcrafts,"* had deceived and sold other nations, but God was not deceived. He would expose her wickedness to all (3:4-7).

God has not changed. As surely as Nahum's prophecy was fulfilled in

612 BC when the Babylonians destroyed Nineveh, God's promise to judge our wicked world once for all will be fulfilled.

Yet even in this book of judgment the Lord's mercy is seen. He is *"slow to anger"* (1:3). His patience waited a hundred years after Jonah's time. He is also *"good, a stronghold in the day of trouble; and He knows those who trust in Him"* (1:7). The *"good tidings"* of Nineveh's destruction was a reminder of His justice and faithfulness, and an assurance that He would ultimately *"restore the splendor of Jacob"* (1:15–2:2 NASB).

THE JEALOUSY OF GOD

To understand God we must understand that He is "jealous," or "zealous" (the same Hebrew word—*qinah*). He will not give His glory to another. But the jealousy of God in the Scriptures must not be confused with common ideas of "jealous" such as "suspicious, distrustful, and fearful of rivalry." Rather it is that combination of unyielding holiness and perfect love which requires the unreserved and exclusive devotion of His creatures, particularly His own redeemed covenant people (Ex. 20:5; 34:14; Deut. 4:24; 5:9; 6:15). The jealousy or zeal of God is at the root of His anger and judgment of sin (Deut. 29:18-20; Ezek. 5:13; 8:3; 16:38, 42; 23:25; 36:5-6; Zeph. 1:18), as well as at the root of His determination to vindicate His own people and carry His promises through to fulfillment and glory (2 Ki. 19:31; Isa. 9:7; 37:32; Joel 2:18; Zech. 1:14; 8:2-3).

The Lord's jealous love causes His *"heart to turn over within Him"* as His inevitable wrath upon Israel's harlotry confronts His unchangeable marriage-covenant love for His beloved (Hosea 11). The jealousy of love is *"the very flame of the Lord"* (Song of Solomon 8:6 NASB). This awesome quality of holy love is most fully seen in the sin-bearing of the Messiah, as God poured out His fury on His beloved One in order to satisfy the demands of His holiness against sin and purify His bride-to-be (Isa. 53:10-11).

We also must hate sin (especially in ourselves) and jealously love God and His people like Phinehas (Num. 25).

HABAKKUK—"THE JUST SHALL LIVE BY FAITH"

The essential requirement to share in the eternal blessings of God's promise is FAITH. In fact, *"without faith it is impossible to please Him"* (Heb. 11:6). Habakkuk, surrounded by Judah's wickedness, cried out to God for justice (Hab. 1:2-4). God answered that He would shortly use the cruel Babylonians to invade Judah and punish her (1:5-11). "This only increased the agony of the prophet, for how could God use a more wicked agent to punish a less wicked people (12-17)?"[1] We often wrestle with similar questions: How can God allow so many innocent people to suffer so greatly? The answer is seen only in the long-range view:

> *The vision is yet for an appointed time; but at the end it will speak, and it will not lie. Though it tarries, wait for it; because it will surely come, It will not*

tarry. Behold the proud, his soul is not upright in him; but the just shall live by his faith (Hab. 2:3-4).

Justice will be done; *"They will be held guilty, they whose strength is their god"* (Hab. 1:11 NASB). After Judah's punishment, wicked Babylon, like Assyria, will receive *"shameful spewing"* in return for her pride, violence, and idolatry (2:6-20). The terrible wrath of *"the Holy One"* will be revealed (3:3-6). In spite of Babylon's grand plans, ultimately *"the earth will be filled with the knowledge of the glory of the Lord, as the waters cover the sea"* (2:14).

In contrast to the pride of the unbeliever, God's righteous one is to live by faith, "a childlike, humble, and sincere trust in the divine message of salvation."[2] Even in the darkest and most hopeless days, we are to be confident and full of joy. Habakkuk 3:17-18 is a graphic definition of true faith:

> *Although the fig tree shall not blossom, neither shall fruit be in the vines; the labor of the olive shall fail, and the fields shall yield no meat; the flock shall be cut off from the fold, and there shall be no herd in the stalls: yet I will rejoice in the Lord, I will joy in the God of my salvation.*

ZEPHANIAH—"THE LORD IS IN YOUR MIDST"

Where Habakkuk demanded faith as the requirement for entering into the benefits of the company of believers, Zephaniah stressed humility and poverty of spirit. In view of the *"Day of the Lord"* coming on Judah, the people were warned, *"Hold thy peace at the presence of the Lord God"* (1:2-7). Joel, Amos, Obadiah, and Isaiah had all spoken of this day, but more than any of them Zephaniah emphasized the world-wide judgment when the Lord *"I will utterly consume everything from the face of the land…man and beast"* (1:2-3). His prophecy was partially fulfilled in the destruction of Jerusalem by the Babylonians in 586 BC and again by the Romans in AD 70, but its final fulfillment is still future.

The same zeal that will devour all the earth *"by the fire of His jealousy"* will *"turn to the people a pure language"* (1:18; 3:9). Out of judgment the Lord will take a remnant of the humble God-fearers who accept correction (2:7, 9; 3:19).

> *In that day…I will take away from your midst those who rejoice in your pride…I will leave in your midst a meek and humble people, and they shall trust in the name of the Lord* (3:11-12).

In the final section of the prophecy we have an amazing look into God's fervent heart of love. We are there after He has fulfilled His promise, and see Him as a victorious warrior in the midst of His beloved people, exulting and rejoicing over them with great joy! And as they are given this glorious prophecy, Zephaniah cries to them (and to us), *"Sing, O daughter of Zion! shout, O Israel; be glad and rejoice with all the heart, O daughter of Jerusalem!"* (3:14).

JEREMIAH—"THE WORD OF THE LORD"

It is hard to imagine more discouraging conditions for serving God than those of Jeremiah, the "weeping prophet." He began during the hopeful reign of the great reformer Josiah, but for 23 years the people refused to listen (25:3). Following Josiah's tragic death (2 Chron. 35:20-27) one disaster after another overtakes Judah and Jerusalem. In quick succession Judah's last four kings, Jehoahaz, Jehoiakim, Jehoiachin, and Zedekiah, are dragged into captivity by foreign monarchs (2 Ki. 23:31–25:21). With them go all the Israelites with any potential value as slaves.

Jeremiah has the thankless task of ministering to the weak, sick, elderly, and otherwise undesirable remnant. He has to tell them that exile is inescapable and that God's will is for them to submit to the invading Babylonians (27:12-22; 28:12-16; 42:11-16). Even as he speaks God's Word to them, his hearers are plotting to kill him (26:7-24; 37:11-16; 38:1-13). He ends his service in Egypt with the remnant of arrogant Jews who have fled there in complete disregard for God's clear warning (chs. 42–44).

Jeremiah was the prophet of the "word of the Lord" (1:2), using phrases like "Thus saith the Lord" over 150 times out of the 350 times such phrases are used in the Old Testament. The basis of Jeremiah's authority was God's word: "Behold, I have put My words in thy mouth" (1:9; 5:14). It was food for Jeremiah's own soul: "Thy words were found and I did eat them, and Thy words became for me a joy and the delight of my heart" (15:16). It was truth which had to be declared, even when it seemed fruitless or brought mocking in return: "In my heart it became like a burning fire" (20:8-9). We can learn much about personal communion with God from Jeremiah as he pours out his frustration over being rejected by the very people he was warning (11:18-23; 12:1-6; 15:10-18; 17:14-18; 18:18-23; 20:7-11).

It is vital to see that the words of all so-called prophets must be tested by the previously revealed scriptures. Many "prophets" were seeing dreams and visions. The Lord said, *"The prophet who has a dream, let him tell a dream; and he who has My word, let him speak My word faithfully. What is the chaff to the wheat?....Is not My word like a fire...and like a hammer that breaks the rock in pieces?"* (23:28-29).

THE VANITY OF EXTERNAL RELIGION

In his so-called "Temple Gate Message" (chs. 7–10), Jeremiah warned the people making their way into the temple of three solemn facts:

"1) Attendance at the house of God was no substitute for real repentance (7:4-20).

2) Observance of religious activities was no substitute for obedience to the Lord (7:21–8:7).

3) Possession of the Word of God was no substitute for responding to what that Word said (8:8-12)."[3]

Jeremiah's Lord has not changed. In the same way today, empty, non-committal religion leads straight to judgment and the wrath of God.

JERUSALEM, THE THRONE OF YAHWEH

But Jeremiah also had the privilege of relaying God's comforting promises to the people. In a most amazing prediction in 3:16-17, he announced that, *"in those days…they will say no more, 'The ark of the covenant of the Lord.' It shall not come to mind, nor shall they remember it, nor shall they visit it, nor shall it be made anymore. At that time Jerusalem shall be called The Throne of the Lord."*

As God's promise is fulfilled in that final day, the ark of the Covenant, the central object in all Israel's worship, would no longer be significant. Instead of God's symbolic enthronement between the cherubim of gold, He Himself would be enthroned in Jerusalem. In this prediction, it became clear that in God's plan the ceremonial institutions of Moses' law would one day be obsolete.

YAHWEH OUR RIGHTEOUSNESS

The *"righteous Branch"* already announced in Isaiah 4:2 and 11:1 is the same son of David foreseen in Jeremiah 23:5-7 and 33:14-22. The special name given to the Messiah is *"The Lord our Righteousness."* So intimately linked are Messiah and His people that this name is shared with Jerusalem in 33:16. Not only does this name indicate that the promised kingdom described in 33:14-22 is to be based on the Lord's righteous character, but that His own righteousness will be given or accounted to them. Much as a bride receives her husband's name and all that goes with it, so Messiah's people receive His name and His righteousness as their own. This is the only basis of true righteousness before God.

"A NEW COVENANT"

The name given to the second half of our Bible was taken from Jeremiah 31:31: *"Behold, the days are coming, says the Lord, when I will make a new covenant with the house of Israel and with the house of Judah."* This great section is the largest piece of Scripture quoted in the New Testament (Heb. 8:8-12; 10:16-17). It is also the subject of at least seven other NT passages dealing with the achievements of the Messiah as Mediator of this covenant (Mt. 26:28; Mk. 14:24; Lk. 22:20; 1 Cor. 11:25; 2 Cor. 3:6; Heb. 9:14-15; 12:24).

This covenant would be *"not according to the covenant that I made with their fathers in the day that I took them by the hand to lead them out of the land of Egypt, My covenant which they broke"* (Jer. 31:31-32). It would be funda-mentally different from the Old Covenant which was engraved on stone. Instead God said, *"I will put My law in their minds, and write it on their hearts"* (31:33). Yet it would not be a new law. God's law does not change; Christ would come not to destroy the Law but to fulfill it. God Himself would write His desire on His people's hearts by His Spirit. The Law, although *"holy, and just, and good"* (Rom. 7:12), was unable to give life. It could only reveal the lawlessness of man and then condemn him. This new covenant would be the work of God through the death and resurrection of the Messiah and the inward regeneration of the Holy Spirit.

While "new" and different from the Mosaic covenant of Mt. Sinai, Jeremiah's covenant was not new in relation to the promise of God to Abraham and David, known by this time also as *"the everlasting covenant,"* *"a covenant of My peace,"* and *"My covenant"* (Isa. 24:5; 42:6; 49:8; 54:10; 55:3; 59:21; 61:8; Jer. 32:39-41; Hos. 2:18-20). Rather it was a renewing, an enlarging and restating of God's unchangeable purpose at the moment of impending destruction for the nation.

CONCLUSION

The New Covenant was made with "the house of Judah and the house of Israel," and it will be completely fulfilled for them nationally at the second coming of Christ. Yet as believers in Christ, we are no longer strangers and aliens but are *"fellow-citizens with the saints, and are of the household of God"* (Eph. 2:19). This is what the Holy Spirit calls "the mystery of Christ":

> ...the mystery of Christ, which in other ages was not made known to the sons of men, as it has now been revealed by the Spirit to His holy apostles and prophets: that the Gentiles should be fellow heirs, of the same body, and partakers of His promise in Christ through the gospel (Eph. 3:4-6).

This incredible treasure, called the *"unfathomable riches of Christ,"* has been guaranteed to us by the New Covenant, sealed and mediated for us by the precious blood of Christ (1 Cor. 11:25; Heb. 8), and written on our hearts *"with the Spirit of the living God"* (2 Cor. 3:3). In light of the surpassing glory of this New Covenant, whatever circumstances we are facing, we should say with Habakkuk:

> I will rejoice in the Lord,
> I will rejoice in the God of my salvation.
> The Lord God is my strength,
> And He has made my feet like hinds' feet,
> And makes me walk on my high places (Hab. 3:18-19).

ENDNOTES

1 Kaiser, TOTT, p. 225.

2 Ibid., p. 227.

3 Ibid., p. 229.

1. (JONAH) What sinful actions and attitudes does the Bible reveal in the prophet Jonah,

    in chapter 1

    in chapter 4

    What do you learn about God's character in chapter 4?

2. (NAHUM) What is your first reaction to Nahum's description of the Lord in 1:1-8? How do you reconcile this with your own ideas of God?

3. On page 168 there is a discussion of the jealousy of God. In the following verses, what is the result of God's jealousy or zeal? Keep in mind that in the Hebrew language "jealousy" and "zeal" are the same word.

    Exodus 20:5; 34:14

    Zephaniah 1:18

    Isaiah 9:7; 37:32

4. (HABAKKUK) What important principle is found in Habakkuk 2:3-4? In your answer consider each of the following three verses where this passage is quoted: Romans 1:17; Galatians 3:11; Hebrews 10:35-39.

5. Write out (or paraphrase in your own words) Habakkuk 3:17-18 in the space below.

    What does this passage teach God's people about overcoming difficulties in their lives? How is it possible to rejoice under such conditions?

6. (ZEPHANIAH) What attitude does the Lord require from His people in these verses: Zephaniah 1:7; 3:11-13?

7. What attitude is revealed in the Lord's words in Zephaniah 3:14-17?
    How does the Lord feel about His people?

8. (JEREMIAH) From the following two verses, what value should the
    Word of God have for us:
    Jer. 15:16; 23:28-29?

    What importance do the Scriptures have in your day-to-day life, prac-
    tically speaking?

9. What importance did the Ark of the Covenant have in Israel's worship
    (if necessary see Study 5, pages 67-76 for details)? According to the
    promise in Jeremiah 3:16-17, how was this to change in the future?

10. In Jeremiah 23:5 and 33:15, how is David's promised Descendant
    referred to?

    In 23:6, we learn that He would also be called by another name. What
    is that name and its importance?

11. The Lord promised in Jeremiah 31:31-34 that He would make a "new
    covenant" with Israel and Judah. What was the "old" covenant (see
    31:32)? Why did it fail? Was there something wrong with the covenant
    (Heb. 8:7-13)?

    How was this "New Covenant" was put into effect (Lk. 22:20; 2 Cor.
    3:6; Heb. 9:14-15)?

    How can you apply this lesson to your own relationship with the Lord
    and His promise?

KINGDOM OF THE PROMISE
EXILIC ERA

Recommended Readings: Lamentations 3:19-38; Ezekiel 1; 11:16-20; 17; 21:25-27; 34; 36:22-36; 37; Daniel 2; 7; 9; 12:1-3

The unthinkable had finally happened. God had destroyed His beloved city Jerusalem, using the cruel Babylonian army. The prophet Jeremiah, in his Lamentations, poured out his anguish at witnessing infants starving (4:4) and women eating their own children (2:20; 4:9-10) during the terrible siege which preceded the city's fall, and then the slaughter (2:20-21), rape, and humiliation (5:11-13) which followed. The deepest source of grief for the prophet is that the Lord Himself has done it (ch. 2:1-9):

> *The Lord has swallowed up and has not pitied…He has thrown down…He has cut off in fierce anger…He has abandoned His sanctuary.*

Let us not miss the point: Sin brings judgment. It steals the joy and glory God desires for His people and leaves only anguish, humiliation, and death. *"He does not afflict willingly nor grieve the children of men"* (3:33). It is the result of sin! Let us listen and learn from Jerusalem: *"The Lord is righteous; for I have rebelled against His commandment: hear, I pray you…and behold my sorrow: my virgins and my young men are gone into captivity"* (1:18).

Their faithlessness was scandalous. Yet in spite of their shameful sin, there was still hope because of the faithfulness of the God of Israel:

> *This I recall to my mind, therefore I have hope. Through the Lord's mercies we are not consumed, because His compassions fail not. They are new every morning; great is Thy faithfulness* (Lam. 3:21-23).

Now that they had entered the long-threatened seventy years of captivity (Jer. 25:11), we find beautiful words of promise, deliverance, and new birth for God's people Israel. Both Ezekiel and Daniel are models for us of living by faith and hope in times of failure and spiritual disaster.

EZEKIEL—THE GOOD SHEPHERD'S REIGN

Ezekiel, a priest by descent, had been carried into captivity with King Jehoiachin in 597 BC, about ten years before the fall of Jerusalem. Following the record of his unique call to service (chs. 1–3), Ezekiel's work has three primary sections:

1. (chs. 4–24) From Babylon, Ezekiel continues to warn Judah of the coming disaster.

2. (chs. 25–32) During the siege of Jerusalem he turns to warn the other nations that judgment will fall on them as well.

3. (chs. 33–48) With no hope left for the old Davidic kings, messages of hope and bright promises of the Good Shepherd's reign take over.

Ezekiel's ministry teems with exotic symbolic actions, allegories and parables, as well as highly symbolic (apocalyptic) language. The governing theme of his messages is given in the opening vision: "The glory of God." The Lord declares, *"I acted for My name's sake, that it should not be profaned"* (20:9, 14, 22), and *"that you shall know that I am the Lord!"* (more than 54 times). This reality needs to govern our lives as well. God is jealous of His own glory. If we claim to be His people, our lives reflect on His name. *"Therefore, whether you eat or drink, or whatever you do, do all to the glory of God"* (1 Cor. 10:31).

We will consider some of the key passages in this prophetic book as the Holy Spirit adds further details to the promise of God.

"THE GLORY OF THE LORD"

Dominating every scene of the book of Ezekiel is the throne of God (1:4-28). This vision, which came to him in Babylonian exile, was the basis of his call as a prophet (chs. 2–3).

> Here is encouragement for all who feel hemmed in and frustrated by circumstances. Ezekiel was cut off from the temple worship in Jerusalem, but in distant Babylon he received such visions of glory as no other priest had ever known. Heaven is often opened when every other road seems closed.[1]

Ezekiel sees a whirlwind coming out of the north (Ezek. 1:4), depicting God's coming in judgment against Jerusalem (43:3). The highly symbolic scene resembles those seen by John (Rev. 1; 4–5) Isaiah (Isa. 6) and Daniel (Dan. 7:9-10; also Ex. 24:9-11). In the center of flashing lightning, gliding wheels and thundering wings, encircled by a brilliant rainbow of color, was the Lord Himself. Enthroned above a glittering expanse over the heads of four *"living creatures,"* He had the *"likeness of a man"* radiating fire and brightness. This was God the Son, who is *"the brightness of His glory"* and *"the image of the invisible God"* (Heb. 1:3; Col. 1:15). For further discussion of the theophanies in the OT, see Appendix 8.

The all-sufficient presence of God would continue to be with His prophet, His promise, the remnant, and the kingdom to come. But in chapter 10, Ezekiel sees the glory of the Lord reluctantly leaving the temple as a result of the horrible idolatry and wickedness within (ch. 8). God's glory did not appear on earth again until the birth of Jesus the Messiah, when *"the glory of the Lord shone about them"* (Lk. 2:9). In his final vision of the kingdom to be established when Christ returns in power, Ezekiel sees the glory of God filling the temple again (43:1-9).

Tracing the story of the glory of the Lord in Ezekiel also provides a good framework for the book as a whole and helps us understand God's prophetic program for Israel, especially for the holy city Jerusalem. A diagram should help clarify this outline:

THE BOOK OF EZEKIEL

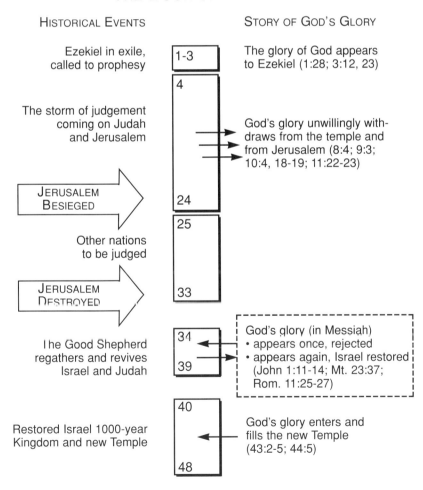

HISTORICAL EVENTS   STORY OF GOD'S GLORY

Ezekiel in exile, called to prophesy | 1-3 | The glory of God appears to Ezekiel (1:28; 3:12, 23)

4

The storm of judgement coming on Judah and Jerusalem — God's glory unwillingly withdraws from the temple and from Jerusalem (8:4; 9:3; 10:4, 18-19; 11:22-23)

JERUSALEM BESIEGED | 24

25

Other nations to be judged

JERUSALEM DESTROYED | 33

The Good Shepherd regathers and revives Israel and Judah | 34 / 39 | God's glory (in Messiah)
• appears once, rejected
• appears again, Israel restored (John 1:11-14; Mt. 23:37; Rom. 11:25-27)

40

Restored Israel 1000-year Kingdom and new Temple | God's glory enters and fills the new Temple (43:2-5; 44:5)

48

YAHWEH THE SANCTUARY (11:16-20)

During the dark years of exile, when God's people were far from even the ruins of the temple, Yahweh would *"be to them as a little sanctuary"* (11:16). Their heavenly Father was even then seeking true worshippers who would *"worship the Father in spirit and in truth"* (Jn. 4:23), irrespective of the setting, whether temple, hall, or chapel. We must continually learn that it is only the presence of the Lord which sanctifies any assembly of His people, regardless of the building, programs, or preachers.

The Lord also promised to restore the people to the land and radically transform their inner beings:

> *I will give them one heart, and I will put a new spirit within them, and take the stony heart out of their flesh, and give them a heart of flesh, that they may walk in My statutes and keep My judgments and do them* (11:19-20).

In familiar words of promise, He says, *"They shall be My people, and I will be their God"* (11:19-20).

THE NEW DAVIDIC KINGDOM AND THE RIGHTFUL KING (17; 21:25-27)

Ezekiel 17 is an allegory picturing the removal by the Babylonian "eagle" of the last wicked Davidic king, Zedekiah, who had relied on Egypt rather than on the Lord. Yet God would have the last word in this history, promising to replant a little twig in Israel which would grow into magnificent cedar, revealing once again God's new World Ruler and Kingdom coming from humble origins (17:22-24; cf. Isa. 9:6-7; Mic. 5:2-4).

God told Zedekiah, whom He called *"profane wicked prince of Israel,"* to remove his crown and told the high priest to remove his turban. The kingdom and the priesthood would be *"no more, until He come whose right it is"* (21:25-27; Gen. 49:10). When that One came who is both king and priest together, God would give the kingdom to Him (Ps. 110; Zech. 6:11-13; Heb. 4:14-16; 7:1–8:2).

THE GOOD SHEPHERD (CH. 34)

The Lord Himself is the Good Shepherd of His people (34:31).[2] He had entrusted His precious flock to undershepherds, the leaders of Israel. But their selfish negligence and cruelty left God's people in exile, *"scattered upon all the face of the earth, and none did search or seek after them"* (v. 6). So the Lord determined to rescue His sheep from the shepherds (vv. 7-10), promising, *"I, even I, will both search my sheep, and seek them out...and I will cause them to lie down. I will...bring again that which was driven away, and will bind up that which was broken, and will strengthen that which was sick: but I will destroy the fat and the strong"* (vv. 11-16).

Then, as previously in Jeremiah 30:9 and later in Ezekiel 37:24, God promises to raise up "David" as their shepherd (v. 24). "God's Servant is that representative person promised to head up the whole group known as the 'seed' of Abraham, Isaac, Jacob, and David."[3] In this *"covenant of peace"* made by God (v. 25) the ancient promise "formula" is found once again:

> *Thus they shall know that I, the Lord their God, am with them, and they, the house of Israel, are My people, says the Lord God* (34:30-31).

THE CLEANSING AND NEW BIRTH (36:22-36)

In this majestic passage God promises to regather Israel and through this to *"sanctify My great name, which was profaned among the heathen"* (v. 23). He would act *"not for your sakes...but for My holy name's sake"* (vv. 22).

But more wonderful than this national restoration would be the inward experience of those who came under the New Covenant by personal belief. These would be cleansed and given *"a new heart...a new spirit"* by the gift of the Holy Spirit (vv. 25-27). Through this work of the Spirit they would fulfill the righteousness of God's law (v. 27), in the restored land given to their forefathers (vv. 28-36).

A REUNITED, RESTORED ISRAEL (37; 40-48)

Through the vision of the "dry bones" in chapter 37 the Lord promises a two-stage national resurrection: Regathering (37:1-8, 11-13) and Reviving (37:9-10, 14). Not only so, but the long-separated tribes ("Joseph" representing the northern ten; "Judah" representing the southern two) would be reunited into *"one nation,"* under *"one king,"* with *"one God"* and *"one shepherd...My Servant David"* (vv. 15-24 NASB). The heart of this *"covenant of peace"* or *"everlasting covenant"* was that the Lord's *"dwelling place will be with them...forever"* (vv. 25-28 NASB).

Ezekiel's message of hope concludes with a detailed description of the renewed land and future glorious temple (chs. 40–48) from which flowed an ever-deepening river of life (47:1-12). Parts of this difficult description may be symbolic rather than strictly literal, but the fact of God's presence among His worshipping people in a new temple and a new Jerusalem, at the center of a renewed heaven and earth, is gloriously certain.

DANIEL—THE PROMISED KINGDOM'S SUCCESS

The old children's chorus urges us, "Dare to be a Daniel!" An exile like Ezekiel, Daniel is a shining example of lifelong faithfulness to God, even among God's enemies and against heavy opposition (chs. 1, 3, 6). But for our study of the promise of God, we will focus on the astounding revelations given to this man of God in chapters 2, 7, and 9–12.

In this book God makes Himself known in a unique way as the great Revealer. *"He reveals deep and secret things...But there is a God in heaven who reveals secrets...and He who reveals secrets has made known to you what will be"*

(Dan. 2:22, 28, 29). Even godless world rulers are brought to confess that *"Truly your God is the God of gods, the Lord of kings, and a revealer of secrets"* (2:47). With Christ Jesus Himself we should thank and praise God for revealing His hidden wisdom in Christ to the hearts of humble people of faith (Mt. 11:25; 16:17; 1 Cor. 2:7, 10). We must avoid becoming so weighed down and dull that we cannot hear the revealing voice of His Spirit (see Paul's prayer in Eph. 1:17-19).

Beginning with the fall of Jerusalem, the nation of Israel came under the domination of four successive world empires. Each rises to rule over many nations, but then weakens and eventually collapses. These are by no means the four greatest empires in world history, but since nations have prophetic significance in the Bible mainly as they enter into conflict with Israel and Jerusalem, it is these four that the visions of Daniel deal with. The maps that follow show the approximate extent of each of these kingdoms at their high point.

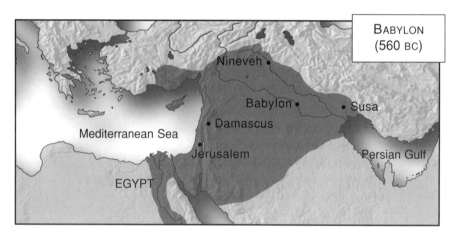

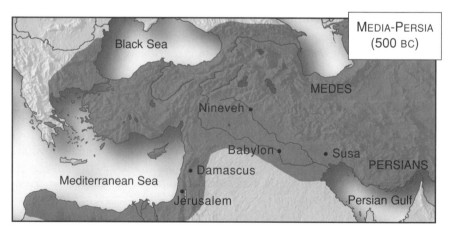

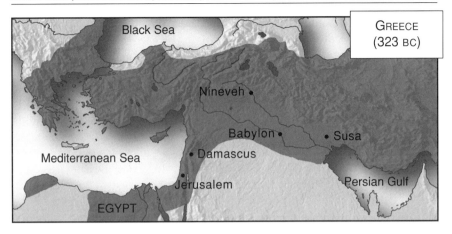

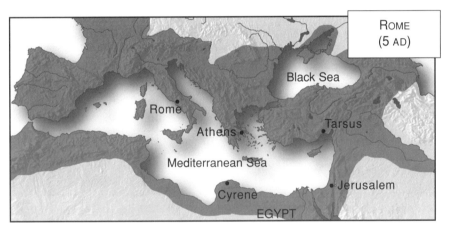

THE "STONE," "THE ANCIENT OF DAYS" AND THE KINGDOM (CHS. 2; 7)

The central theme of the book of Daniel is the everlasting sovereignty of God, who rules now over the proud kingdoms of man, and will one day destroy them completely, enthroning His Anointed as King over all the earth and bringing in His eternal Kingdom.

> *He is the living God, and steadfast forever; His kingdom is the one which shall not be destroyed, and His dominion shall endure to the end* (Dan. 6:26; compare 2:20-21, 44; 4:3, 34; 7:14).

This theme is presented most graphically in two fascinating revelations. Nebuchadnezzar's dream in chapter 2 and Daniel's vision in chapter 7 are parallel revelations. Together they predicted a series of four world empires which would rule Jerusalem through a period of time referred to by Jesus Christ as *"the times of the Gentiles"* (Lk. 21:24). This period began with the Babylonian invasion and will be dramatically ended by the establishment of God's own glorious kingdom on the earth.

The four parts of the massive image seen by Nebuchadnezzar correspond to the four beasts seen by Daniel in his vision. These represented the four empires mentioned above. The critical point was reached in Nebuchadnezzar's dream when the *"stone cut out without hands"* (Messiah) arrives to break *"in pieces...and fill the whole earth"* at which time God will set up a kingdom *"which shall never be destroyed"* (2:34, 44). In Daniel's vision this point was reached when *"One like a Son of Man"* comes and receives dominion over all nations from the *"Ancient of Days"* (7:13-14). These parallel scenes will be fulfilled when the Lord Jesus Christ returns *"in the clouds of heaven"* to judge and reign over all the earth (Mk. 14:61-62).

A COLOSSAL IMAGE & THE STONE (2:31-35)	4 BEASTS & THE SON OF MAN (7:1-14)	THE INTERPRETATION (2:36-45; 7:15-28)
1. Golden head	Winged Lion	Babylonian Empire
2. Silver breast & arms	Bear (in 8:20 a Ram)	Media-Persian empire
3. Bronze belly & thighs	Leopard/four heads (in 8:21-22 a Goat)	Alexander's Greek empire & 4 generals who followed
4. Iron legs/ Clay & iron feet	Dreadful Beast/ Ten horns, one horn	Roman empire[4]/ Western Confederacy, Antichrist
5. The heavenly Stone crushing the image, then filling the earth	Son of Man given an eternal kingdom by the Ancient of Days	Jesus the Messiah at His second coming in power to receive His kingdom

The proud kingdoms of man will confront the blazing judgment of the Highest One, the Ancient of Days. In spite of great accomplishments, they will all be revealed as parts of one satanic, idolatrous system; beastly, savage, and sensuous in nature. In place of the idol the true Stone of Israel, the Lord from heaven, and in place of the beastly world rulers the true Son of Man, will take the throne once and for all. With Him in dominion will be *"the saints of the Most High"* (7:18, 22, 27). This is the *"holy seed"* or remnant (Isa. 6:13; also Num. 24:7; Isa. 60:12; Mic. 4:7). The outcome is sure. Thus God's people are commanded to remain separate from this condemned world system which is presently under the power of Satan:

> *Do not love the world or the things in the world for all that is in the world— the lust of the flesh, the lust of the eyes, and the pride of life…is passing away…but he who does the will of God abides forever* (1 Jn. 2:15-17).

THE SEVENTY WEEKS (CH. 9)

When he noticed that the seventy-year exile predicted in Jeremiah 29:10 was nearly over, Daniel *"set his face to the Lord God to seek by prayer and fasting"* (9:1-19 NASB). As he was praying, the angel Gabriel appeared to him and outlined the future of Jerusalem and the nation of Israel under the figure of seventy "weeks" or periods of seven years, divided into sets of 49 years (7 "sevens"), 434 years (62 "sevens"), and 7 years (1 "seven").

This remarkable summary of prophetic history begins with an outline of God's great purposes for His chosen people and the holy city Jerusalem (v. 24). The six-point plan included complete deliverance from sin and guilt, the conclusion of prophetic activity, and the coming of the righteous kingdom with its anointed sanctuary. God promised to…

- *finish the transgression*
- *make reconciliation for iniquity*
- *seal up the vision and prophecy*
- *make an end of sins*
- *bring in everlasting righteousness*
- *anoint the most Holy.*

To understand these verses, we must try to correctly identify the various personages and peoples referred to:

"Thy people" = the Jews
"Messiah the Prince" = the Lord Jesus Christ
"the people of the prince that shall come" = the Romans
"the prince that shall come" = the Roman Beast, Antichrist

From the decree of Artaxerxes in 445 BC to rebuild Jerusalem (Neh. 2:1-8) to the Messiah's first coming, specifically his entry into Jerusalem as king, would be 483 (7+62 "7"s) years (v. 25). Messiah would then be *"cut off"* describing His crucifixion and rejection by Israel. Then the Romans and their "prince" would destroy the city and temple (this occurred in AD 70). An era of war and desolation for Jerusalem of undetermined length would follow, continuing until the 70th "week," the climactic seven years preceding the return of Messiah to set up His kingdom over all the earth (vv. 26-27). This prediction provides a key to the main events of biblical prophecy. The main elements of its (premillenial) interpretation can be diagrammed as shown on the following page:

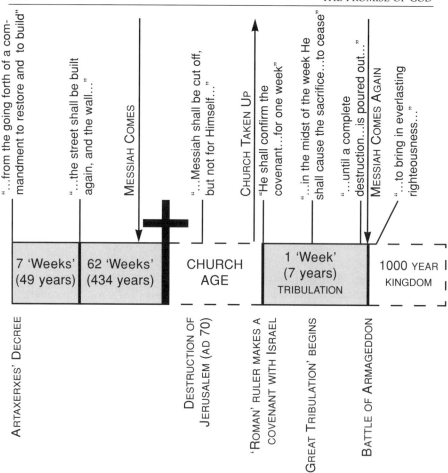

THE BOASTFUL *"LITTLE HORN"*

Against God's holy remnant would arise a final enemy known as the *"little horn"* (7:8, 24-25), the *"prince"* (9:26b-27), or self-willed *"king...speaking monstrous things against God"* (8:23-26; 11:36–12:1). Like the kings of Babylon and Tyre before him, the Greek general Antiochus who desecrated the temple in 168–165 BC (ch. 8:9-14; 11:21-35) was another forerunner of the final *"Antichrist"* in this satanic *"seed"* (Gen. 3:15; 1 Jn. 2:18).

THE FUTURE RESURRECTION (12:1-3)

When this evil one has done his worst, resulting in God's judgment and *"a time of trouble such as never was since there was a nation"* (the famous *"Great Tribulation,"* Mt. 24:21), then God will deliver His remnant and introduce His everlasting kingdom (12:1). His promises will be fulfilled to all His *"holy ones,"* many of whom He will raise from the dust to inherit eternal life (vv. 2-3).

CONCLUSION

Biblical prophecy is fascinating. Understanding the general outline and even some of the details of God's timetable gives us greater appreciation for the Word of God.

However, the reason for this revelation is not to amaze us or satisfy our curiosity, but rather stimulate us to more faithful expectancy and fervent service. *"The people who know their God shall be strong, and carry out great exploits"* (Dan. 11:32).

Above all, *"the testimony of Jesus is the spirit of prophecy"* (Rev. 19:10), which means that even in times such as Ezekiel and Daniel lived, we are called to boldly testify that Jesus is the Christ, the rightful King and only Saviour of the world. Many have been slain and many more will be slain in the future because of the Word of God and this testimony, but their future is certain:

> *Those who are wise shall shine like the brightness of the firmament, and those who turn many to righteousness like the stars forever and ever* (Dan. 12:3).

ENDNOTES

1 W.P.W. McVey, cited in the "Choice Gleanings" calendar.

2 See the following references: Gen. 49:24; Ps. 23; 78:52-3; 79:13; 80:1; 95:7; Isa. 40:11; 49:9-10; Jer. 31:10; Zech. 11; 13:7.

3 Kaiser, TOTT, p. 241.

4 "By the division of the [Roman] empire by the emperor Theodosius (AD 395) it was parted into two sections, the western empire with its capital at Rome itself, and the eastern [Byzantine] empire with its capital at Constantinople [Istanbul]. Numerous expositors think that this was signified by the two legs of Nebuchadnezzar's image." Erich Sauer, *Triumph of the Crucified,* Eerdman/Paternoster, p. 132.

1. (LAMENTATIONS) What lessons can we learn from the Fall of Jerusalem about the consequences of sin and the possibility of returning to the Lord from these verses?
   Lam. 1:18; 3:33

   Lam. 3:21-23

2. (EZEKIEL) Read the accounts of the visions of God given to the following prophets in their books: Ezekiel (1:4-28), Isaiah (6:1-7), Daniel (7:9-14) and John (Rev. 1:12-18; 4:1-5). What features do these visions have in common?

   What effect did these visions have on the men who saw them? Why were they so affected?

3. For what does the Lord condemn the leaders of Israel in Ezekiel 34: 1-6?

   What is the ultimate solution to this ongoing problem, according to Ezekiel 34:11-16, 23-24?

4. Write (or paraphrase) Ezekiel 36:25-27 in the space below.

   What key features of the New Covenant (see Jer. 31:31-34) can you find in these verses?

5. In Ezekiel 37:15-28, God promises to do something great for Israel. What will He do? Has this promise been fulfilled yet?

(DANIEL) Before answering questions 6 and 7, review the chart explaining the two great visions in Daniel, on page 182.

6. Read Daniel 2:31-45. What kind of kingdom will the Lord establish and how will it affect the existing kingdoms of the world (v. 44)?

7. Read Daniel 7:1-28. To whom will the kingdom of God be given (vv. 13-14, 27)? What will be the extent of this dominion?

8. How did Daniel discover that the period of exile was nearly over (Dan. 9:2)? What was his response (9:3-20)?

   What can we learn about prayer from Daniel's example?

9. Daniel 9:24-27 contains a detailed prophecy concerning the time of Messiah's death and future glory. What does the angel tell Daniel will be done for his people and the holy city?

   If one "week" equals 7 years, how many years would it be from the decree (v. 25) until Messiah was "cut off" (v. 26):

   7 (7's) + 62 (7's) =   years?

   450 BC (date of the decree) + 483 years =   AD

10. What great promises does Daniel receive in verses 1-3 of chapter 12?

11. What practical applications can you make from this lesson to your own relationship with the Lord?

TRIUMPH OF THE PROMISE
POST-EXILIC ERA

14

Recommended Readings: 1 Chronicles 29:11-12; Haggai 2:1-9, 20-23; Zechariah 3:8; 6:9-13; 12:10–13:7; 14; Malachi 3:1-3; 3:16–4:6

C enturies before his birth, a great Gentile king was chosen to fulfill part of God's plan. In this extraordinary prophecy, this Persian monarch was even called by name:

> I saith of Cyrus, He is My shepherd, and shall perform all My pleasure: even saying to Jerusalem, Thou shalt be built; and to the temple, Thy foundation shall be laid. For Jacob My servant's sake, and Israel Mine elect, I have even called thee by thy name: I have surnamed [given a title of honor] thee, though thou hast not known Me.
> I have raised him up in righteousness, and I will direct all his ways: he shall build My city, and he shall let go My captives, not for price nor reward, saith the Lord of hosts (Isa. 44:28–45:13, KJV).

Now as the seventy years of exile drew to an end, in order *"that the word of the Lord spoken by the mouth of Jeremiah might be accomplished, the Lord stirred up the spirit of Cyrus king of Persia…"* (2 Chron. 36:22-23; Ezra 1:1-4). The king issued a proclamation that whoever was willing among God's people should go and rebuild the temple in Jerusalem. God moved the heart of this king to carry out His purposes and fulfill His promises.

Together, the histories of Ezra, Nehemiah, Esther, Chronicles, and the prophecies of Haggai, Zechariah, and Malachi make up the final note of revelation in the Old Testament. They move from the despondency of conditions in Israel after their return from the seventy years of Babylonian Exile to the complete triumph of God's Person, word and work.[1]

The great problem of the era was the pitifully small and weak condi-

189

tion of the restoration when compared to the grandeur of earlier days or to the glory that was still expected. Everywhere were the reminders of defeat. Everything was wrong. In spite of the high hopes which accompanied the return from Babylon, it was a *"day of small things."* Where were they to turn? The answer was to God's GRACE. All He had promised would indeed be accomplished, yet it would be *"not by might, nor by power, but by My Spirit,"* and *"crying 'Grace, grace to it'"* (Zech. 4:6–7). This is foundational: God's promise is entirely based on His grace. It is possessed by faith, not by man's success or religious works.

The focus of these books is the house of God, the temple, which was the symbol of God's presence with them. Solomon's great temple had been destroyed by the Babylonians following the sad withdrawal of the glory of the Lord (Ezek. 10). The first remnant under Zerubbabel set about rebuilding a smaller version of the temple. The often-discouraged workers were urged on by the visionary prophets *Haggai* and *Zechariah*, who tried to show them that their efforts, however feeble, were part of the mighty work of God whose promise would not fail. Men must now look up, believe, and work! And so they did. The temple was finished and a second group of returnees led by *Ezra* arrived to support and extend the restoration work. This time national repentance and spiritual revival was brought about through the effective reading and teaching of the Law of God (Ezra 9–10).

Some years later, *Nehemiah* and a third group of returnees took up the work, rebuilding the city walls and reorganizing the temple worship. *Malachi's* searching message of the need for purity came during this period. See Appendix 4 for the full chronology of this period.

Each of these three returns brought a new challenge and a fresh work of God by His Spirit. This period can be diagrammed as follows:

THREE RETURNS FROM EXILE

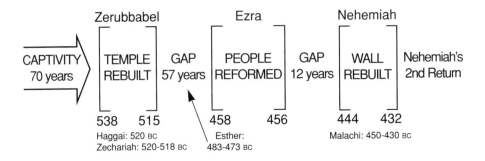

The work facing these returnees was extremely difficult and discouraging. Rebuilding ruined structures is often far more frustrating work

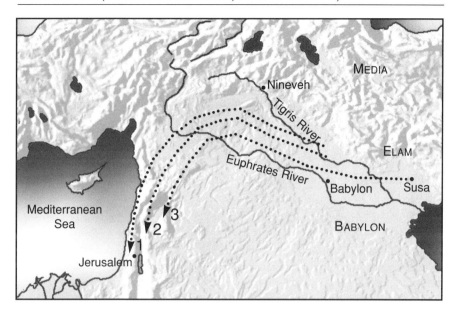

than building new ones. Rubble must be cleared away while usable materials must be cleaned up and reused. This is true in rebuilding local churches as well. Often it is easier to abandon the work and start afresh elsewhere. But the Lord is the God of restoration: *"The Lord will again comfort Zion, and will again choose Jerusalem"* (Zech. 1:17). If we are called to rebuild, let us do so with the zeal and confidence that comes from Him.

1 & 2 Chronicles: The Kingdom is the Lord's

The Books of 1 and 2 Chronicles, originally one Book which concluded the Hebrew Bible, trace the history of the kingdom of God from Adam to the end of the Exile. At first glance the Chronicles may seem to be little more than a repetition of Samuel and Kings, but closer inspection reveals a marked difference in purpose. The Books of Samuel and Kings emphasize the historical and political (royal history) while Chronicles emphasizes the spiritual (temple history). In Chronicles...

- Only the reign of David and his dynasty are given. The northern kingdom and kings of Israel are mentioned only as they affect Judah. God's heart is in His promise, and this promise is in David's Son.
- The tragic stories of Amnon, Absalom, and Adonijah; and Solomon's unfaithfulness (2 Sam. 13-19; 1 Ki. 2, 11) are passed over. While God must judge sin in His people, His grace will ultimately triumph.
- The focus is on the ark and on the ordinances connected with the temple, with an emphasis on joy, music, and prayer in times of revival and worship (1 Chron. 15–16; 22–26; 28–29; 2 Chron. 23:18-19; also Ezra 3,

6; Neh. 8, 12) Without the spiritual realities of holiness, joy, and wor-ship, the nation was no different than any other on earth. So it is today. The Father still seeks worshippers (Jn. 4:23; Phil. 3:3).

• Greater detail is given of reforms under some of the good kings (2 Chron. 14–17; 19–20; 29–31; 34–35). When these kings searched out and returned to the Law of God with a *"perfect heart,"* God was with them wholly. Hanani the prophet challenged King Asa with this prin-ciple:

The eyes of the Lord run to and fro throughout the whole earth, to show Himself strong on behalf of those whose heart is loyal to Him (2 Chron. 16:9).

Thus in Chronicles the Holy Spirit gives us a spiritual commentary on Israel's history. We see God's activity in events, where before the human cause had been emphasized.[2] This teaches us that we must be spiritual people, seeing, obeying, and trusting the unseen God in every part of our lives.

In thanksgiving for Israel's wholehearted offering for the temple con-struction, David blessed the Lord, *"All that is in heaven and in earth is Yours; Yours is the kingdom, O Lord…and You reign over all…In Your hand it is to make great and to give strength to all"* (1 Chron. 29:11-12). The kingdom is the Lord's. David and his failing *"house"* were merely vice-regents. The genealogy from Adam (chs. 1–9) and the promise to David (1 Chron. 17:14; see Study 8) "make it clear that all mankind was affected by the enormity of God's eschatological work."[3]

EZRA–NEHEMIAH: THE WORK IS THE LORD'S

Originally one book, Ezra and Nehemiah begin with the decree of King Cyrus to rebuild the temple in Jerusalem (2 Chron. 36:22-23; Ezra 1:1-4). In the history of the three successive returns (see diagrams pp. 190-191 and Appendix 4), certain vital principles for the work of the Lord emerge:

The centrality of the Scriptures. Ezra's sweeping reforms came through his ministry of the Word of God (Ezra 10:3; Neh. 8-9). Like the blessed man of Psalm 1, *"Ezra had prepared his heart to seek the law of the Lord, and to do it, and to teach in Israel statutes and judgments,"* and because of this, he could say, *"the hand of my Lord his God was upon me"* (7:6-12, 28; Neh. 2:8, KJV). An enduring work of God will be led by men of God using the Word of God (2 Tim. 3:16-17).

The importance of prayer. At each critical point, repentance, confes-sion, fasting, and sincere prayer paved the way for the Lord's work (Ezra 8:23; 9; Neh. 1; 2:4; 9). God has amazingly linked His own sovereign pur-poses to the prayers of His saints (see Dan. 9 for another example.)

The requirement of holiness. The prayers and actions of Ezra and Nehemiah display a deep sensitivity to sin. Holiness demands separation:

from marriage to unbelievers (Ezra 9:1-4; Neh. 13:23-29); from love of money (Neh. 5; 13:10): in fact from all defilement of body and spirit.

The need for hard work. *"The people had a mind to work"* (Neh. 4:6). They persisted in the tough work of rebuilding, against both external opposition and internal discouragement (Neh. 3–4). At times they labored until the stars came out (4:21). Knowing that it was God's work, their attitude was, *"I am doing a great work, so that I cannot come down"* (6:3).

ESTHER: THE PROVIDENCE OF GOD

The Book of Esther was likely written by the same "chronicler" (perhaps Ezra the scribe) who is believed to have compiled Chronicles, Ezra, and Nehemiah under the hand of God's Spirit. As in the book of Ruth, the emphasis in Esther is on the providential hand of God.

> One of the remarkable features of the book is that the name of God is not found in it…[Instead] His presence and power are clearly manifested through a series of designed coincidences. Even if Jehovah's name is not explicitly associated with those who voluntarily stayed in Babylon instead of returning to their own city and land…they were still His people, and He would protect them from the anti-Semitism (inspired by the devil) which sought to exterminate them. God is the author of all history, even if He does not sign His name at the bottom of every page.[4]

God's providence for His people can be seen, for example, in:

1) Esther the Jewess becoming queen *"for such a time as this"* (ch. 2; 4:14).
2) Mordecai hearing and exposing the plot to murder the king (2:21-23).
3) The lot allowing nearly a year for Haman's plot to be thwarted (3:7). "Even superstition was chained to the divine chariot wheels."[5]
4) Mordecai's assurance that if Esther remained silent, *"Enlargement and deliverance arise to the Jews from another place"* (4:14).
5) The king's insomnia and the reading of the record of Mordecai's loyalty to him (6:1-2).
6) The certainty of Haman's men that he would not overcome Mordecai since he was from *"the seed of the Jews"* (6:13).
7) Summary: *"The month which was turned…from sorrow to joy"* (9:22).

HAGGAI: GOD'S SIGNET RING

To stir up His distracted and discouraged people, God spoke through the prophet Haggai four times over a four-month period (1:1; 2:1, 10, 20). First He met their flippant excuse that the time was not right to build the temple with a searching question, relevant today for local churches: *"Is it time for you yourselves to dwell in your paneled houses, and this temple to lie in ruins?…Consider your ways!"* (Hag. 1:2-5). Amazingly, the leaders and the people *"obeyed…and they came and did work"* (1:12-15).

Haggai then gave them a vision to work by. To encourage those who had seen greater days and the more glorious first temple, the Lord said, *"Be strong...and work; for I am with you...and I will fill this temple with glory...The glory of this latter temple shall be greater than the former"* (2:1-9). They should not despise this small beginning; in God's eyes it was one with the glorious future house of His promise (Isa. 60; Ezek. 40–48).

Zerubbabel, as the Davidic ruler, represented the glorious future Servant of the Lord, Messiah. To bring in that day, God would *"shake the heavens and the earth...destroy the strength of the kingdoms of the heathen,"* and establish him *"like a signet ring,"* the Seal of divine authority and faithful covenant love (2:6-7, 21-23; Song of Sol. 8:6; Isa. 42:6; 55:3).

ZECHARIAH: GOD'S CONQUERING HERO

No book in the Old Testament is as intensely Messianic as the book of Zechariah. Its precise prophecies and apocalyptic visions add many details to the emerging portrait of God's coming Shepherd-King. At the same time these stirring visions helped to motivate the weary workers who were rebuilding the temple.

With eight night visions (1:7–6:8) and two burden messages (9–11; 12–14), the priest-prophet Zechariah traced the growth of God's kingdom from its humble beginnings to its triumphant victory over every opposing force.[6]

Between the "night visions" and the "burdens," the Lord stirs up the remnant to work on the temple using a startling coronation ceremony, crowning Joshua the high priest as king (6:9-15), and answering their question about fasting (7–8). The sure triumph of God's promise in His Messiah shines brightly throughout. This structure can be diagrammed as shown below:

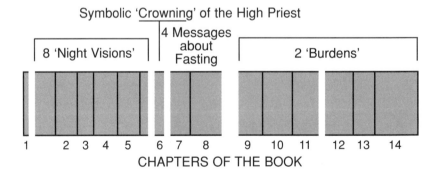

Symbolic 'Crowning' of the High Priest

8 'Night Visions'   4 Messages about Fasting   2 'Burdens'

1   2   3   4   5   6   7   8   9   10   11   12   13   14
CHAPTERS OF THE BOOK

"BEHOLD, A MAN WHOSE NAME IS BRANCH!"

The eight night visions summarize both the future judgment of the nations which were still *"at ease"* (1:7-21; 5:1–6:8; seen in 1:18-21 as four horns, the same world-powers of Dan. 2 and 7), and the future glory of Zion through the cleansing and empowering of God's Spirit (chs. 2–4). At the heart of God's plan is One whom He calls *"My Servant the Branch"* (3:8) who is also *"the Stone on which are seven eyes,* (3:9, NAS)*"*[7] through whom Zion's iniquity will be removed *"in one day"* (3:9-10; Dan. 2:34-5, 45).

In 3:8 we meet again one of the most suggestive titles given to the Messiah in the Hebrew scriptures, the "BRANCH," or "SPROUT," This draws our attention to the One who would grow out of the root or lineage of God's promise. The four different uses of this title in the Scriptures correspond well to the four views of Christ in the gospels:

- *"David a righteous BRANCH"* (Jer. 23:5; 33:15)—The Davidic King (Mt.)
- *"My Servant the BRANCH"* (Zech. 3:8)—The Servant (Mk.)
- *"The Man whose name is BRANCH"* (Zech. 6:12)—The Son of Man (Lk.)
- *"The BRANCH of the Lord"* (Isa. 4:2)—the Son of God (Jn.)

The crowning of the high priest in chapter 6 symbolized the reign of the "Branch," who as God's sole Mediator will rule as both Priest and King (6:9-13; Ps. 110:1, 4). Following the eight night visions, this was the climax of the series of visions, and pointed to the crowning of Messiah as true King after the judgment of the evil world forces.

The densely-packed prophecy to the high priest Joshua in 6:12-13 gives us a seven-fold résumé of this glorious " *Branch."*

1. *He will branch out from where He is* indicates His humble beginnings, as previously predicted in Isaiah 53:2-3.
2. *He shall build the temple of the Lord. Even He shall build the temple of the Lord,* carrying out the will of God to dwell among His people. In fact, both His own physical body (Jn. 2:19), and His spiritual body, the church (1 Cor. 3:16-17) would be the visible temple of the invisible God.
3. *He shall bear the glory*—both the glory which He had with God before the foundation of the world and the glory He received as the reward of His sufferings (Jn. 17:5, 24).
4. *(He) shall sit*—which the priest serving in the temple never did. But He, having offered one sacrifice for sins for all time, would sit down at the right hand of the majesty on high (Heb. 1:3; 10:12).
5. *And (He will) rule on His throne.* God would install His Son as high King, and give Him the very ends of the earth as His possession (Ps. 2:6-8).
6. Most revolutionary, *He shall be a priest on His throne.* The throne of Messiah is a mercy seat, where He intercedes for His people as their priest even as He rules them.
7. *The counsel of peace shall be between them both*—probably indicates the uniting of the separate offices of priest and king in one Person. It may

also refer to the covenant between Father and Son which forms the basis of God's eternal purpose for man.

THE FASTING QUESTION (CHS. 7–8)

Two years after Zechariah received his eight night-visions, the people of Bethel sent their leaders to the priests and prophets in Jerusalem to seek God's favor. They asked whether they should continue to weep and fast in the fifth month as they had been doing for seventy years throughout the exile (7:1-3). Four times *"the word of the Lord"* came to the prophet (7:4; 7:8; 8:1; 8:18), bringing both rebuke and encouragement. The Lord repeats several of the key themes of the first chapters, driving home the certainty that His promise will be fulfilled:

Ch. 1–2	Ch. 7–8
1:4-6	7:7, 11-14 (listen to the words of the former prophets)
1:14	8:2 (The Lord is exceedingly jealous for Jerusalem)
1:16; 2:10	8:3 (The Lord will return to Zion and dwell there)
2:4	8:4-5 (Jerusalem will again be filled to overflowing)
2:11	8:20-23 (The nations will come to Jerusalem, seeking God)

A) Their intent (7:4-7). The question of fasting or not fasting was not so important. The real question was, and still is, more fundamental: *"When you fasted...did you really fast for Me—for Me? When you eat and when you drink, do you not eat and drink for yourselves?"* (7:5-6). God always examines our intent or motive.

B) Their hearts (7:8-14). The Lord had told His people exactly what He wanted from them: *"Execute true justice, show mercy and compassion everyone to his brother. Do not oppress the widow or the fatherless, the alien or the poor. Let none of you plan evil in his heart against his brother"* (7:9-10; see also 8:16-17). He reminded them of the disastrous results when their forefathers *"made their hearts like flint"* and rejected the words of the former prophets (7:11-14).

C) God's heart (8:1-17). Yet because God's faithfulness was greater than theirs, His plan would go on: *"I am zealous for Zion with great zeal...I will return to Zion, and dwell in the midst of Jerusalem"* (8:2-3). Because nothing is too hard for Him, the Lord promised a great regathering from both east and west, and once again declared His plan to dwell among them (8:4-8). This clearly refers to a future regathering connected with Messiah's second coming, since in Zechariah's day the first regathering had already occurred. Referring to the glorious age when the earth will be full of the knowledge of the Lord, Isaiah says, *"in that day...the Lord shall set His hand again the second time to recover the remnant of His people"* (Isa. 11:11).

D) God's intent (8:18-23). Finally returning to the question of fasting, the Lord assures His people that He intends greater things for them than they know the fasts will become *"joy and gladness and cheerful feasts…many peoples and strong nations shall come to seek the Lord of hosts in Jerusalem"* (8:19-23). Men from every language will seek God through the Jews.

"THE BURDEN OF THE WORD OF THE LORD"

Two "burdens" make up the remaining chapters of Zechariah. The first message (chs. 9–11) emphasized the first coming of the Messiah, while the second (chs. 12–14) looks forward to His glorious return. Through these six chapters run four series of remarkable prophecies. Specific events from the return from exile to beyond the second coming of Messiah are predicted, some of them four times over, as shown below:

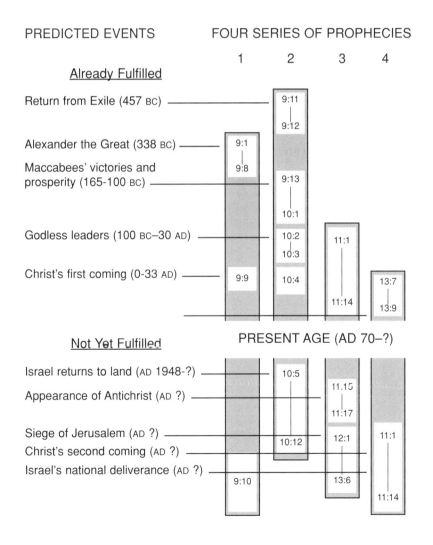

"BEHOLD, YOUR KING!"

In bright contrast with the world's wicked rulers (9:1-8), Zion's coming King would be *"righteous, endowed with salvation and...humble,"* entering Jerusalem on a donkey (9:9). Yet He would reign in peace over all the earth at His second coming (9:10). Again we see an example of the "prophetic fore-shortening" so characteristic of the Old Testament prophets. Within the space of two verses both comings of Christ are clearly predicted. As always His sufferings precede His glory:

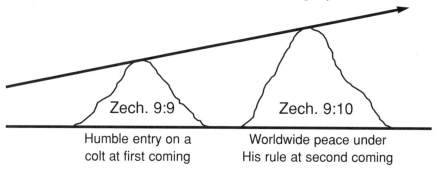

Humble entry on a   Worldwide peace under
colt at first coming   His rule at second coming

"AWAKE, O SWORD, AGAINST MY SHEPHERD!"

God will not leave His people in the grasp of useless shepherds forever, but would deliver and care for them (9:16–10:12). The doomed flock would suffer under many worthless shepherds, culminating with Antichrist (11:1-9; 15–17), and the Lord, the true Shepherd, would be betrayed for thirty pieces of silver, the price of a slave (11:12-13; Ex. 21:32; Mt. 27:1-10). But this very *"smiting"* of the Good Shepherd by the Lord's *"sword"* of judgment at Calvary would provide the basis of a cleansing *"fountain opened to the house of David and to the inhabitants of Jerusalem for sin and for uncleanness"* (see 13:1-7).

In that day the Lord would pour out *"the Spirit of grace and supplication; then they will look on Me whom they pierced. Yes, they will mourn for Him"* (12:10-14; see also Isa. 53). This awesome realization will finally bring the lost sheep of the house of Israel back to the Lord.

"BEHOLD, THE DAY OF THE LORD COMETH!" (CH. 14)

A decisive battle remained to be fought by the Lord. In that day He would gather all the nations as they attempt to deal once and for all with the troublesome Jews (14:1-2). All the nations of earth will unite in a final siege of Jerusalem (12:1-9; 14:1-3). Then with great convulsions of nature the Lord Messiah Himself will descend in blazing glory to fight against the nations. (For New Testament accounts of some of these same climactic events, see Mt. 24:15-31; 2 Thess. 1:6–2:12; and Rev. 19:11–20:6.)

As shown in the diagram to the right, *"His feet will stand on the Mount of Olives, which faces Jerusalem on the east. And the Mount of Olives shall be split in two, from east to west, making a very large valley; half of the mountain shall move toward the north and half of it toward the south"* (14:4). Christ will return to this same hill from which He ascended to glory (Acts 1:6-12).

Zechariah bursts out with great joy, *"Then the Lord, My God, will come, and all the [saints] with Him…and the Lord will be King over all the earth"* (14:5-11). This is the day awaited by God's people for so many ages, and in fact by the whole creation:

> *The earnest expectation of the creation eagerly waits for the revealing of the sons of God…the creation itself also will be delivered from the bondage of corruption into the glorious liberty of the children of God* (Rom. 8:19-22).

Messiah will establish the long-promised kingdom of world peace

Lev. 23:	Name of Feast	Meaning & Fulfillment
1) vv. 4-5	"Passover"	Christ's sacrificial death as the Lamb of God (1 Cor. 5:7)
2) vv. 6-8	"Unleavened Bread"	The sanctification of Christ's redeemed people (1 Cor. 5:8)
3) vv. 9-14	"Firstfruits"	Christ's resurrection as the "firstfruits" of who will be raised (1 Cor. 15:20)
4) vv. 15-22	"Weeks/ Pentecost"	Holy Spirit's coming and the first harvest of souls (Acts 2:1-4)
5) vv. 23-25	"Trumpets"	Up-taking of the saints (1 Thes. 4:16-17), gathering together God's elect (Mt. 24:31)
6) vv. 26-32	"Day of Atonement"	Israel's national repentance and conversion (Zech. 12:10–13:1)
7) vv. 33-44	"Booths"	Joy of the 1000-year messianic Kingdom (Zech. 14:16)

and holiness. We are told a number of time that the nations will go up to Jerusalem *"to worship the King, the Lord of hosts, and to keep the **Feast of Tabernacles**"* (14:16-19). This was the final feast of the Hebrew calendar, commanded by God in Leviticus 23. These seven festivals pictured key events in God's prophetic timetable, as summarized on the previous page.

This final scene of all nations celebrating the Feast of Booths assures us that, in spite of the raging opposition of God's enemies and all the failure of God's own people, in the end God's promise will triumph and His "house" will be built. The Lord will dwell among His people in a far more glorious way than when He tabernacled in their booths in the wilderness.

MALACHI: GOD'S MESSENGER OF THE COVENANT

One final prophet, Malachi, was sent to the half-hearted, doubting remnant, especially to their immoral priests. In this book the Lord answers a series of arrogant complaints (1:2, 7, 12-13; 2:17; 3:7, 8, 13-15), the worst of which was, *"Where is the God of Judgment?"* (2:17). This brought a simple but searching response:

> *The Lord, whom you seek, will suddenly come to His temple, even the Messenger of the covenant, In whom you delight. Behold, He is coming...But who can endure the day of His coming? And who can stand when He appears? For He is like a refiner's fire* (Mal. 3:1-2).

Again we see an example of how the two comings of Messiah merge into one in predictive prophecy.

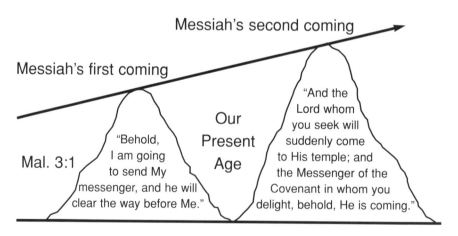

From this amazing promise we can learn the following truths:

1. The coming One would be Yahweh Himself, it was *"His temple."* The One whose way the messenger (John the Baptist) would prepare was the Lord.

2. The Lord's appearing would be through His Mediator, *"The Messenger ("Angel") of the Covenant."* (See Appendix 8.)

3. His appearing would be terrible for *"all the proud, yea, and all that do wickedly,"* but full of joy for *" you that fear My name "* (3:16–4:2). As a refiner separates the worthless dross from the gold, a launderer cleans the filthy garment, or a farmer eliminates the chaff from his wheat (4:1), Messiah would purify His people, particularly the priests (1:6–2:9; 3:3). Only those whose heart has been cleansed by faith in God's promise could *"abide the day of His coming."* For them, *"the Sun of Righteousness will rise with healing in its wings"* (4:2).

Before He came, the Lord would send a forerunner, "Elijah," to prepare the hearts of the people (3:1; 4:5), just as Isaiah had predicted (Isa. 40:1-6). As the two comings of Messiah merge into one in prophetic writing, so it is with His forerunner. At Jesus' first coming, John the Baptist *"before Him in the spirit and power of Elijah,"* but was ultimately rejected and martyred, as his Master was soon afterward. Before Messiah's second coming "Elijah" will again come and *"restore all things"* (Mt. 17:10-13).

The promise would not fail. Yes, God's holiness required judgment, and Israel would have been consumed long ago had it not been for God's unchanging love (3:6). But because of God's faithfulness to His covenant, through the atoning work and righteous reign of His Messiah, a worldwide kingdom and pure worship unknown in history past or present will be glorious reality in the age to come:

> *From the rising of the sun, even to its going down, My name shall be great among the Gentiles; in every place incense shall be offered to My name, and a pure offering; for My name shall be great among the nations, says the Lord of hosts* (1:11).

CONCLUSION

To cooperate with and serve God effectively, we must know what He is doing. From these post-exilic books we've seen that God's focus is His "house." Today His house is not built of cut stone and timbers but of men and women, *"living stones,"* who, *"are built on the foundation of the apostles and prophets, Jesus Christ Himself being the chief corner stone…are being built together for a dwelling place of God in the Spirit"* (1 Pet. 2:5; Eph. 2:20, 22).

The question is, do we love His house, the church? If we do we will imitate Christ, who loved the Church and gave Himself up for her (Eph. 5:25). We will give top priority to the local assembly rather than our own projects, ministries, or homes. We will sacrifice and work hard to build it up. Knowing that *"the fire will test each one's work, of what sort it is,"* we will seek God's help to build with lasting materials, which He calls *"gold, silver and precious stone"* (1 Cor. 3:12-13). Zeal for His house will consume us as it did Him (Jn. 2:17).

The present heavens and earth are like temporary scaffolding around

God's mighty building project. They will only remain until the work is finished. Then the Lord Jesus will tear them down; He will *"shake not only the earth, but also the heaven...removing of those things that are shaken, as of things that are made, that those things which cannot be shaken may remain"* (Hag. 2:6; Heb. 12:26-27). Let's not waste our time, money, and energy investing in the scaffolding, but rather pour them out unreservedly into the work of His house.

ENDNOTES

1   Kaiser, TOTT, p. 49.

2   See for example: 1 Chron. 10:13-14; 11:9; 21:7; 2 Chron. 10:15; 12:2; 13:18; 14:11-12; 16:7-9; 17:3-5; 18:31; 20:30; 21:10; 22:7; 24:18, 24; 25:20; 26:5, 7, 20; 27:6.

3   Kaiser, p. 261.

4   MacDonald, OTD, p. 318.

5   Ibid.

6   Ibid., p. 253.

7   The seven eyes represent the seven-fold Spirit of God upon the Messiah for His world-wide work, see Isa. 11:1-5; Rev. 1:4; 3:1; 4:5 and especially 5:6)

1. (CHRONICLES, EZRA, NEHEMIAH) What kind of people is the Lord looking for to strongly support (2 Chron. 16:9; Ezra 7:9-10)?

   Are you one of these people? If not, what do you need to do to become one?

2. Choose either David's psalm of thanksgiving in 1 Chronicles 16:7-36 or his prayer of rejoicing and dedication in 1 Chronicles 29:10-20, and summarize the key points in your own words.

3. How did the Scriptures contribute to the revival of spiritual life in Israel, according to the following two passages:
   2 Chron. 34:14-32
   Neh. 8

4. Examine Ezra's prayer in Ezra 9 and Nehemiah's prayer in Nehemiah 1. What common features do these two prayers have? How can we deepen our prayer life based on these examples?

5. (HAGGAI) Both Haggai and Malachi rebuke the people of Israel. Identify the sinful attitudes against which they spoke in these passages:
   Hag. 1:2-4, 9
   Mal. 1:6-14

   What do we need to do to avoid falling into the same sins?

6. How does the Lord encourage the people who were discouraged by comparing their work with the greater days of the past? What assurances did He give them (Hag. 2:1-9)?

7. (ZECHARIAH) What two important offices (roles) will be combined for the first time in the coming "Branch" (Messiah) according to Zechariah 6:9-13? Consider Psalm 110:1, 4 in your answer.

8. What extraordinary qualities will the ultimate King of Israel have (Zech. 9:9-10)? Who will he be (Zech. 14:3-11; compare Acts 1:6-12)?

9. Look carefully at Zechariah 12:10; 13:1 and 13:7. What will form the basis of the cleansing from sin promised there?

    Who is the one who was "pierced" by Israel and "smitten" by the Lord's "sword" of divine judgment?

    How were these two aspects of Messiah's death fulfilled historically (see Jn. 19:31-37 and Mt. 27:45-46)?

10. (MALACHI) Carefully read Malachi 3:1. Can you identify the two whose coming was foretold there? If you have difficulty, see Mark 1:2, 7, 9.
    "My messenger" is

    "The messenger of the Covenant" is

    What is the relationship between these two servants of God (see Lk. 1:17; 3:1-17 and Jn. 3:30)? Why was this relationship necessary?

11. How can you apply this lesson to your own relationship with the Messiah? What promises can you appropriate for yourself or for the "house of God" which you are helping to build?

THE PROMISE FULFILLED
PRESENT AND FUTURE ERAS

Recommended Readings: Lk. 1:69-73; 24:44-49; Acts 2:22-39; 3:18-25; 3:16-41; 26:6-8; Gal. 3:6-29; Eph. 3:6-7; Heb. 6:9-20; 1 Pet. 1:10-12; 2 Pet. 1:3-4, 16-21; Rev. 1:6-7; 21:1-8; 22.

We have now surveyed the OT from Genesis to Malachi and seen that the Scriptures reveal a single plan of God to bless all mankind. A picture has emerged of a divine "seed" which would continually be at enmity with, and would finally crush, the "seed" of Satan. This "seed" was sometimes the one unique individual and sometimes the whole line of descendants through whom God's purposes would be fulfilled.

Age by age new details were added to the picture. There would be a redeemed **People** and a holy Nation among who God would dwell; there would be a **Land** and a **Rest**; an everlasting **Kingdom** and a Righteous **King**; a glorious Temple and a **Priest** according to the order of Melchizedek. From the seed of Abraham and David would sprout a **Branch**, an anointed One or **Messiah** known as **Emmanuel**, the **Shepherd**, the **Cornerstone**, the **Servant**, the **Despised One**, the coming **Mighty God** and the **Messenger of the Covenant**. There would be an atoning Sacrifice, the eternal blessing of free **Salvation,** a New **Covenant** of peace in which God's Law would be written on new hearts and spirits, a final Judgment of the nations in the "Day of the Lord," a **Restored Israel** with its glorious capital city of Jerusalem, and ultimately **New Heavens and a New Earth**.

"THE PROMISE" IN THE NEW TESTAMENT

In the New Testament era this singular yet inclusive plan was known as "the promise of God." "For the New Testament writers, this one promise of God epitomized all that God had begun to do in the Old Testament and that He continued doing in their own new era."[1] Paul declared to the Jews of Pisidian Antioch, *"We declare unto you glad tidings, how that the promise which was made to the fathers, God has fulfilled this …in that He raised up Jesus* (Acts 13:32-33). Again, on trial before King Agrippa for his apostolic work of spreading the gospel of Jesus Christ, said, *"I stand and am judged for the hope of the promise made by God to our fathers"* (Acts 26:6).

Without question, "this one promise can be identified as that which was given to Abraham and repeated to Isaac, Jacob, and David."[2] A careful study reveals *"the promise of God"* was used along with the word *"covenant"* to refer to at least five major NT truths:[3]

- The coming of Jesus as the Messiah
  (Lk. 1:69-73; Acts 3:25-26; 13:23, 32-33; Rom. 15:8)
- The gospel of salvation by faith alone and its blessings
  (Rom. 1:2-3; 4:1-25; 2 Cor. 3:6-11; Gal. 3:6-29; 4:23, 28; Eph. 2:12; 3:6-7)
- The doctrine of redemption from sin by the blood of Christ
  (Mt. 26:28; Mk. 14:24; Lk. 22:20; 1 Cor. 11:25; Heb. 10:29)
- The gift of the Holy Spirit in new fullness
  (Lk. 24:49; Acts 1:4-5; 2:33-39; Gal. 3:14; Eph. 1:13)
- The hope of the resurrection and eternal life
  (Acts 26:6-8; 2 Tim. 1:1; Titus 1:2; Heb 6:9-15; 10:23, 36; 2 Pet. 1:3-4; 3:4, 9, 13; 1 Jn. 2:24-25)

JESUS CHRIST THE FULFILLMENT OF GOD'S PROMISE

The fulfillment of God's promise is found in God's Messiah, Jesus Christ. *"For all the promises of God in him are yea, and in him Amen, unto the glory of God by us"* (2 Cor 1:20). He claimed to be the central focus and the fulfiller of the Old Testament: *"Beginning at Moses and all the Prophets, He expounded to them in all the Scriptures the things concerning Himself…all things must be fulfilled which were written in the Law of Moses and the Prophets and the Psalms concerning Me"* (Lk. 24:27, 44; see also Mt. 5:17; 13:14; 21:42; 26:56; Mk. 14:26-27; Lk. 4:20-21; 22:37; Jn. 5:39-47; 15:25). His apostles also repeatedly made the same claim for Him (Acts 3:18; 10:43; 13:29; 17:2-3; 1 Cor. 15:3-4 Rom. 1:2; 1 Pet. 2:5-6).

Some of the fulfillment of God's promise is linked with Jesus' first coming, and with the accomplishments of His death, resurrection, exaltation, and present mediation in heaven. Much still awaits His second coming in power as the King to establish His kingdom in place of the present kingdoms of man.

As the extensive chart in Appendix 5 clearly demonstrates, Jesus fulfilled a great number of OT prophecies in a remarkably specific way. These concerned His birth, His nature, His ministry, His suffering, and death, and His resurrection and exaltation. Many more which concern His second coming and glory remain to be fulfilled.

As we noticed in Study 1, the greatest evidence of the divine nature of God's Word is the fulfillment of prophecy. Only the true God can unfold the future with perfect accuracy: *"I am God, and there is no other…there is none like Me, declaring the end from the beginning, and from ancient times things that are not yet done, saying, My counsel shall stand, and I will do all My pleasure"* (Isa. 46:9-10).

If one cannot see from examining these undeniable fulfillments of prophecy that Jesus is the promised Saviour of the world, is only because he is unwilling. Christ told the Jews who were resisting Him, *"The Scriptures…are they which testify of Me. But you are not willing to come to Me that you may have life"* (Jn. 5:39-40).

GOD'S PROMISE FULFILLED IN THE PRESENT ERA & THE AGE TO COME

It is clear to all Christians that Jesus is the Messiah (the "Christ") promised in the O. T. Like the Samaritans, *"We believe, not because of what you said, for we ourselves have heard Him and we know that this is indeed the Christ, the Saviour of the world"* (Jn. 4:42). In Christ we *"are complete"* (Col. 2:10). In this one Seed the whole Seed has been made righteous and blessed eternally. Christ is the last Adam, and in Him a new creation has begun (Rom. 5:12-21). Just as we lost, sinful men *"have borne the image of the man of dust, we shall also bear the image of the heavenly Man"* (1 Cor. 15:45-49). "We share already in some of the benefits of the age to come; yet the greater part of that same unified plan still awaits a future and everlasting fulfillment."[4]

> Meanwhile, like an ever-rolling wave, the central current of God's basic promise sweeps steadily onward toward that final shore when the Great Controller of the flow of earth's history shall gather up all the various waves of prophecy to Himself in complete fulfillment.[5]

All of Christ's people agree with the apostle: *"He who did not spare His own Son, but delivered Him up for us all, how shall He not with Him also freely give us all things?"* (Rom. 8:32). All of God's promises are sure in Christ. Nevertheless, believers differ concerning how, and to whom, and when these *"exceeding great and precious promises"* (2 Pet. 1:4) are fulfilled. To answer these questions we will look briefly at three areas where the disagreement is sharpest: The Law of God, the People of God, and the Kingdom of God. For further discussion on major viewpoints, see Appendix 6.

THE PROMISE AND THE LAW OF GOD

The law of God given at Mount Sinai is an expression of God's moral nature. He requires "complete conformity to that holy nature"[6] as His inflexible standard for His people: *"Be holy, for I am holy"* (1 Pet. 1:16). God gave His law to Israel through Moses (Ex. 19; Jn. 1:17) and it is known as *"the Law of Moses,"* distinct from the eternal "law of God" (1 Cor. 9:9, 21). In the book of Hebrews it is the *"first covenant"* (8:7, 13; 9:1, 18) while

God's Promise is called the *"new"* or *"better covenant"* which Jesus has mediated by His blood (6:13-19; 7:18-22; 8:6-13; 9:14-15; 12:24).

But are believers not under God's law today? How do we fulfill His holy requirements? It is important to understand the relationship of the Law of Moses to the Promise (especially in Rom. 4, Gal. 3, and Heb. 6–10). First of all, the Law was not given to the nations, but only to Israel. God declared to Israel *"His covenant which He commanded you to perform, the Ten Commandments"* (Deut. 4:13).

Secondly, while this Law is *"holy and just and good"* (Rom. 7:12), it was not given as a means of salvation (Gal. 3:11–21). Rather it was given to "intensify man's knowledge of sin, to reveal the holiness of God, and to lead the sinner to Christ"[7] (Rom. 3:19; 7:7, 13; Gal. 3:22-24). The Law can only condemn and curse those who are under it (Gal. 3:10; 2 Cor. 3). But God gave it to Israel for a specific interval, in order that the privileged people might learn that they were no different from other men, *"all under sin, that the promise by faith in Jesus Christ might be given to those who believe"* (Gal. 3:22). God's promised salvation and holy new life is not based on law-keeping, but on His redeeming grace in Christ and the mighty inner work of the Holy Spirit, all of which is received and maintained only by faith (Rom. 8:1-4; Gal. 3:13-14; 5–6).

Thus the believer is *"not under the law, but under grace"* (Rom. 6:14; 7:6; Gal. 5:18), and is to *"Stand fast therefore…and do not be entangled again with a yoke of bondage,"* but by faith and love fulfilling ***"the law of Christ"*** and keeping *"the commandments of God"* (Gal. 5:1, 5-6; 6:2; 1 Cor. 7:19). That is, law-keeping does not secure salvation, but the salvation given in Christ enables the believer to fulfill the righteousness of the law through the Holy Spirit's supernatural power.

Many other questions arise about the relationship of Christians to the OT. It is clear that a great transition has taken place, and the changes are not insignificant. See Appendix 7 for a fuller discussion of the differences between the Testaments.

THE PROMISE AND THE PEOPLE OF GOD

To whom are God's promises given? Have the many promises made to Israel been fulfilled to the Church? Has the Church replaced Israel forever as the people of God? It is obvious that in one sense "the people of God are one, since all will be related to Him through the same covenant of salvation. But…this fundamental unity in a relation to God through Christ does not eliminate the distinctiveness of Israel as a special nation called of God for a unique ministry in the world as a nation among nations."[8]

The "church" is a spiritual organism which did not begin until the NT era. During His ministry on earth, Jesus spoke of His church as still future (Mt. 16:18). Following His ascension and exaltation Christ became *"head over all things to the Church, which is His body"* (Eph. 1:19-23). God is now *"to take out of them [the Gentiles] a people for His name"* whose *"citizenship is in heaven"* (Acts 15:14; Phil. 3:20 NASB).

The following diagram will help clarify and bring together the overall picture of God's purpose for Israel, the nations, and the Church. In the diagram, the downward arrows represent major judgments of God. The black lines moving from left to right represent Israel, the nations and the church as they separate and join each other. The gray band beginning with Abraham represents the blessing of God, which the apostle Paul calls *"the root and fatness of the olive tree"* (Rom. 11:17).

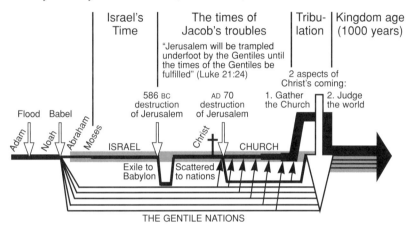

THE GENTILE NATIONS

In the Church, both believing Jews, who are those *"natural branches"* which have not been *"broken off,"* and Gentile believers, as the ingrafted branches *"of a wild olive,"* partake together of the rich root of God's blessing through Christ (Rom 11:16-24). Yet Israel and the Church remain distinct entities in God's program. In the kingdom era, shown on the right of the diagram, there is some merging of the two as the heavenly Bride (the Church) comes with the Lamb to reign on earth. While Christ reigns as King of Israel after Israel's national conversion, His spiritual "body," the Church, will be His "royal family." Israel will apparently function as a priestly nation among the nations, channeling their promised blessings from Jerusalem to all the earth.

Whatever the future relationship between Israel and the Church may be, in the present the distinction is clear. The following quotation sums up the relationship,

> This present work of God in the Church is distinct from the…OT prophetic picture of the Messianic kingdom in which Israel has a pre-eminent position among the nations…The nations come to know God without merging into or becoming a part of Israel. Israel remains a nation [with] the role of the priestly member in the number of earthly states (Ex. 19:6; Isa. 2:2-4; 61:6-9; Mic. 4:1-3)."[9]

The NT word "Israel," with a few exceptions, always means the Jewish nation. *"The Israel of God"* in Galatians 6:16 is sometimes cited to show that the Church is God's "new Israel," but it is better to see it as a reference to believing Jews, who are a *"remnant"* kept by God's grace from the *"partial hardening [that] has happened to Israel"* (Rom. 9:6; 11:5, 25).

The Church participates fully in the spiritual blessings of the New Covenant: forgiveness of sins, a new heart and spirit, the presence of God's Spirit, an eternal inheritance (Acts 2:16ff; Titus 3:5; Heb. 8:7-13; 9:15). Yet unfulfilled promises of blessing for "the house of Judah and the house of Israel" clearly do remain.

In Christ, Gentiles are made *" fellowheirs, of the same body, and partakers of His promise...through the gospel"* (Eph. 3:6). Yet while *"wild branches"* (Gentiles) have been grafted into the *"fatness of the olive tree"* of God's promise, from which the *"natural branches"* (Israel) have been broken off, it is only *"until the fullness of the Gentiles has come in"* (Rom. 11:25; see vv. 16-26). There is awesome blessing yet to come for the whole world through Israel's *"fulfillment"* or *"acceptance"* (11:12, 15). *"All Israel shall be saved"* because *"the gifts and calling of God are without repentance"* (11:26-29).

THE PROMISE AND THE KINGDOM OF GOD

When does the Kingdom of God come? God's *"dominion is an everlasting dominion"* (Dan. 4:34) and *"His kingdom ruleth over all"* at all times (Ps. 103:19), but God has also promised to establish His rule on earth at a specific time in world history (Dan. 2:44; 7:23-27). When He began His ministry, Jesus Christ announced: *"The time is fulfilled, and the kingdom of God is at hand. Repent, and believe in the gospel"* (Mk. 1:14-15). Is it therefore true that "the kingdom promises are comprehensively fulfilled in the church, not in restored Israel?"[10] Personally, I do not believe that they are.

The main views of how and when the mediatorial kingdom of Christ "comes" can be diagrammed as shown below. Of course there are significant variations within these views which are not represented here. But the general picture is clear enough:

1. Christ returns before
   ("Pre-Millennial" View)

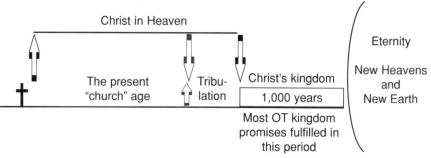

2. Christ returns
("Post-Millennial" View)

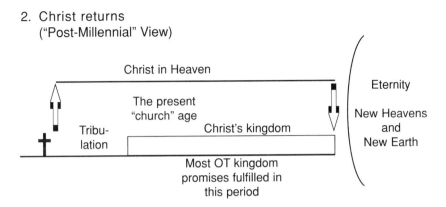

Which view is correct? I believe that the first or "premillenial" view best summarizes the biblical evidence. The key to this question lies in the two separate comings of Jesus Christ. Do the Scriptures link the promised kingdom of God with His First or His Second Advent? The answer is: with both! But the nature or form of the kingdom corresponds to Christ and His people's relationship to the kingdoms of men following each coming.

In the present era, the kingdom is spiritual, inward, and invisible, corresponding with Christ's enthronement in heaven, which is also invisible to the world. All who are born again and delivered from Satan's kingdom of darkness enter that kingdom (Jn. 3:3, 5; Mt. 12:28-29; Acts 26:18; Col. 1:13). Christ's servants, as their Lord before them, summarized their message as *"the things concerning the kingdom of God"* (Acts 8:12; 19:8; 20:24-27; 28:23, 31; Col. 4:11). This is a spiritual reign in the believer's heart which is worth our whole life (Mt. 6:33; 13; Rom. 14:17; 1 Cor. 4:20; Rev. 1:9).

In the age to come, the kingdom will be not only "spiritual," but outward and visible, corresponding with Christ's majestic presence on earth. Following the judgment, *"the righteous will shine forth as the sun in the kingdom"* (Mt. 7:21-23; 13:43; 25:31-34; Col. 3:4). With Christ, the saints will judge the world and rule the nations for a thousand years (1 Cor. 6:2; Rev. 2:26-27; 20:4-6). This establishing of the kingdom of God on earth is linked with Christ's return in glory and was foreshadowed by His transfiguration (2 Tim. 4:1; Mk. 9:1-8; 2 Pet. 1:16-19). It will be the long-awaited *"times of restoration of all things, which God has spoken by the mouth of all His holy prophets since the world began"* (Acts 3:20-21; Rom. 8:18-23). Many details of this age are filled in by the OT prophets.

Like the nobleman in His parable, Christ has gone *"to a far country to receive for himself a kingdom, and to return"* (Lk. 19:12). Our Lord has been rejected by Israel and by the world, whose consensus is, *"We will not have this Man to reign over us"* (Lk. 19:14). In the meantime He is seated *"at My right hand, until I make Thine enemies Thy footstool"* (Ps. 110:1 KJV; Heb. 10:12-13).

For this reason, in our present age we are to honor kings (1 Pet. 2:13-14) and obey the authorities (Rom. 13). God's people are dragged before kings and rulers who oppose Christ (Lk. 21:12; Acts 12, 23-28). Rather than reigning, the apostles are counted as *"the filth of the world"* (1 Cor. 4:8-13). In total contrast, the coming of the Son of Man will *"break in pieces and consume all these kingdoms"* so that *"all people, nations, and languages, should serve Him"* and His holy ones (Dan. 2:44; 7:14, 27; Rev. 11:15-18).

CONCLUSION

The fact that different views exist about how certain aspects of the promise are being fulfilled should never obscure the glorious good news of God. The Saviour of the world has come! Jesus of Nazareth took the words of the prophet Isaiah on His lips to tell why He had come (Lk. 4:18-21; Isa. 61:1-3):

> *The Spirit of the Lord is upon Me,*
> *Because He has anointed Me*
> *To preach the gospel to the poor;*
> *He has sent Me to heal the brokenhearted,*
> *To proclaim liberty to the captives*
> *And recovery of sight to the blind,*
> *To set at liberty those who are oppressed;*
> *To proclaim the acceptable year of the Lord.*

Then He boldly and directly told His listeners, *"This day is this scripture fulfilled in your ears."* The promised Seed has come. As the apostle Paul told the Jewish leaders, *"Nor is there salvation in any other, for there is no other name under heaven given among men by which we must be saved"* (Acts 4:12). We are looking for the return of the One who testifies,

> *Behold, I am coming quickly, and My reward is with Me, to give to every one according to his work. I am the Alpha and the Omega, the Beginning and the End, the First and the Last...I am the Root and the Offspring of David, the Bright and Morning Star. And the Spirit and the bride say, "Come!"* (Rev. 22:12-13, 16-17).

May God strengthen us to eager, faithful service in these unparalleled days, which may well be the last hour of earth's long night. And may we *"hold fast the confession of our hope without wavering, for He who promised is faithful"* (Heb. 10:23).

ENDNOTES

1 Kaiser, TOTT, p. 264-265.

2 Ibid., p. 264.

3 Ibid., p. 265.

4 Ibid., p. 269.

5 Richard D. Patterson, Commentary on Joel, *Expositor's Bible Commentary,* Vol. 7, p. 258.

6 John S. Feinberg (Editor), *Continuity and Discontinuity: Perspectives on the Relationship Between the OT & NT,* Exact reference unavailable.

7 Ibid.

8 Ibid.

9 Ibid.

10 Ibid.

1. Comment on some of the aspects of God's promise in the Old
    Testament that have been most meaningful to you in this series of
    studies (see the Introduction to this final study).

2. Why does the New Testament begin the way it does in Matthew 1:1?

    How are the announcements of Jesus' birth linked to the Old
    Testament promises (Lk. 1:32-33, 55, 69-73, 76)?

3. In your own words, write out below the Lord's point in Luke 24:27
    and 24:44.

    What is the significance of Jesus' claim in these verses?

4. Why is the fulfillment of Old Testament prophecy so important for
    our faith (See Isa. 46:9-10 and Appendix 5)?

5. Explain why the Law of Moses was given, basing your answer on
    these verses: Romans 3:19; 7:7, 13; Galatians 3:22-24).

    How is the Law related to God's Promise? Carefully read Galatians
    3:15-24 before answering.

6. What blessings does the Church of Christ receive through the fulfill-ment of God's promise to Abraham according to the following verses?
    Eph. 3:6; Gal. 3:6-7

    Mt. 26:28

    Lk. 24:49; Gal. 3:14

    Heb. 6:9-15

    Acts 26:6-8

7. How is the kingdom of God present in the era in which we now live (Jn. 3:3, 5; Mt. 12:28-29; Acts 26:18; Col. 1:18; Rom. 14:17; Rev. 1:9)?

8. As citizens of the kingdom of God, how are we to behave toward established human authority (1 Pet. 2:9-25)?

9. How will the kingdom of God be present in the future age (Dan. 2:44; 7:14, 27; Rev. 11:15-18)?

    What will the position of believers be then (1 Cor. 6:2-3)?

10. If a friend asked you, "What is this Kingdom of God that Jesus is always talking about in the Gospels?" how would you answer?

11. What does God expect from us in light of His solemn oath and the unchangeability of His purpose (Heb. 6:9-20)?

12. How can you apply this lesson to your own relationship with the Lord and His people (consider Heb. 10:23-25)?

Appendices

ORDER AND DIVISIONS OF THE HEBREW HOLY SCRIPTURES[1]

"THE LAW OF MOSES" (The *Tôrah* = 5 books)
1. Genesis
2. Exodus
3. Leviticus
4. Numbers
5. Deuteronomy

"THE PROPHETS" (The *Nevî'îm* = 8 books)

A. FORMER PROPHETS
1. Joshua
2. Judges
3. Samuel (1 &2)
4. Kings (1 &2)

B. LATTER PROPHETS
1. Isaiah
2. Jeremiah
3. Ezekiel
4. The Twelve
    (from Hosea through
    Malachi = 1 book)

"THE PSALMS" (The *Writings* or *Ketûvîm* = 11 books)
1. Psalms
2. Job
3. Proverbs
4. Ruth
5. Song of Solomon
6. Ecclesiastes
7. Lamentations
8. Esther
9. Daniel
10. Ezra–Nehemiah
11. Chronicles (1 & 2)
    (The final book of the
    Hebrew Scriptures)

---

1 Wm. MacDonald, *Believer's Bible Commentary*, Old Testament, Nelson, p. 20.

Messianic Psalms Quoted
in the New Testament

Psalm	Reference in the New Testament
* 2	Acts 4:25-26; 13:33; Heb. 1:5; 5:5
* 8	Mt. 21:16; Heb. 2:6-8; 1 Cor. 15:27
* 16	Acts 2:25-28; 13:35
18	Rom. 15:9
* 22	Mt. 27:46, 39, 35; Mk. 15:34, 29, 24; Lk. 23:34; Jn. 20:25, 24; Heb. 2:12
* 40	Heb. 10:5-7
* 41	Jn. 13:18
* 45	Heb. 1:8-9
68	Eph. 4:8
* 69	Mt. 27:34, 48; Mk. 15:23, 36; Lk. 23:36; Jn. 2:17; 19:28-30; Rom. 15:3; 11:9-10
89	Acts 13:22
95	Heb. 3:7-11, 15, 17; 4:3, 5, 7
97	Heb. 1:6
* 102	Heb. 1:10-12
* 109	Mt. 27:39; Mk. 15:29; Acts 1:20
* 110	Mt. 22:44; 26:64 Mk. 12:36; Lk. 20:42-43; Acts 2:34-35; 1 Cor. 15:25 Heb. 1:13; 5:6; 6:20; 7:17, 21; 10:12-13
* 118	Mt. 21:9, 42; 23:39 Mk. 11:9; 12:10; Lk. 13:35; 19:38; 20:17; Acts 4:11; Jn. 12:13; 1 Pet. 2:7
132	Acts 2:30
144	Heb. 2:6

* Psalms marked with the asterisk refer directly to the Messiah Himself, while the others refer more generally to the Messianic Kingdom.

KINGS AND PROPHETS OF THE KINGDOMS OF JUDAH AND ISRAEL

Verse	BC	Kings of Judah	Kings of Israel	BC	Prophets
1 Ki.					
12:1	931	Rehoboam	DIVISION OF THE KINGDOM		
12:16			Jeroboam		
15:1	913	Abijam			
15:9	911	Asa			
15:25	910		Nadab		
15:33	909		Baasha		
16:8	886		Elah		
16:15	885		Zimri		
16:21	885		Omri		
16:29	874		Ahab	(874-845)	Elijah (I)
22:41	873	Jehoshaphat			
22:51	853		Ahaziah		
2 Ki.					
2:1				(845-790)	Elisha (I)
3:1	852		Jehoram		
8:16	848	Jehoram		(848-841)	Obadiah
8:25	841	Ahaziah			
9:1-2	841		Jehu		
11:1	841	Athaliah			
12:1	835	Jehoash			
13:1	798		Jehoahaz	(830)	Joel
13:10	793		Jehoash		
14:1	796	Amaziah			
14:23	793		Jeroboam II	(793-753)	Jonah (I)

(CONTINUED ON NEXT PAGE)

Verse	BC	Kings of Judah	Kings of Israel	BC	Prophets
2 Ki. 15:1	790	Azariah (Uzziah)		(790-715)	Hosea (I)
				(762)	Amos (I)
15:8	753		Zechariah		
15:13	752		Shallum		
15:17	752		Menahem		
15:23	742		Pekahiah		
15:27	752		Pekah		
15:32	750	Jotham		(750-680)	Micah (I)
16:1	732	Ahaz		(741-681)	Isaiah
17:1	732		Hosea		
17:6	722	DESTRUCTION OF SAMARIA			
18:1	715	Hezekiah			
21:1	697	Manassah		(663-654)	Nahum
21:18	642	Amon			
22:1	640	Josiah		(627-582)	Jeremiah
				(622-612)	Zephaniah
23:31	609	Jehoahaz			
23:34	609	Jehoiakim		(606-604)	Habakkuk
24:8	598	Jehoiachin			
24:18	597	Zedekiah		(593-571)	Ezekiel
25:1	586	DESTRUCTION OF JERUSALEM		(586-585)	Lamentation of Jeremiah
Jer. 5:12	605	70 YEAR EXILE		(537)	Daniel
Ezra 1	538	Zerubbabel (first return)		(520)	Haggai
				(520)	Zechariah
Ezra 7	458	Ezra (second return)			
Neh. 2	444	Nehemiah (third return)		(450-430)	Malachi

(I) = Prophets sent to Israel. All others sent to Judah

Note: Dates taken from *The Bible Knowledge Commentary,* Walvoord & Zuck, Victor, 1985

CHRONOLOGY OF EZRA, NEHEMIAH, AND ESTHER

DATE (BC)	EVENT
538	Cyrus's decree to rebuild temple (2 Chr. 36:22-23; Ezra 1:1-3)
537	Zerubbabel's expedition to Jerusalem (Ezra 1–2)
536	The altar built and foundation of the temple laid (Ezra 3)
535	Work on the temple halted by opposition (Ezra 4)
520	Ministry of Haggai and Zechariah (Ezra 5:1-2; Haggai 1:1; Zech. 1:1)
520	Decree of Darius to resume work on the temple (Ezra 5:3–6:12)
516	Temple completed (Ezra 6:13-15)
486	Reign of Ahazuerus (Xerxes, son of Darius) begins (Esther 1:1-2)
479	Esther crowned queen (Esther 2)
466	Jews rescued by Esther (Esther 3–10)
458	Ezra's expedition to Jerusalem (Ezra 7–10)
445	Artaxerxes' decree to rebuild Jerusalem (Neh. 2:1-8; Dan. 9:25)
444	Nehemiah's first journey to Jerusalem (Neh. 1–12)
444	City walls completed (Nehemiah 6)
430	Ministry of Malachi
420	Nehemiah's second journey to Jerusalem (Neh. 13)

(Dates are approximate)

OLD TESTAMENT PROPHECIES
FULFILLED BY JESUS CHRIST

MESSIANIC PROPHECIES	OT PROPHECY	NT FULFILLMENT
CONCERNING HIS BIRTH		
Born of the Seed of woman	Gen. 3:15	Ga. 4:4; Mt. 1:20
Born of a Virgin	Isa. 7:14	Mt. 1:18-25; Lk. 1:26-35
Seed of Abraham	Gen. 22:18	Mt. 1:1; Ga. 3:16
Son of Isaac	Gen. 22:12	Mt. 1:2; Lk. 3:34
Son of Jacob	Num. 24:17	Mt. 1:2; Lk. 3:33
From the tribe of Judah	Gen. 49:10; Mic. 5:2	Mt. 1:2; Lk. 3:33; Heb. 7:14; Rev. 5:5
From the line of Jesse	Isa. 11:1	Mt. 1:6; Lk. 3:32
From the house of David	2 Sam. 7:12; Jer. 23:5	Mt. 1:1; Rom. 1:3; 2 Tim. 2:8
Born at Bethlehem	Mic. 5:2	Mt. 2:1-11; Lk. 2:4-7
CONCERNING HIS NATURE		
His pre-existence as Creator	Mic. 5:2; Ps. 102:25 Isa. 9:6; 44:6; 48:12	Jn. 1.1, 8:58; Col. 1:17 Heb. 1:8-12; Rev. 1:17
Would be called Lord	Ps. 110:1; Jer. 23:6	Mt. 22:43-45; Lk. 2:11
Would be Immanuel	Isa. 7:14	Mt. 1:23
Would be a Prophet	Deut. 18:18	Jn. 6:14; Acts 3:22-26
Would be King and Priest	Ps. 110; Zech. 6:11-13	Jn. 1:49; He. 7; Rev. 19:16
Anointed with Holy Spirit	Isa. 11:2; 42:1; 61:1	Lk. 4:1, 14-21; Acts 10:38
His zeal for God	Ps. 69:9	Jn. 2:15-17

MESSIANIC PROPHECIES	OT PROPHECY	NT FULFILLMENT
CONCERNING HIS MINISTRY		
Preceded by a Forerunner	Isa. 40:3; Mal. 3:1	Mk. 1:1-9; Jn. 1:23
Ministry to begin in Galilee	Isa. 9:1	Mt. 4:12-17
Ministry of miracles	Isa. 61:1	Lk. 7:18-23; Acts 2:22
Teacher of parables	Ps. 78:2	Mt. 13:34-35
Would come to the Temple	Mal. 3:1	Mt. 21:12; Jn. 2:13-16
Enter Jerusalem on donkey	Zech. 9:9	Mt. 21:6-11; Lk. 19:35-37
CONCERNING HIS SUFFERING AND DEATH		
483 years after decree	Dan. 9:25-26; Neh. 2	10 Nisan AD 33
Betrayed by a friend	Ps. 41:9	Mt. 10:4; 26:49-50
Sold for 30 pieces of silver	Zech. 11:12-13	Mt. 26:15; 27:3-10
Forsaken by His disciples	Zech. 13:7	Mk. 14:27, 50
Silent when falsely accused	Isa. 53:7	Mt. 27:12; 1Pet. 2:21-23
Smitten and spat upon	Isa. 50:6	Mt. 26:67; Lk. 22:63
Mocked	Ps. 22:7-8	Mt. 27:39-43
Wounded for our sins	Isa. 53:5	Mt. 27:26; 1Pet. 2:24-25
His hands and feet pierced	Ps. 22:16; Zech. 12:10	Lk. 23:33; Jn. 20:25,27
Crucified with thieves	Isa. 53:12	Lk. 22:37; Mk. 15:27-28
Interceded for His enemies	Isa. 53:12	Lk. 23:34
Rejected by own people	Isa. 53:3	Jn. 1:11; 19:14-15
Hated without a cause	Ps. 69:4; Isa. 49:7	Jn. 10:31-32; 15:25
Clothing to be gambled for	Ps. 22:18	Jn. 19:23-24
Given vinegar for His thirst	Ps. 22:15; 69:21	Jn. 19:28-30; Mt. 27:34
His forsaken cry	Ps. 22:1	Mt. 27:46
Committed His spirit to God	Ps. 31:5	Lk. 23:46
His bones not broken	Ps. 34:20	Jn. 19:33
His heart broken	Ps. 22:14	Jn. 19:34
His side pierced	Zech. 12:10	Jn. 19:34
Darkness at noon	Amos 8:9	Mt. 27:45
Buried in rich man's tomb	Isa. 53:9	Mt. 27:57-60

MESSIANIC PROPHECIES	OT PROPHECY	NT FULFILLMENT
CONCERNING HIS RESURRECTION AND EXALTATION		
His resurrection	Ps. 16:10; Isa. 53:10	Mt. 28:6; L.k 24; Jn. 20; Acts 2:23-32; 1Cor 15
His Ascension	Ps. 68:18	Lk. 24:50-51; Acts 1:9
Exalted to right hand of God	Ps. 110:1; Isa. 52:13	Acts 2:33-36; Heb. 1:3, 13; Eph. 1:20; Phil. 2:9-11
"Stumbling Stone" to Jews	Ps. 118:22; Isa. 8:14	1 Pet. 2:8; Rom. 9:30-33
"Light" to all the nations	Isa. 49:6	Acts 13:47-49; 26:23
"Cornerstone" of church	Isa. 28:16; Ps. 118:22	1Pet. 2:6; Eph. 2:20
Regather and save Israel	Isa. 59:15-60:22	Rom. 11:25-29
Return to judge and rule over Messianic Kingdom	Ps. 2; Isa. 11:1-10; Dan. 7:13-14; Zech. 14	Mt. 25:31; Lk. 21:25-31; Acts 3:19-21; Rev. 1:7; 20:4

If one cannot see from this listing that Jesus is the promised Saviour of the world, is only because he is unwilling. As the Lord told the Jews who were resisting Him, *"The Scriptures...testify of Me. But **you are not willing to come to Me** that you may have life"* (Jn. 5:39-40).

DISPENSATIONAL AND NON-DISPENSATIONAL VIEWS OF GOD'S PROMISE

6

There are two Testaments; no one questions that. How do they form one Bible? In evangelical, fundamental circles, traditionally two answers have dominated the scene: Covenant Theology and Dispensationalism."[1]

Simply put, Covenant Theology (or non-dispensationalism) sees the promises made to Israel in the OT as being spiritually fulfilled through the NT Church. Thus, for example, believers in the Church today are spiritual Israel, and there is no national future ahead for ethnic Israel. Christ is presently reigning in heaven on the throne of David, and the kingdom promises are fulfilled in the invisible, spiritual kingdom of God. Thus the history of the kingdom "is primarily salvation history."[2]

Dispensationalism, on the other hand, makes a clear distinction between Israel and the Church, and maintains that ethnic Israel, to whom unconditional promises were made, still has a central place in God's plan as a nation. Christ, while reigning spiritually now in the hearts of His people, will establish the promised kingdom in visible, material form at His second coming. Thus the history of the kingdom of God includes not only inward spiritual salvation, but also an ultimate mediatorial rule of Christ over the social, economic, and political realms of the earth's nations.

"Non-dispensationalists begin with NT teaching as having priority, and then go back to the OT."[3] They argue that "the OT is...provisional, the shadows, whereas the NT is...reality. A major reason for holding this is that so much of the OT system is removed as unnecessary with the coming of Christ."[4] Therefore they see the way the NT writers used the OT as the pattern for handling all OT prophecy and promise (for example, Joel 2:28-32 in Acts 2:14-21; Amos 9:11-12 in Acts 15:16-18; Hos. 11:1 in Mt. 2:15). To them NT application of promises given to Israel indicates their cancellation to Israel.

"Dispensationalists...demand that the OT be taken on its own terms rather than reinterpreted in the light of the NT."[5] They maintain:

1) The NT uses OT passages in a variety of ways. "This underscores that there is no single NT pattern of OT usage."[6] Thus no certain rule of interpretation can be derived in this way.

2) "NT application of the OT passage does not necessarily eliminate the passage's original meaning...the NT writer merely offers a different application of an OT passage than the OT might have foreseen; he is not claiming that the OT understanding is now irrelevant. Double fulfillment, then, is necessitated by the NT's application of the passage to the Church and by maintaining the integrity of the OT's meaning."[7]

3) "If an OT prophecy or promise is made unconditionally to a given people and is still unfulfilled to them even in the NT era, then the prophecy must still be fulfilled to them. While a prophecy given unconditionally to Israel has a fulfillment for the Church if the NT applies it to the church, it must also be fulfilled to Israel. Progress of revelation cannot cancel unconditional promises...OT civil and ceremonial laws and institutions are shadows and are explicitly removed in the NT. But unconditional promises are not shadows, nor are the peoples to whom they are given."[8]

In summary, the various ways of understanding the relationship between the two Testaments can be seen in terms of a scale of continuity and discontinuity. The more one sees continuity between the Law of Moses and the Law of Christ, between Israel and the Church, and between the kingdom promised to David and the present spiritual rule of Christ over His people, the more clearly one takes a Covenant Theology (amillennial or post-millennial) position. Likewise, the more one sees discontinuity between these things and expects a future fulfillment of many of the OT promises at, and after, the second coming of Christ, the more one takes a Dispensational (premillenial) position.

ENDNOTES

1 John S. Fienberg (Editor), *Continuity and Discontinuity: Perspectives on the Relationship Between the OT & NT,* Crossway, p. 110.

2 Ibid., p. 85.

3 Ibid., p. 75.

4 Ibid.

5 Ibid.

6 Ibid.

7 Ibid.

8 Ibid.

Differences Between the Testaments

Has God Changed His Mind?

A serious consideration of the Old Testament inevitably raises questions about its relationship with the New Testament. In the course of these studies we have tried to show how the Hebrew scriptures prepared the way for the coming of Jesus the Messiah and for the NT scriptures which reveal Him. Yet certain significant questions may seem unanswered to the skeptical or inquisitive reader. In particular it may be asked why God seems to have changed His mind on certain issues in the New Testament period. Or to put it another way, is God really consistent between the two Testaments? The issues involved here may be divided into two related areas:

1) Why does the standard of behavior or holiness required in the OT sometimes seem lower than that in the NT? Why are social evils like slavery, polygamy, and "holy war" permitted or condoned? For example, how is it consistent for God to command Israel on certain occasions to ruthlessly exterminate their pagan enemies, when in the NT He commands His people to love and pray for their enemies and persecutors? In this group of issues we must consider why the New Testament standard of behavior seems to be higher, stricter, or more "spiritual."

2) Why are certain restrictions or commandments which are found in the Old Testament no longer applicable in the New Testament? Why, for example, is the eating of pork (and other "unclean" foods) forbidden in the Law of Moses and then later permitted by the New Testament? Why is so much of the legislation of the OT, especially the detailed ceremonial and civil aspects of the law, no longer enforced in the NT? In this group of issues, the New Testament seems to be looser or less restrictive than the Old. Has God changed His mind on these issues?

A full treatment of these two broad questions is beyond the scope of this book, but we should at least notice four key principles which will enable us to answer these questions satisfactorily.

PRINCIPLE # 1
SCRIPTURE SOMETIMES RECORDS WITHOUT COMMENT ACTIONS WHICH GOD DOES NOT SANCTION.

We must not confuse what the Bible records with what it sanctions or commands. Many instances of this are seen in the OT especially. Man's sinfulness is faithfully recorded, and God's prophets are not excluded. God's grace covered the sins of these men and women of faith, but His truthfulness prevented anything short of realistic records. Not every action of men of faith is to be imitated or made into a pattern. Noah, Abraham, Isaac, Jacob, Moses, and David are all recorded in God's roll-call of faithful saints (Heb. 11:7-32), but in the OT we find the record of their sins, among which are drunkenness, lying, unbelief, deception, polygamy, murder, and adultery.[1] The immediate record of these acts do not always contain a statement of God's disapproval, though they are condemned in other passages of Scripture.

In thinking about behavior that seems more strongly restricted in the NT than in the OT (such as polygamy and violence), remember that the mere fact of actions being recorded, even repeatedly, does not indicate God's approval. At most it shows His tolerance.

Nor does His approval of a person in a particular situation mean that the person's every action pleased Him. The pagan prostitute Rahab in Jericho is praised for her faith in the God of Israel, but this does not mean that prostitution is acceptable or that her use of deception to protect the Israelite spies is a good pattern for believers to follow.

PRINCIPLE # 2:
BIBLICAL REVELATION IS PROGRESSIVE.

As was stated in our introductory study, and developed throughout the following chapters, God has revealed His will gradually, over long periods of history. It is thus no surprise to find progress toward a fuller, deeper, or higher standard of conduct in the later parts of the Bible. We see the same process in the progressive training of a child. Of course, if this change were in the reverse direction, the situation would be seriously disturbing. That is, if standards became more "primitive," superficial, or outward in nature, we would have a real problem.[2]

Yet we must remember that while there is development and "growth" in the gradual revelation of God's Word to mankind, there is also "perfection of revealed truth at all stages in the process.[3] Recall Kaiser's illustration of the acorn and oak tree quoted on page 20. While much less developed, the seed and first growth is no less perfect than the full-grown tree. In the same way, while much of the richness and spiritual depths of God's truth were revealed only much later in the New Testament, the earliest revelation contained the very same truth in less developed, but nonetheless perfect seed-form.

Having said this, the fact that God's revelation was revealed gradually helps answer the questions above, and allows us to understand the following two facts more clearly:

1) God tolerated certain things in His people (e.g. polygamy, divorce) in earlier ages which He later clearly forbid.

2) God required certain external rituals (e.g., animal sacrifice, the temple rituals) which He later removed.

A final point should be made here. God deals with people on the basis of the knowledge of His will that they have received. *"For unto whomsoever much is given, of him shall be much required: and to whom men have committed much, of him they will ask the more"* (Lk. 12:48). This also helps explain why God tolerated certain behavior in Old Testament believers that He later explicitly forbids. They had received less than we have, and therefore less was asked of them.

PRINCIPLE # 3
OLD TESTAMENT REVELATION IS LIMITED IN SOME SIGNIFICANT WAYS.

The Old Testament was not the final chapter in God's truth; it rather anticipated the New Testament revelation to follow. "There are several acknowledged limitations present that usually can be explained by the fact that the progress of revelation is set in the process of history, and to that degree limited thereby in the good plan and pleasure of God."[4] We can identify the following four limitations:

A) HISTORICAL LIMITATIONS

The reality of the Fall is the background of all God's work in history. Vast social evils such as idolatry, slavery, and inter-tribal warfare were part of the fabric of Israel's world. The Lord Jesus specifically tells us of things permitted in Israel due to the *"hardness of your hearts,"* which was the result of the Fall (Mt. 10:2-9). *"Who in times past suffered all nations to walk in their own ways…And* **the times of this ignorance** *God overlooked; but now commands all men everywhere to repent"* (Acts 14:16; 17:30). During these "times of ignorance" God was preparing the way for the coming of the Saviour of the World. Thus while not leaving Himself without witness, He worked gradually in the fallen world, revealing Himself to one nation which was no less fallen than any other. This historical reality provides the context for much OT legislation.

B) NATIONALISTIC LIMITATIONS

Most of the laws and commands of the Old Testament are directed specifically to the nation of Israel. The Covenant at Mount Sinai, within which were the Ten Commandments, the Tabernacle instructions and all of Israel's ceremonial and civil law, was made with that nation alone: *"You only have I known of all the families of the earth; therefore, I will punish you for all your iniquities"* (Amos 3:2). Israel was God's nation on earth, a true theocracy, where the Lord was enthroned among His people, and in which His Word was not only their moral standard, but also their civil law. This unique era ended as God withdrew from Israel and judged them. A new era began, which Jesus referred to as *"the times of the Gentiles"* (Lk. 21:24).

The form of God's government over the world has clearly changed at certain points in human history, though His character and will for man has not. In this new era God began to deal with individual disciples and gatherings of believers in all the nations of the world, building what He calls His "ekklesia" (church or assembly).Thus for example, these individuals and churches are called to obey the civil authorities of the nation where they live, not the civil law of the nation of Israel. Therefore, in considering many of the OT injunctions, we must keep this nationalistic limitation in mind.

C) Legalistic limitations

"The Law lacked an inner source of motivation or something to compel me to achieve what it commands. While the whole essence of the Law can be summarized in love, it cannot in itself produce that love."[5] This is all due to the imperfection and weakness of man. The Law was more like a guardian to supervise children or a yoke to keep oxen in line (see Gal. 3:23–4:3 and Acts 15:10). The Law was not in itself deficient, but it could not be the means to produce real obedience to God's commandments.

D) Materialistic limitations

Unquestionably there was a greater emphasis on material prosperity as evidence of God's blessing in the OT era. The "spiritual" blessings revealed in the NT were not very evident before Christ came. This higher calling of rejoicing in the Lord in every circumstance, assured of an eternal inheritance and heavenly treasure, is to a great extent realized only after the resurrection of Jesus from the dead. In this mighty event He *"brought life and immortality to light through the gospel"* (2 Tim. 1:10).

PRINCIPLE # 4
The coming of Christ has transformed all relations between God and man.

The coming of Christ is the central event of all history, as most calendars remind us year by year. Therefore to expect any less than a massive advance or a whole new era is to underestimate the greatness of what the New Covenant brought. If as the NT records claim, the One who has come to earth through virgin birth, lived a unique and absolutely perfect life, died a sacrificial death, risen from the dead, and ascended again into heaven is the Lord and supreme Lawgiver Himself, it should hardly surprise us to find some major changes in the order of things.

The OT records the era of promise and carried with it many temporary or preliminary *"shadow of good things to come"* (Heb. 10:1). But the NT is the record of the fulfillment of the promises, and thus the reality has come. The Holy Spirit of God has come to dwell and reign in each believer's inner being, replacing external rituals and rites with spiritual worship and joyful service of God our Father. This inner dynamic makes possible and compulsory a deeper, fuller obedience to the will of God in every area—marriage, personal holiness, relationships with enemies, etc. Thus what God tolerated in OT saints He no longer overlooks, and forms or rituals useful as visual illustrations of God's truth have given way to the reality of free worship in the Spirit of God (Phil. 3:3). In the same way Jesus as the Lamb of God ended animal sacrifice, so also all other aspects of that ceremonial law were fulfilled in Him.

Specific Questions

I believe that almost all of the specific questions about differences between the Testaments may be analyzed in the light of these four principles and satisfactorily answered. Let us attempt a brief answer to several specific issues before concluding this appendix:

Divorce

Why was divorce permitted in the OT for more situations than in the NT? This question is specifically answered by the Lord Jesus in Matthew 19:1-9. He makes it clear that the easier provisions for divorce found in the Law of Moses (Deut. 24:1-4) was only an accommodation by God to the hardness of their hearts, but took them back to the original plan of God found in Genesis 2:23-24. He then told His disciples that as of now divorce for any reason other than sexual immorality is in fact adultery. Even in the OT God stated His real attitude to this issue: *"I hate divorce!"* (Mal. 2:16 NASB).

Polygamy

While a number of OT saints, especially kings like David and Solomon, had multiple wives, the NT explicitly forbids polygamy, disallowing men who are not *"the husband of one wife"* from leading or serving in the church (1 Tim. 3:2, 12). Like divorce in the OT, polygamy was tolerated by God, though never sanctioned or expressly permitted. In fact the OT principle given to Adam—*"they two shall become one flesh"*—clearly established monogamy as the pattern for all marriage. As noted in the first principle above, we must not confuse what the Bible records with what it sanctions or commands.

SLAVERY

At no point in the Old or New Testament is slavery expressly forbidden. The Law of Moses contains clear guidelines protecting the human dignity and value of slaves. In fact the very first provisions of the so-called Book of the Covenant given to Moses on Mount Sinai protect the rights of slaves as human beings (Ex. 21:2-11). The New Testament addresses believing slaves and slave-owners as equals in God's sight, while not expressly condemning the institution of slavery (Col. 3:22; 4:1).

Nevertheless the principles upon which slavery was eventually abolished (to a large extent by the extended efforts of devoted Christian leaders), are clearly presented in both the Old and New Testament. All men and women are made in the image of God, and are created and redeemed for free, loving service of God and one another. Job affirmed his essential equality with his slaves and their right to "file a complaint" against him to God, saying, *"Did not He who made me in the womb make them? Did not the same One fashion us in the womb?"* (Job 31:15). In summary, slavery is just one more wretched result of the Fall.

"HOLY WAR"

Israel is commanded by God to utterly destroy certain cities of their enemies, killing every man, woman, and child (e.g., Deut. 20:17). Jesus commands His disciples in the NT to love and pray for their enemies. It is interesting that the general NT principle for dealing with our enemies in love because vengeance belongs to God is in fact quoted directly from the Old Testament (Rom. 12:17-21 quotes Prov. 25:21-22). We may say three things about this issue:

1) Israel as a nation was God's instrument of judgment on the pagan nations of Canaan whose wickedness has gone beyond bounds. In the same way God later used other nations to wipe out Israel when they sinned. God was dealing with nations as nations in that era. Warfare was unavoidable when God's theocracy was established among idolatrous nations.

2) Such total destruction was strictly limited to nations living within the land God was giving to Israel, and the purpose was clearly stated: *"That they teach you not to do after all their abominations, which they have done to their gods; so you should sin against the Lord your God"* (Deut. 20:18). There was no other way of dealing with rampant idolatry and to keep it from infecting God's people. Of course they failed to carry this command out fully and the results were precisely as God had warned.

3) These NT commands do not deal with national or governmental actions, but rather with individuals who persecute, misuse, or hate us. The holy warfare of God's people today is limited to the unseen "spiritual" realm, using spiritual weapons (Eph. 6:10-18). No nation or army on earth

can rightly claim to be God's nation today. His is an international "nation."

FORBIDDEN FOODS

Pork and other foods were clearly declared "unclean" and forbidden in the OT (see Lev. 11). Just as clearly the Lord Jesus as the Lawgiver declares "all foods clean" and edible (Mk. 7:18-19; 1 Tim. 4:3-5). In addition to clear health benefits, the dietary laws in the Mosaic Law were designed to teach obedience to God's Word regarding what was clean and unclean. These commands in Leviticus 11 about which of *"all the beasts"* they may eat resemble God's command to Adam in Genesis 2:16-17: *"Of every tree of the garden you may freely eat; but of the tree of the knowledge of good and evil you shall not eat..."* The issue was not inherent cleanness or uncleanness, but obedience to God's Word. *"To the pure all things are pure, but to those who are defiled and unbelieving nothing is pure; but even their mind and conscience are defiled"* (Titus 1:15).

God no longer is requiring such dietary restrictions. Acts 10:15 makes it clear that these dietary provision were closely linked with Israel as God's unique people among all others, and that status was changed by the Lord Himself in this era. God's Word to Peter is clear: *"What God has cleansed, no longer consider unholy."*

DEATH PENALTY

Quite a number of actions were punishable by death under the Law of Moses. The enforcement of these laws was carried out by the civil authority of the kingdom of Israel. But in the NT we find no such commands for the Church of God. Instead we are clearly told that civil government *"beareth...the sword"* and is *"God's minister, an avenger to execute wrath on him who practices evil"* (Rom. 13:4). This indicates that the death penalty and other civil punishments are to be enforced only by governments. The most serious punishment God's people can administer in the household of God is to put a person out of the church (1 Cor. 5:9-13).

ANIMAL SACRIFICE

All the animal sacrifices of the OT were symbolic of the ultimate sacrifice of Christ as the Lamb of God on the cross (Heb. 10:1-10). Therefore the symbols have ceased to be required.

TEMPLE RITES

All of these rites such as ritual washing, lighting the holy lamps, burning incense, etc. were also symbolic of aspects of the Christian's worship such as inner cleansing, the Holy Spirit, prayer, etc. The temple itself has given way to the temple of the believer's body and the local church (1 Cor. 6:19; 3:16-17).

HOLY DAYS AND FESTIVALS

Again these festivals were symbolic of the fullness to come in Christ. Believers today are specifically told, *"Let no one judge you in food or in drink, or regarding a festival or a new moon or sabbaths, which are a shadow of things to come, but the substance is of Christ"* (Col. 2:16-17).

CIRCUMCISION

A final aspect of the Law of Moses that has been fulfilled by the work of Christ is circumcision. Circumcision represented the cutting off of the sinful nature in the covenant relationship with God. Even under the Law the primary importance was the inward circumcision of the heart. Israel was promised, *"The Lord your God will circumcise your heart and the heart of your descendants, to love the Lord your God with all your heart and with all your soul, that you may live"* (Deut. 30:6).

In Christ this has been accomplished: *"In Him you were also circumcised with the circumcision made without hands, by putting off the body of the sins of the flesh, by the circumcision of Christ"* (Col. 2:11). Therefore for a believer, "Circumcision is nothing and uncircumcision is nothing, but keeping the commandments of God is what matters" (1 Cor. 7:19).

TITHING

For the NT believer who is no longer under Moses' Law, giving a specific percentage of his or her income is not a legal obligation. Still the principle of giving financially to God's work is unchanged: *"On the first day of the week let every one of you lay something aside...as God has prospered him"* (1 Cor. 16:2). Believers are called to give very generously, not as a law, but because of the abundant grace of Christ, who is God's indescribable gift to us (2 Cor. 8:1-9).

CONCLUSION

We have tried to show that when certain principles are kept in mind, the changes seen between the Old and New Testaments are in fact evidence of the progressive revelation of God's unchanging purpose. God has worked in the real environment of sinful men, preparing them over the centuries for the coming of Christ. A careful look shows that there is no inconsistency whatsoever. God has not changed His mind, yet His multi-faceted wisdom is far beyond our simplistic judgments. We should rather worship Him along with the apostle:

Oh, the depth of the riches both of the wisdom and knowledge of God!
How unsearchable are His judgments and His ways past finding out!
For who has known the mind of the Lord? Or who has become His counselor?

Or who has first given to Him and it shall be repaid to him?
For of Him and through Him and to Him are all things,
To whom be glory forever. Amen (Rom. 11:33-36).

ENDNOTES

1 See Gen. 9:20-27; 12:10-20; 16:1-6; 27:1-40; 29:15–30:24; Ex. 2:11-12; 2 Sam. 11:1-27.

2 This is one reason Christians reject the Quran as divine revelation. When compared with the Bible, we find no advance upon New Testament teaching. In fact we find just the opposite. The Quran is much closer (at least superficially) to the Old Testament than to the New, in emphasizing external religious rites such as circumcision, annual fasts, prescribed alms-giving, prayers toward a particular location (Mecca), annual pilgrimages, etc. It also teaches such things as jihad (holy war), permits polygamy and slavery. Thus it represents at best a move backward, completely out of sequence with the progressive revelation in God's Word. (Of course in many fundamental ways the Quran conflicts with the OT as well. Many extensive studies are available. For a good summary, see *The Islamic Invasion,* Robert Morey, Harvest House Publishers, Eugene, Oregon, 97402.)

3 Walter C. Kaiser, *Toward Old Testament Ethics,* Zondervan , p. 61.

4 Kaiser, p. 38.

5 Kaiser, p. 36.

GOD'S APPEARANCES IN THE OLD TESTAMENT; THE "THEOPHANIES"

8

The following overview has been adapted from chapter 2 of H. C. Hewlett's excellent book, *The Glories of our Lord.*[1]

Theo-phany means God-appearing. Throughout the Old Testament we read of God appearing to mortal men, changing the course of their lives and bringing them to their knees in trembling worship. For example, the elders of Israel *"saw the God of Israel"* (Ex. 24:10). Yet we are told just as clearly that *"No man has seen God at any time"* (Jn. 1:18). How do we reconcile these two truths? H. C. Hewlett gives a straightforward answer: "Such glimpses of God given to men were partial."[2] These men were privileged to see not God the Eternal Father in His essential Being, but the image or form of God.

The NT makes it clear that the one seen in this way was God the Son, who is called *"the image of the invisible God"* (Col. 1:15), and *"the brightness of His glory, and the express image of His person"* (Heb. 1:3).

In these appearances the Son of God did not actually take on a body and become man as He did later in His "Incarnation." In Bethlehem He partook of flesh and blood in reality and for all eternity. He lived among men as the God-man and even now He combines in His Person both a human nature and a divine nature. But until that epochal miracle He only had appeared visibly in the likeness of a son of man.

THE ANGEL OF THE LORD

Most frequently God appeared as a glorious being known as *"The Angel of the Lord."* There are many angels of God, but only one singular "Angel of the Lord." He "wields divine authority, bears divine names, and receives divine worship."[3] The narratives which record His appearances to various OT characters make His identity clear: This "angel" is the Lord, Yahweh, Himself.

To Hagar

Genesis 16:7-11 says that *"the Angel of the Lord found* [Hagar]*"* and that He talked to her. But Hagar knew that she had not seen any ordinary angel, but God Himself, *"Then she called the name of the Lord who spoke to her, Thou art a God who sees; for she said, Have I even remained alive here after seeing Him?"* (Gen. 16:13 NASB).

To Abraham

In Genesis 22, after Abraham demonstrated his willingness to sacrifice his son Isaac, *"the angel of the Lord called unto him out of heaven"* and stopped him from killing the boy. He said, *"Now I know that you fear God, since you have not withheld your son, your only son, from Me"* (v. 12). The second time He said, *"By Myself I have sworn, says the Lord, because you have done this thing...blessing I will bless you, and multiplying I will multiply your descendants...In your seed all the nations of the earth shall be blessed, because you have obeyed My voice"* (vv. 16-18). The "Angel" who swore this oath to Abraham was clearly God Himself (see Heb. 6:13-14).

To Jacob

A comparison of two accounts of the Lord's first appearance to Jacob leaves no doubt as to the identity of this Angel. At Bethel, the *"Lord stood above"* the ladder in Jacob's famous dream and told the patriarch, *"I am the Lord God of Abraham your father"* (28:13). Jacob awoke and set up his stone pillow as a memorial of this event and anointed it with oil, saying, *"This is none other than the house of God"* (28:17-18). Years later, after the Lord appeared to him in another dream to send him back to Canaan, Jacob described it to his wives in these words: *"The Angel of God spoke to me in a dream...'I am the God of Bethel, where you anointed the pillar"* (31:11-13). Clearly then, "the Angel of God" who appeared to Jacob was God Himself.

After wrestling with *"a man"* all night, Jacob said *"I have seen God face to face, and my life is preserved"* (Gen. 32:24, 30). This "man" named him "Israel" there, saying, *"You have striven with God...and prevailed"* (32:28 NASB). The prophet Hosea recalls this event in Jacob's life with this parallelism:

> *...by his strength he had power with God:*
> *Yes, he had power over the angel, and prevailed.*

Once more before his death, while blessing Joseph's two sons, the patriarch speaks of the Lord's involvement throughout his life:

> *And he blessed Joseph, and said: God, before whom my fathers Abraham and Isaac walked, The God who has fed me all my life long to this day, the Angel who has redeemed me from all evil, bless the lads* (Gen. 48:15-16).

So the Angel of the Lord was indisputably the God of Abraham, Isaac, and Jacob.

TO MOSES

The memorable encounter at the burning bush adds further certainty to this identity. Who was it that appeared and spoke to Moses from the bush?

> *The angel of the Lord appeared to him in a flame of fire from the midst of a bush...*
> *God called to him from the midst of the bush, and said...*
> *I am the God of your father, the God of Abraham, the God of Isaac, and the God of Jacob. And Moses hid his face; for he was afraid to look upon God* (Ex. 3:2, 4, 6).

TO ISRAEL

Who went in front of the Israelites in the pillar of cloud?

> *The Lord went before them by day in a pillar of a cloud, to lead the way...* (Ex. 13:21).
> *The angel of God, who went before the camp of Israel, moved and went behind them; and the pillar of the cloud went from before them, and stood behind them* (Ex. 14:19).

In the time of Joshua, the Lord, who had established His covenant with Israel, came to Bochim and gave them a summary of how He had led them:

> *The Angel of the Lord came up from Gilgal to Bochim, and said: "I led you up from Egypt and brought you to the land of which I swore to your fathers; and I said, 'I will never break My covenant with you'"* (Jud. 2:1).

TO THE JUDGES

During the era of the judges, the Angel of the Lord visited first Gideon and later the parents of Samson. The conversation between the angel and Gideon makes his identity clear, though Gideon was unaware of this at first:

> *There came an angel of the Lord, and sat under the terebinth tree...the angel of the Lord appeared to him, and said to him, "The Lord is with you, you mighty man of valor!"*
> *...the Lord turned to him, and said, "Go...have not I sent you?"*
> *And he said to Him, "Oh my Lord, how can I save Israel?"*
> *...And the Lord said to him, "Surely I will be with you, and you shall defeat the Midianites as one man"* (Judges 6:11-16).

Gideon wanted to be sure that it was the Lord speaking with him, so he asked permission to make an offering to Him there. The Angel of the Lord gave directions and Gideon set out his sacrifice on a rock. The Angel touched the meat with his staff and fire consumed the offering. Gideon's appalled reaction again makes clear the essential deity of this "Angel": *"Alas, O Lord God! For I have seen the Angel of the Lord face to face"* (6:22).

The episode in chapter 13 is quite similar. The Angel of the Lord appeared to the barren wife of Manoah to announce the birth of a special son they would name Samson. She described Him as *"A Man of God...His countenance was like the countenance of the Angel of God, very awesome"* (13:6). After the angel appeared the second time, Manoah, not realizing that He was the angel of the Lord, wanted to offer Him a meal (a kid), but the angel refused, saying, *"I will not eat your food. But if you offer a burnt offering, you must offer it to the Lord"* (13:16).

When Manoah asked the angel's name, the answer was, *"Why askest thou thus after my name, seeing it is **Secret** [Wonderful]?"* (13:18), the very name applied to the Messiah who would be born to Israel:

> *For unto us a child is born, unto us a son is given: and the government shall be upon His shoulder: and His name shall be called Wonderful, Counselor, the mighty God, the everlasting Father, the Prince of Peace* (Isa. 9:6).

The angel then *"did wondrously"* ascending to heaven in the flame of the altar as Manoah made his offering to the Lord. *"Then Manoah knew that he was an angel of the Lord"* and like Gideon, he said to his wife, *"We shall surely die, because we have seen God"* (13:22). He was right—they had "seen" God. A mere angel of God would never receive worship offered to God.

THE ANGEL'S PROTECTIVE CARE OF ISRAEL

Repeatedly the Angel of the Lord intervened to guide and guard the people of Israel. In the following passages He:

- *"Stood in the way as an adversary against"* the false prophet Balaam who was coming to curse Israel (Num. 22:22-35).
- Came to Joshua as *"Captain of the host of the Lord"* to take full command of Israel's armies for their upcoming battles. He received Joshua's prostrate worship and told him to remove his shoes because *"the place where you are standing is holy"* (Josh. 5:13-15).
- *"Encamps all around those who fear Him, and delivers them"* (Ps. 34:7).
- Destroyed the Assyrian army that in attacking God's people was in fact *"rage against Me"* (Isa. 37:29, 36).
- Identified with and delivered them in their difficulties: *"In all their affliction He was afflicted, and the angel of His Presence saved them"* (Isa. 63:9).

THE ANGEL OF THE COVENANT

The Angel of the Lord was presented as the one whose way was to be prepared by God's messenger. In Malachi 3:1, two messengers or "angels" are predicted, the first of whom will clear the way for the second.

> *Behold, I send My messenger, and he will prepare the way before Me. And the Lord, whom you seek, will suddenly come to His temple, even the Messenger of the covenant, in whom you delight. Behold, He is coming.*

This Angel of the covenant is *"the Lord,"* who will come to His own temple. The New Testament begins with the crystal-clear declaration that the first messenger was John the Baptist, and the second (the Angel of the covenant) was Jesus Christ, the Son of God (Mk. 1:1-4). His first coming brought the gospel of salvation, but His second coming will bring the terror of judgment. In Malachi's words, *"But who can endure the day of His coming? And who can stand when He appears? For He is like a refiner's fire and like launderer's soap"* (Mal. 3:2).

THE LORD'S APPEARANCES TO THE PROPHETS

In this final group of "theophanies" there is no reference to the Angel of the Lord. Rather we are shown the radiant visions given to certain prophets of the Lord Himself.

TO ISAIAH

In the temple, Isaiah *"saw the Lord sitting on a throne, high and lifted up, and the train of His robe filled the temple."* Angelic seraphim worshiped Him, calling out, *"Holy, holy, holy, is the Lord of hosts: the whole earth is full of His glory"* (Isa. 6:2-3). Isaiah's commission follows the cleansing of his iniquity with a burning coal taken from the altar. The great significance of this vision is revealed in John's Gospel, where we are told that the One whose glory Isaiah had seen and written of (in both Isaiah 6 and 53) was the Lord Jesus Christ (Jn. 12:36-41).

TO EZEKIEL

The prophet Ezekiel received an extraordinary vision of the glory of God, which is recorded in the first chapter of his prophetic book. Above an expanse extending over the outstretched wings of glorious beings was *"the likeness of a throne…and upon the likeness of the throne was the likeness as the appearance of a man above upon it"* (Ezek. 1:26). The description which follows concludes with these beautiful comforting words:

> *Like the appearance of a rainbow in a cloud on a rainy day, so was the appearance of the brightness all around it. This was the appearance of the likeness of the glory of the Lord* (Ezek. 1:28).

To Daniel

God on His throne is the center of the heavenly courtroom scene of Daniel 7:

> *I watched till thrones were put in place, and the Ancient of Days was seated; His garment was white as snow, and the hair of His head was like pure wool. His throne was a fiery flame, its wheels a burning fire; a fiery stream issued and came forth from before Him. A thousand thousands ministered to Him; ten thousand times ten thousand stood before Him* (Dan. 7:9-10).

The One with the appearance of a man reappears in this scene as well:

> *I was watching in the night visions, and behold, One like the Son of Man, coming with the clouds of heaven! He came to the Ancient of Days, and they brought Him near before Him. Then to Him was given dominion and glory and a kingdom, that all peoples, nations, and languages should serve Him. His dominion is an everlasting dominion, which shall not pass away, And His kingdom the one which shall not be destroyed* (Dan. 7:13-14).

Jesus Christ applied this prophetic vision to Himself as the Son of Man, warning the leaders of Israel that He would return to take His place the throne of the kingdom of heaven (Mt. 26:64).

Conclusion

The cumulative effect of these many appearances of God to men is staggering. Found throughout the OT from the first to the last book, they present the holy God of glory drawing near to His sinful creatures to reveal Himself to them and to unfold His great unchangeable purpose. Above all they pave the way and prefigure the greatest wonder of all, which C. S. Lewis called the "Grand Miracle."[4] God the eternal Son became the perfect Mediator between God and men, coming into the world in the likeness of sinful flesh to save sinners:

> *The Word became flesh and dwelt among us, and we beheld His glory, the glory as of the only begotten of the Father, full of grace and truth...No one has seen God at any time. The only begotten Son, who is in the bosom of the Father, He has declared Him* (Jn. 1:14, 18).

Endnotes

1 H. C. Hewlett, *The Glories of Our Lord*, Gospel Folio Press, P.O. Box 2041, Grand Rapids, MI, 49501-2041, pp. 19-26.

2 Ibid., p. 19.

3 Ibid., pp. 20-21.

4 C. S. Lewis; *God in the Dock*, "Miracles."

Index of Scripture Verses

Throughout the course of these studies over 2500 verses have been referred to. This index lists every place in the book where each reference is found. References which are found in the endnotes, diagrams, or questions have been marked with an "f," "d," or "q" after the page number.

INDEX OF SUBJECTS AND PROPER NAMES

OT = Old Testament; d = diagram; f = footnote; q = question; proper names are in *ITALICS*

Index of Charts, Maps, Diagrams and Illustrations